# RACKET BOY

# RACKET BOY

Philip George

Copyright © 2023 Philip George

The moral right of the author has been asserted.

Apart from any fair dealing for the purposes of research or private study, or criticism or review, as permitted under the Copyright, Designs and Patents Act 1988, this publication may only be reproduced, stored or transmitted, in any form or by any means, with the prior permission in writing of the publishers, or in the case of reprographic reproduction in accordance with the terms of licences issued by the Copyright Licensing Agency. Enquiries concerning reproduction outside those terms should be sent to the publishers.

Matador
Unit E2 Airfield Business Park,
Harrison Road, Market Harborough,
Leicestershire. LE16 7UL
Tel: 0116 2792299
Email: books@troubador.co.uk
Web: www.troubador.co.uk/matador
Twitter: @matadorbooks

ISBN 978 1805141 266

British Library Cataloguing in Publication Data.
A catalogue record for this book is available from the British Library.

Printed and bound in the UK by TJ Books LTD, Padstow, Cornwall
Typeset in 11pt Minion Pro by Troubador Publishing Ltd, Leicester, UK

Matador is an imprint of Troubador Publishing Ltd

For my George

# CONTENTS

| | |
|---|---|
| Foreword | ix |
| Acknowledgements | xiii |
| | |
| Freedom | 1 |
| Divergence | 18 |
| Education Nearly Complete | 33 |
| Out of Reach | 52 |
| Still I Rise | 69 |
| Rumble in the Jungle | 83 |
| Rule the Waves | 103 |
| 'You Can Say That Again' | 119 |
| The Veil Drops | 137 |
| Meritocracy | 154 |
| Freedom Come, Freedom Go! | 173 |
| Cui Bono | 193 |
| Built on Dreams | 212 |

| | |
|---|---|
| The Open Road | 228 |
| Truth is a Tricky Business | 243 |
| The Ballad of East and West | 258 |
| Am I Not a Man and a Brother? | 276 |
| Somehow, I Reached the Shore | 296 |
| The Great Hedge | 316 |
| The Trials of Philip George | 332 |
| A Little Respect | 352 |
| Full Circle | 370 |
| Seat of Justice | 389 |
| Home | 409 |
| Tranquillo | 429 |

# FOREWORD

I first met Philip George, then our new next-door neighbour, when he had just returned from a long trip abroad. He was sitting in our lounge and chatting with my wife about his recent experiences in Argentina. From that very first meeting, I realised I was in the presence of a quite extraordinary person.

The house, situated on a new "country park" estate, was once part of the Moor Hospital, a nineteenth-century institution in Lancaster. It had opened in 1816 and was visited in 1857 by Charles Dickens and Wilkie Collins and had originally been the home of the hospital director and was later split to make two properties. By way of hard work, enterprise and good fortune, Philip George then owned a property on the site at which he had been trained and employed in his first years in England as a psychiatric nurse. He quickly became a close and valued friend. At some point during the next year or two, as we got to know more about his life and travels, we said to him, 'You ought to write a book about all that.' And here it is.

The book explores the author's life from his childhood in Malaya of Indian parents, his father being the field conductor of a large rubber plantation. Included in these earlier chapters are memories of schooldays and boyhood adventures, his developing sporting interests and exciting family visits to Kerala in India. He explores very revealingly and tenderly his relationship with his parents and his father's determination that he should be successful in his schooling, along with his love for his supportive and clever mother, who is always there to advise.

Philip arrived in the UK with just £20 in his pocket to begin his hospital training and later undertook further study and work in banking. He continued his studies at university, gaining a degree in law and joining a firm of solicitors in Morecambe, Lancashire, later becoming President of the Lancaster and Morecambe Law Society and a Solicitor of the Supreme Court of England and Wales.

Along with his narrative are his experiences of considerable success in playing badminton, running marathons, world travel and cycling through Vietnam, with a range of interesting contacts and encounters on his journeys. A train journey in Spain involved him as a target in an attempted robbery where he fought off the attackers, and one of the most riveting episodes is concerned with the tragic kidnapping and murder of one of his clients in the jungles of Ecuador. He travels to the country to secure compensation for the family and for the driver, also murdered.

The author has a remarkable memory and is able to bring to life many incidents and personal experiences with great freshness and detail. Such memories include his brilliant Chinese badminton coach, swimming across a crocodile-infested river, the dreariness of a hotel-enforced stay in Moscow and visits to Aix and Arles, made famous by Cézanne and Van Gogh. His experiences of two marriages are reflected upon, as is his great friendship with his senior law partner and constant support Geoffrey Knowles.

He later returns on a visit to Malaysia and finds many of his old places destroyed, the rubber trees of Prang Besar ripped out, the glory of his father's life's work changed forever but finds some consolation in meeting old friends.

The book is thus written in an engaging and pacey style, along with close observation and probing of social and racial experiences during his life in the UK and especially his thoughts on the wider historical issues of slavery and racism. One of the central themes of this wonderful book is the author's fluctuating feelings of conflict between the East and the West and his efforts to fuse different cultures and values. Because of this, there is an often occurring exploration of Britain's former role in India and Malaysia and his final decision to leave a highly successful life in the

UK and, rather than return to Malaysia or even India, to find a new home in San Romano, Italy.

It has been a great pleasure to be a friend of the author's for many years. We have enjoyed much discussion and exploration of many joint interests; in particular, Formula 1 motor racing and a love of Italy.

Ray Haslam

# ACKNOWLEDGEMENTS

Adrenaline and adventure have been my mainstays, with the racket being my gateway to freedom. I craved pace, and pace loved me, to make for a life that hasn't been ordinary. I'd heard it mentioned enough times by friends to start thinking, yes, let's chronicle my intrepid journey. Why spare readers the excitement, motivation and lessons they could pick up?

There had been a couple of aborted attempts at getting my memoirs written. I even enrolled in a creative writing course at Lancaster University, but the project got kicked into the long grass each time. I wanted professional assistance from a writer with an Eastern outlook who understood the East and the West and the fusion of its wonders, which is what my life story is about. And it had to be someone who could instinctively relate to my sentiments and expressions, especially with my tendency to stray from sports to history to politics to the law to just about anything, and very often slip into obscure jargon.

My light-bulb moment came around the start of 2021 during a BBC Radio 4 discussion on the importance of maintaining positivity to avoid COVID 19-induced negative effects. ...*set a new goal... gives you focus and a sense of control...* was all the motivation I needed.

Telling myself not to waste a good crisis, I called my childhood friend, Rajeevan Kunjamboo, in Malaysia, which resulted in an introduction to Geetha K, a budding author flushed from the release of her first novel, a memoir-ish historical fiction. Geetha entered my life like a gift wrapped and sent from heaven, as I keep saying to her embarrassment.

During our first FaceTime chat in February 2021, she wanted to know how I set myself apart from others to make my little mark in Middle England, especially in the 1970s, and I explained how it was all inadvertent. There was no charting of my life; I just went along like a nowhere man with the world at my command! I told Geetha how I slowly learnt "to be the sponge, to absorb everything, to open my mouth– although it was very difficult – and never let failures and setbacks pull me down for too long". I would go on to find out that the lady listening intently possessed all those qualities in abundance, along with plenty of patience, insight and enthusiasm.

## ACKNOWLEDGEMENTS

We bonded over sports, animals and our common roots, stemming from Malaya's rubber estates, love of Malaya's countryside, food and mish-mash of cultures and customs. Just like that, *Racket Boy* lifted off with weekly FaceTime discussions and note-taking between Tuscany and Kuala Lumpur, following Geetha's clearly outlined narrative arc encapsulating my three lives: Malaya, England, Italy.

From lockdown-induced melancholia and a feeling of travelling in the slow lane as opposed to racing on the *autostrada*, as I liked it, I was once again alive to the mountains! It was back-to-school type homework time for me, having to dig deep into my trove of moleskins (my diaries over the years of my active legal practice), photographs, and the deep recesses of my memory bank to produce as many detailed, accurate nuggets as I possibly could, considering I was almost seventy years of age. Curiously, my writer was not in the habit of scrupulous note-taking as is my habit, let alone recording our sessions, which frequently ran into hours. Geetha's ability to weave chapters based on my Ariston washing machine ramblings and rough scribbles is indeed a testimony to her skill for questioning and extracting pertinent details, and even more remarkably, her ability to listen.

As I was discovering one soulmate, my other was fast deteriorating. George, my Labrador shadow companion of fourteen and a half years, had lost the function of both hind legs for more than a year and required full-time care. Our top-floor master bedroom was gathering dust as we'd moved to the ground level, and to a futon bed, so George could continue to sleep with me. In November 2021, yielding to my vet's advice, George was put to sleep after his paralysis took a turn for the worse. George breathed his last in my embrace, following which we shared the futon for one last time. In the morning, I carried him to the pre-dug grave engulfed by memories of the first time I carried him aged two weeks. I laid him inside, curled up and serene, covered him with earth and lined it with large stones. The grief was no different to the one time I agreed to the termination of my baby.

Consolation comes from having buried George on the terrace of my garden overlooking the Apuan and Apennine peaks he so loved to roam during the better part of his life. I call the mountains "Michelangelo", for it was from here that the great Italian Renaissance artist sourced his Carrara marbles to carve his magic. One other great satisfaction I have is that Geetha and George got to meet each other, albeit in video meetings.

To my ritual of daily runs, I added a visit to George's grave to share my unspoken thoughts and soak in the majesty of Michelangelo. It was my breakthrough. Sometimes I'm joined by Scuisi, my neighbour's cat, and the friendly dove I christened Che, so friendly he once pecked away at my infected toe like a doctor scraping skin off a stubborn corn! George, Scuisi and Che make up my Holy Trinity; my spiritual connection with them isn't different to the one established during my childhood encounter with a loin-clothed aboriginal man locals called the Sakai. This book could not have taken shape if Geetha did not understand my Sakai spirit.

# ACKNOWLEDGEMENTS

In mid-2022, following approximately fifteen months of work, the draft manuscript of *Racket Boy* was completed. I prepared to return to my country of birth after ten years, with two aims: retracing the foundation years that provided me with the tools to survive parochial Middle England, even as my personality changed expression over the decades and I wrestled with a conflict of loyalty between the East and the West. And, more importantly, to meet Geetha in person.

Vaccinated, masked, maintaining a safe distance from people, the world had undergone a massive overhaul; yet, no vortex could dampen my momentous meeting with my co-writer. Geetha turned out to be just as attentive, intelligent and compassionate in the flesh, on top of being an incredible ambassador for her country. I say it for the record again; she was gift-wrapped and sent from heaven!

My deepest appreciation also goes out to my vast network of friends, many of whom are more family to me, having journeyed far with me. Their unstinting support in providing constructive feedback and comments in the form of emails, WhatsApp messages or hours of telephone and in-person conversations right from the draft stages of the manuscript has been most useful and enjoyable. My sincere thanks to Prof Ray and Ann Haslam, Marion and Terry Middleditch, Anthony Rickard Collinson, Kathryn Bevan, Kate Bottomley, Anna Wilkins, Sandra Ferarri and Suzie Sanders.

My special gratitude goes out to Ray and Ann who, over the years, were instrumental in making sure I embarked on this project. I'm grateful for their friendship and concern for me. Ray in particular for his unwavering interest in the progress of my book and for agreeing to write the foreword.

This book is a dedication to the towering personalities responsible for my making: my late parents KP George and Kunjamma George, Coach Chan and the late Geoffrey Knowles.

Philip George

## ONE

# FREEDOM

On a big *padang* in Kuala Lumpur, Malaya was preparing to be independent. Home Counties Englishmen, however, were to continue ruling the plantations and workers of much of the country, including the piece of tropical haven I called home.

The Prang Besar Rubber Estate, set in the Ulu Langat district in Selangor, was so named by its British founders, for they had served in the Great War. They were beneficiaries of the colonial government's policy of alienating tracts of land to serving British officers to encourage rubber cultivation.

It is memories of Prang Besar (Big War) I continue to keep close to my heart, and from where my story begins, with my most vivid early memories coming from the period when Malaya was transitioning. The year was 1957.

*Merdeka* was all the grown-ups wanted to talk about. The chatter was ceaseless and everywhere. From the vast manicured gardens of the whitewashed manager's bungalow atop the estate's tallest hierarchal hill; the less grand bungalows in the following tiers occupied by assistant managers; the modest cottagey homes like mine on its surrounding flatter hills; the estate's office, factory, smoke office, science labs, nursery and co-op grocery shop scattered along the base of the sprawling hill; to the rows of basic coolie/labour lines housing about four hundred families who did most of the toiling to meet the demands of the burgeoning manufacturing and automobile industries of Britain and North America.

I was a five-year-old not known for obedient conduct, the first child of KP George and Kunjamma George, delivered in a wooden makeshift hut by an elderly *amah*, in Mary Estate, Sungai Tinggi, Kuala Selangor, where my father worked at the time, in 1952.

My only sister, Mary (Shanta), was also born in Mary Estate, but my brothers Mathew (Viji), George (Prasad) and Thomas were all born in Prang Besar Estate. My parents came from Kerala, sixteen years apart, and were of Orthodox Malayali Syrian Christian descent. I was named Philip George after my paternal grandfather and given the pet name Mohan – we all had Indian pet names, except Tom. If one calls me Mohan, it means we go back to childhood.

The regular social gatherings of estate clerks and conductors at my house increased as 31st August 1957 neared.

I was too small to be enamoured with the man everyone called Tunku, or the new flag he was going to raise in place of the Union Jack in the field preparing for history that would one day be known as Dataran Merdeka. But I knew of Tunku because Papa was always preaching his virtues with estate and church friends.

Conversation, I realised, had shifted from communist insurgencies and the constant dangers posed by guerrilla leader Chin Peng to the valiant prince politician, the nation's first prime minister, Tunku Abdul Rahman.

In the late afternoon of the 30th of August, Papa, my father's Chinese assistant "Lucky Strike" Tan and I were heading to Malaya's most famous ground to watch its man of the moment. The men looked smart, especially Papa in his black suit, tie, his hair slicked back with Brylcreem, Hitler moustache sharper than usual and smelling of Old Spice I wished I could splash on too.

Mummy had lathered me from head to toe more vigorously than usual in Chandrika soap – the Made in India wonder bar's herbaceous perfume withstanding the buckets of water poured over my head. She then dressed me as if to match Papa's style, in a long-sleeved white shirt, new shorts, and clean canvas Bata shoes. 'It's a moment in history,' she breathed, eyes looking over me, hands clipping a gold watch bracelet around my puny wrist, never mind that I couldn't yet tell the time.

After two hours of "the Federation of Malaya, Malayan

Union, Communist Party, Alliance Party, Tunku, Chin Peng, royals, bargains, political deals, ethnic relations, citizenship..." during which time the two men had puffed away a packet of Lucky Strike between them, Papa parked his Morris Minor outside the High Court area, where we joined streams of people heading to the field, also the cricket ground of the Selangor Club (now Royal Selangor Club).

It is my strongest early childhood memory because it was the first time I saw such a large gathering of people. The pomp and ceremony did not faze me. If anything, I felt reassured amid the throng where every single face looked immensely happy!

The gaiety of a nation on the threshold of freedom showed on the crowds in resplendent *kebayas, kurungs*, saris, *songkets, cheongsams*, Western wear and, to my utter fascination, two heavyset black turbans. The sun was beginning to set, bringing out every colour to focus, carrying with it an air of assimilative power and optimism.

I did a lot of staring, my bubbling mind in absolute wonder. Up until then, I might have spotted the older ladies in my friend Ah Chong's house (his father was the estate clerk) in Chinese costume; there was also the Malay *makcik* in *baju* and sarong who came from a neighbouring village to help Mummy with the washing... but never had I seen such a huge congregation of Malaya's races in their traditional attire.

When the big moment arrived at the stroke of midnight, I was no longer Mummy's neat, new handiwork; neither did Chandrika soap's strength last. We were up at the front of the stage, jostling among cheering, clapping, tearing Malayans on the cusp of witnessing history. Nothing could compare to the radiant figure on the stage turned out in princely Malay attire, bearing the proudest of smiles. He lifted a hand and the crowd responded with extraordinary receptivity.

The Father of Independence was bringing together a newborn nation. Independence, in his own words, spurred by a leaking roof he attributed to British spite. As Chief Minister of the Federation of Malaya before he became Prime Minister, Tunku was not given a car or an official residence, but rather a house in quite a state… 'the roof leaked so badly I had to shove my bed from one end of the room to another. It was then that I vowed that I would drive the British out.'

Back in Prang Besar Estate, celebrations were in full swing. The temple bell clanged longer than usual for there was a special prayer, followed by the slaughter of goats and a gathering at the estate hall where all labourers were fed biryani and *payasam* to mark the auspiciousness of the day. The toddy shop did a roaring trade, and later there was a double delight of MGR and Sivaji Ganesan films, courtesy of Shaw Bros, that normally came on a Thursday from KL in a van carrying two imposing black movie projectors.

The independence euphoria lingered for long after, but not for me. I had more important work at hand. I too was gearing myself to break free, from the bit role of a mere spectator to becoming a legitimate *player*. I was determined to have my own badminton racket – enough of watching and cheering the elders. Papa had dismissed my request for a proper racket. 'Too young,' he reasoned. And so I sawed boards off an old EveryDay milk powder wooden crate and nailed them onto a plank for my first racket; since I had no feather shuttlecock, I gathered scrap latex to make little rubber balls instead.

I spent hours hitting against a wall as my opponent, quickly improving my athleticism and reflexes. That moment I stepped onto our common grass court, rudimentary racket and rubber ball in hand for my first proper match, it was not for a casual game. I was prepared for some serious Eddy Choong-style acrobatic jumps and smashes, a battle-ready warrior primed to trounce opponents, for all I was no more than three and a half feet tall! It likely sparked the invention of my circuit board, something that stayed with me long after I left Malaysia and throughout my adventures around the world.

I revelled in gladiatorial displays and by age eight, all I wanted was to be the world badminton champion. What I thought or felt did not matter to my parents, for whom good education was the only passport to success. In the eyes of Papa and Mummy, badminton was pointless, not something to crow about at the Syrian Orthodox Church in Brickfields, KL, where my family attended service every Sunday. Not that I hold any rancour against my late parents. If anything, I still feel Mummy's prayers, and my heart remains full of love and gratitude for the many hardships both underwent; the sacrifices they had to make to give my siblings and me a definite head start in life.

My father, Kalayil Puthuparampil George, the fourth

of nine children, was born in Ayroor, Kerala. In 1935, aged seventeen, he arrived in Port Swettenham, Malaya, armed with elementary Indian school education, head filled with ambition, heart with fire to make something of his life in Malaya. It wasn't poverty that drove him to Malaya – his family-owned land and properties – rather, it was a scarcity of jobs and the promise of immediate work with high wages under the British-managed plantations. Hardworking, resourceful, fastidious, a natural-born charismatic person, KP George began as a manual labourer in Neville Garden Estate before moving to other estates, doing all types of work. Soil digger, rubber tapper, conductor, clerk…

In the process, he built a strong network of connections, especially with private Chinese planters and smallholders who became his drinking buddies, and his advisory committee. The Chinese enjoyed the way KP George held court, delivering nuggets amassed from the *Reader's Digest*, the *Straits Times*, film magazines, or his insatiable call to venture. During the Japanese occupation of Malaya from 1942 to 1945, my father learnt the Japanese language, which put him in good stead with the new occupiers, got him employment as a storekeeper and spared him the atrocities meted out to many Malayans. One day, when he was somewhat the worse for drink, I heard him telling Lucky Strike Tan he'd played spy by passing on secrets to the Brits.

A great source of pride and fulfilment for my father and his Malayali community was when they appealed to the Sultan of Selangor and successfully obtained a lease into perpetuity (with peppercorn rent) in Brickfields. On this site, they built the St Mary Syrian Orthodox church in 1956. In my adulthood, I would visit the church on every return trip, watching it being dwarfed by skyscraper after skyscraper as Brickfields turned into a gold mine.

As the church was being constructed, the church elders did what church elders of the time did to ensure the clan remained within its fold: a suitable alliance was arranged, my parents were introduced, and their marriage took place in that same year. Notably, my father refused a dowry for my mother's hand.

My mother, Komatt Kunjamma, had only arrived in Malaya the year before and was twenty-three upon marriage, ten years younger than her husband. She was born in Kumbanad, Kerala, and in contrast to my father was an only child. When she was three, her father, a drawing master in a school, died of pneumonia in a boat on the River Pamba, en route for treatment in a local dispensary. Three years later, her mother was struck on the head by a falling coconut and died from a brain haemorrhage. She was left under the care of her wealthy maternal grandparents, who owned a large house and abundant land with cash crops, but after their deaths, my mother's relatives took advantage of the situation to fraudulently claim her inheritance. Thereafter, she was brought up by other relatives, obtaining basic education before leaving Kerala with an uncle already settled in Malaya.

Being dark-skinned in a relatively lighter-complexioned community added to my mother's list of liabilities. Orphan, dark, no inheritance. What she did have in abundance was the tenacity to face challenges flung at her, a quality my firebrand father would recognise and learn to respect from their periodic confrontations. For her part, she stood by her husband to the end, even on occasions when she did not agree with his impulsive decision-making, driven perhaps by his voracious pioneer spirit. My father was stern and serious, his word the law in the house. A twitch of his bushy brows would render most people speechless; yet, far from being subservient, Mummy ensured her voice was heard when needed. Importantly, she held the purse strings.

The wee hours in verdant Prang Besar Estate, encircled by forested hills, were cold. Windows clouded in mist, bushes and grass wet with dew, the air fresh and crisp. Until bossy cockerels from cages and branches announced the first ray of sunlight, nothing could arouse me from underneath my *kambli* blanket, its pokey wool giving the feel of being wrapped in porcupine skin. On the rare occasion I was awoken by some muffled kitchen activity or the cry of one of my little brothers or the waft of bubbling coffee in Mummy's percolator, I'd remain under my *kambli* picturing Papa getting ready for his field conductor rounds with preliminary muster – donning his shirt, shorts, sweater and muffler to contain the morning chill and knee-length socks over rubber shoes to head to the labourer lines. His attendance de rigueur was proof to the Englishman of his reliability. 'See you later.' I'd hear his standard parting line, which meant his nipping home at 9.30 am for coffee and a curry puff or corned beef. Then he'd whack to life his AJS or Norton, either of his big, heavy motorbikes, and thunder away into the dark of dawn.

Similarly well wrapped, the labourers would walk for miles in poor vision, huddled in groups – better the protection against a skulking cobra or python, or worse, a pouncing tiger. Prang Besar Estate's hilly terrain covered more than two thousand acres of densely planted rubber trees. Sometimes a Massey Ferguson trailer tractor was despatched to transport tappers to their lines. Always loaded to the brim, the men and women would be offloaded at the bottom of hills from where they trudged up carrying tapping knives, metal buckets and lunches in tiffin cans to split into teams under a *kangany* (supervisor).

The English bosses carried out periodic inspections in their Land Rovers, sparing themselves of distasteful labour, including the mental pressure of day-to-day operations of the estate, delegated to my father and his subordinates. It was abhorrent for them to don their Bombay Bowlers for the march down to the austere labourer huts to sort out a row in the lines, as happened about once a month; high on toddy, which invariably sparked a drunken brawl, it was the only time the labourer workforce caused trouble. Fortunately, a single hard "clip" was enough to knock them out before a dunk under the tap cooled them off.

As I think it over, I see how the privileged and sub-privileged classes (my family included) of Prang Besar Estate, a part of Harrisons and Crosfield Ltd, London, prospered from the fortunes latex gifted them, while the mainstay of the plantation, its servile class of labourers (and their descendants) – the ones who came most in contact with the prized commodity of the time – remain, to this day, its biggest casualties.

Papa also did the check roll: the daywork book with yields per field and per rubber tapper to be worked out, neatly written and placed on manager Mr Mackintosh's table by 7.30 am on the first day of each month. Or face Mackintosh's wrath. The stress and pain on my father's face on the last night of each month, the anguish on my mother's when things went wrong, her dark complexion deflecting the crimson that would have otherwise shown up, are lingering memories. The swellings, however, couldn't be camouflaged, nor the occasional sorrow beneath my mother's bespectacled eyes.

My mother spun about our airy brick bungalow with its clay tiles and glass slate windows… preparing meals, making beds, rolling up mosquito nets encasing each bed, cleaning kerosene lamps (electricity from the main supply was cut off at 9 pm), tending to gardens. It was left to me and Shanta to help her with chores and minding the little ones. My sister was three years younger than me, while the age gaps with my brothers were much bigger – Prasad by seven years, Viji by nine, and I was eleven when little Tom was born. The downside was I had no opportunity to truly bond with my brothers. I was in my last year of primary school when Prasad even began school, and I never saw Tom in school uniform till the day they all winged away to Kerala without me.

The adults in Prang Besar were slaves to afternoon siestas. The whole of the estate and all its domestic animals would lull themselves into a deep silence. No one came a-calling during these hours, a rule not observed by children, of course. While my siblings entertained themselves within our compound, my free hours were never spent indoors. The entire estate was one big playground, and it was usual for boys to only return home when the ubiquitous blood-red hibiscus adorning every garden had closed up their petals.

All I was interested in was sports and roaming the breadth of the estate with my friends, mainly barefooted but always in Japanese slippers (flip-flops) when we zipped around on our bicycles. There was just so much open ground for hours of football, badminton, kite-flying, top-spinning or rounders, when the girls would join us. If it wasn't someone's grassy yard or garden, then we played on the huge field with a slope bordered by two coconut trees to hang the cinema screen once a week, when we would bring our folding chairs to sit on the elevated part of the "venue" with the other clerks, conductors, their families and children. The labourer families were spread on the slope and grass below.

I attended the Kajang primary school, thirteen miles from Prang Besar, and went by school bus. The English children travelled by car to missionary schools in KL or Port Dickson, and the labour-line children walked up to the estate Tamil school. My father bore the heavy burden of educating his children in good schools, besides arranging for tuition classes for me at additional cost – with no success. As I was the eldest child, he expected me to set a blazing example, but my failure to play by his rule book irked him and it did not accommodate for a congenial upbringing. On report card signing day, I unfailingly ended up with parts of my body sore and discoloured. My worst memory was the time when a fed-up class teacher, who knew very well what I was up to with my "I forgot", "Father was busy" excuses, wrote a note for Papa and sent it through my friend and classmate Rajeevan. Heart beating in my ear, I watched Papa, stirred from his siesta by Rajeevan's arrival, his bushy eyebrows twitching over his thick-rimmed black spectacles, glaring at the red marks on my report card. It triggered a tsunami, set off by a stentorian MOHAN… one of many storms of my schooldays!

It was a societal norm to regard the English man as superior. Anyone who dared show nerve was inevitably put in their place, as my father would experience numerous times over the course of his career.

The deference the English elicited from locals was carefully cultivated by the elite oligarchy living in secluded compounds with grass tennis courts, luxuriant gardens, trimmed lawns, servants, drivers, sentry posts with uniformed Gurkha security guards and pedigree Alsatians. Their social exclusivity meant we were not allowed anywhere near their compounds or to play with their children.

It was much the same with the Indian workers, where factionalism kept those in supervisory and administrative roles segregated from menial labourers. We Malayali children were told the labour lines bordering a Hindu temple, toddy shop and Tamil school were off-limits. It was a rustic settlement landscaped by orange marigolds and scented jasmines, plantains and *neem*; where naked children ran after chickens, spinning mongrels tangled with aimless brown goats, soft-eyed Indian cattle responded to names; where radios blared the same song from each house and babies were slung up in voluminous saris hanging from timber beams under a common shelter, all looked after by *one ayah* as their mothers laboured on the estate as weeders, sweepers or servants of the planters or executive staff.

I made stealthy trips down the lines to the strong smell of dung, my nose absolutely perking up to the even stronger whiff of wood smoke, for some fun with the Tamil boys in their shrinking attire, oily hair and little lumps of muscles from chopping, splitting, stacking up rubberwood. Sitting on upturned sturdy metal "latex" buckets (tappers walked miles balancing buckets of latex on a hard pole), I ate tapioca and tinned sardines with them, tomato sauce from the tin all but vanished in onions and masala ground on stone grinders, probably the second most important utensil in every household after the wood fire stove. Matching the simple, delicious food were the boys' wild tales of tiger, snake or Sakai encounters if one "dared go deep into Limau Manis". The toughness of the Tamil boys, their fearlessness and wild optimism rubbed off on me – all qualities I would need to survive my early years in England when the tables were turned and I became the uncouth youth from the colonies.

Those escapades, coupled with constant warnings from our elders to never trespass into Limau Manis, a mountainous equatorial rainforest on the fringe of Prang Besar Estate, kindled my longing for exploration.

Inspired by the daring of the Tamil boys, my friends and I began taking our expeditions beyond the expanse of Prang Besar, itself a rugged jungle gym of gravel roads, mud paths and a roaring river. Our covert Limau Manis trips took place mainly on a Saturday morning. When the coast was clear, I would click my tongue to make a woodpecker sound – our "gang signal" – and the boys would assemble with their bicycles, having carefully checked the brakes were in order.

Once out of familiar estate territory, beyond the sporadic *attap* huts forming small Malay villages along the way, the real excitement began as the forest beckoned. Trees hosting wild ferns and vines were fierce and tall, their drooping boughs ideal base for a nap. I'd heard Papa say Limau Manis was a Red Army hideout during the Malayan Emergency, easy to see why.

We cycled under a busy canopy of foliage and overgrowth to an accompaniment of fluttering, hoots and shrieks until the base of the hill. From there, it was pushing our bicycles up a mile or so of dirt track to the summit, from time to time checking on each other.

In what today feels like a mythical playground, we roamed, swam, looked out for wild animals – hoping for a tiger or elephant sighting (never happened) – did Tarzan-like swinging from vines, walked on fallen trees over its rushing river and returned home hot, sweaty, sometimes covered in mud, always totally exhausted. As for Sakai sightings, there was a watershed.

My friends were ready for home, but I felt a strong pull towards the thicker part of the forest further uphill, which up until then we'd avoided out of fear. No one dared follow me, so I went for a little exploration by myself. Transported to a different vibration, the forest felt responsive and my legs were being guided. Almost immediately, I heard a heavy rustle from a few feet ahead… bushes parted and there emerged a very lean brown native armed with a blowpipe and arrows. The piece of murky loincloth covering his modesty the same shade as his skin gave the impression he was naked. As his narrowed eyes pierced into me, I stiffened, aware of the enormous power of his presence – of a man who drew his energy from the forest, looking at this clothed child, an inhabitant of the orderly rubber plantation lording over his wiped-out former habitat. The Sakai gurgled and gave a fleeting nod, a gesture I instinctively returned. The unspoken communication was as subtle as it was strong, and he was gone. Having made my spiritual connection with Limau Manis, I returned to my friends, a lilt of happiness filling my heart.

My Prang Besar years were the effulgence of bliss, providing me with the type of schooling no modern structure can afford. I did not realise it then, but just observing and being a part of the natural world of Limau Manis helped me understand the workings of the world that would one day turn me into an introspective spirit. I would go as far as to claim it was the Malayan jungle that lured me back for a timely return from England in 1986 when I managed to squeeze in a trip to what remained of Prang Besar Estate… and to Limau Manis, which to me represents the true heartbeat of Malaya.

I had my chance to say my final goodbye just three days

before the estate, villages, hills and forests were bulldozed to make way for Putrajaya, Malaysia's new administrative capital.

TWO

# DIVERGENCE

Memories of my schooldays are deeply divided, going back to my cramped shed-like kindergarten in Kajang town, which has miraculously survived the bulldozer.

Filing back from playtime one day, I noticed a coin on the floor, picked it up and put it in my pocket. The teacher asked if anyone had found a coin since the girl sitting next to me had complained of losing hers.

The fresh build-up of sweat I was experiencing had nothing to do with the intense games I'd just left behind.

'Empty your pockets…' ordered the teacher, her eyes fixed and searching.

My squirming and shamefaced expression ensured

there was no need for that from the fifteen or so young bottoms lifted off rows of long wooden benches.

'Give it back! Say sorry!' the hulking figure hollered, wagging a thick wooden ruler taller than my six-year-old self.

Then, for the longest thirty minutes, I was made to stand face down by the teacher's side, feeling every pair of eyes screaming THIEF! To complete my "lesson", the teacher informed my father. No self-respecting Indian parent would entertain a child's word over a teacher's – the school and the teacher were temple and God respectively, a deeply entrenched community mantra.

What the teacher did was turn an embarrassing memory into a permanent scar, one that has stayed with me, along with my father's cautionary message, delivered in no uncertain terms to my slap-stung face, to hand anything back which did not belong to me.

Another hard lesson was driven home that day. Empathy for the underdog. A quality I used to great effect in my decades as a civil litigator in England and Wales – an assiduous campaigner for due process to the point where a judge once scolded me, 'My dear Mr George, truth is a tricky business, *and* it is often in the middle,' when I was acting for an abused female client in a matrimonial dispute.

I'm not disputing the value of that day's lessons, but my kindergarten teacher could have employed a kinder approach to teaching her unplanned lesson. I'm reminded of my mother's handling of the woman from the labour line, one dirty child with a runny nose on her hip, another one tugging her overused sari, pleading for her delinquent husband sacked by my father for cutting off the sciatic nerve of a rubber tree in a hungover daze to be reinstated. Mummy had stern words for the woman, sterner still for the sheepish husband, but the unit left the happier. There was also a time in India when my hunched grandmother, with no formal education or training, no paper, slate or chalk, ever so patiently guided my clumsy fingers over and over again on the sand in her front yard to form words in Malayalam. Without a raised word or weapon.

The influence of such simple acts of kindness must have shaped my social conscience and made me, at nine or ten years of age, without my parents' knowledge, skip school to board a bus from Kajang town to a remote village, in time for the final rites of a school friend's father.

I wriggled my way through a crowd of jostling males to watch my Hindu friend become a cremator. My sobbing friend was being supported by a handful of solemn, shirtless men bearing a strong resemblance to him. With only a wet *dhoti* draping his small waist, his normally centre-parted hair a drenched mass from a bathing ritual, his forehead and arms plastered with ash, my friend set fire to the kerosene-doused pyre that immediately released a tang of wood smoke. I knew the rubberwood pile housed my friend's dead father, although all that was visible were dry cow dung cakes slapped onto a white shroud. Crackling, spewing, the fire raged; searing an everlasting memory.

Kajang Primary Boys' School was a coveted English medium school back in the day. My favourite part of the school was its two uncovered cement badminton courts set on a wide expanse of green terracing, with interconnected terraces and covered corridors. From age seven, I was regularly challenging my estate friends to hit with me in groups; there was a time when I played against six on the opposite side and came out tops, so you can imagine my joy at the chance of playing on a proper badminton court.

Schools then were adamant about putting children into streams – to be moulded into boys and girls befitting the tailored education system's ideal of "success". An ideal unsuited for my nature.

English teachers refusing to consider any variation to a subjective question simply did not work for me. I would not limit a composition on *My Holiday* to an insipid expansion of points provided by the teacher. To me, "the smell of a freshly cracked durian by a roadside stall reminding me of my father's Rémy Martin brandy" was a very real holiday experience… as was the sheer joy of riding in my father's "shiny black Made in England Austin Cambridge registration BE8816, running on petrol, four manual forward gears, a reverse gear on the dashboard, carpet matting topped by rubber ones by Mummy to keep the footwells clean from the estate's mud roads".

*Out of topic Philip George* screamed Teacher's red ink.

I fared no better in other subjects, mainly because I wasn't ready for rigorous self-discipline. My mind was constantly drawn to the outdoors. Every downpour made me wish I could fling away my shoes for football on the field; the screech of the ubiquitous parrots in our school gardens took me to cycling in Limau Manis.

I found history meaningful, though, but long before learning it as a subject in school, Papa was my disseminator of history and political tutelage. It was in our living room that I learnt during the Second World War the Japanese Imperial Army had put to sleep the idea of British superiority from the time its soldiers cycled down the jungle roads of Malaya to batter Churchill's "fortress Singapore" while the British awaited a sea invasion *because the Japanese couldn't possibly come through Malaya's impassable jungle!*

'They sank *two* British ships off Kuantan in the South China Sea,' Papa would say, with more animation than any history teacher, about the capital ships *HMS Repulse* and *HMS Prince of Wales* that took the lives of more than a thousand men.

Admittedly, the system of that era did ingrain in teachers the mastery to provide rounded education focused on academia, sports and life skills. As well as harness challenging charges like me and instil loyalty to country and institutions. Chinese, Malays, Indians, Eurasians, we played together and visited each other's houses, especially during festival times. We rallied and roared in support of national teams representing Malaysia in football or badminton, and nobody had reservations about attending funerals, weddings, even religious festivals of other races.

The only time in my life I was in an A class was in standard one, as streaming based on academic report cards only began in standard two, which meant I was banished to the E class the following year to remain in the "lower echelon" until standard 6E, a great cause of frustration and embarrassment to my father, who wouldn't take pride in my badminton or athletics skills or appreciate that I excelled as a Cub Scout. In my father's estimation, I was headed down the road of the most likely candidate to bring shame to his proud Malayali community.

After-school loitering was by the main road at the entrance of the school, squatted by rough and ready Chinese and Indian Muslim *kaka* hawkers selling dried *sotong, ice kacang* and an array of colourful cool drinks topped with Dutch Lady condensed milk. My daily pocket money of ten cents just about covered it, although as I grew older, I would sell toast with South African blackcurrant jam, made for me by Mummy, to my friends for some extra money.

It was home for lunch by two. Once or twice a week, I used to stay back for sports or extra private tuition. On these occasions, I went back using the evening school bus and would reach home to the smell of mosquito oil spray fused with Papa's cigarette smoke or burning candles whenever the estate generator was not functioning. Bathing in the dark bathroom meant you had to keep your senses peeled and feet nimble to scoot if you stepped on any slimy, stealthy visitor, so it was always a splash-and-dash shower, also because I'd be ravenous by then. Once changed into a nightshirt and shorts, it was prayers with the family before tucking into Mummy's rice, vegetables and *sambar* or fish curry of the kind that always left a lingering aroma on well-licked fingers.

I wasn't particularly clever at any form of brainwork that didn't compel my interest. Neither did I have the confidence to raise my hand or shout out the correct answer, as exemplified by the front-row candidates.

One such front-row passenger was a tall, large-built Ceylonese boy called Bryan Pereira, with whom I'd cross swords frequently. Bryan lived not too far from school, opposite the Kajang General Hospital, which I frequently visited for sports knocks and cuts. For falling off trees, snake bites, rusty nails, dirty broken bottles, I was taken to the Menon "dresser", like the time I electrocuted myself on our Electrolux table fan amid Papa giving me a talking-to about my poor schoolwork. I absent-mindedly inserted my Venus lead pencil into the speed control, blacked out, slumped to the floor and had to have Mr Menon attend to me. It took about three hours for me to regain consciousness to find Mummy in tears and Papa fuming, 'You STUPID boy!'

Bryan was, like me, good at sports, and we competed fiercely in badminton, football, *speak raga*, rugger and athletics. Unlike me, though, he was a top-of-the-class student, a favourite of headmistress Mrs Richards and the teachers, especially sports master Mr Balachandran and discipline master Mr Thurairajah.

Confident, cocky Bryan was not impressed whenever I took him on and would use his academic superiority to heckle me. We'd drag old scores into adulthood, two established lawyers once memorably having a major brawl in KL's Royal Selangor Club (Bryan was its then president!) only to finally bin our pointless animosity decades later – again in the same historic club – during a personal pilgrimage I took after completing the manuscript of this book.

Then there was Aziz and his Malay clique calling me *keling* and challenging me to fights, once resulting in Aziz sustaining cut lips and a black eye. It caused him to run to his father, who came to school and reported me to the headmistress.

My defence of the boys' constant name-calling and slurs was brushed aside by Mrs Richards, who gave me no quarter facing expulsion... only reprieved following the intervention of Miss Vijaya, our Civics teacher, who also ensured the incident did not reach my home, at least not straight away. Miss Vijaya was one of few teachers in all of my school life to not regard me as a waste of space. That incident and many others made it into my travelling report card, diligently recorded by class teacher after class teacher, for my father's attention.

But really, with bullies and teachers giving instructions like *slap kid next to you if he makes noise*, how was a restive spirit like me not going to get into serious trouble?

Early into primary school, I awakened to the realisation winners are seldom called names – a much higher chance of *you stupid boy*, as was the case with me.

Dodging out of the way from strutting bullies, teachers always pulling me up to do sums on the blackboard, hitting me on the back of my head when I unfailingly wrote the wrong answer (those wooden aluminium-capped blackboard dusters thumped like bricks), prefects chasing me to the jungle (I could run!), dragging me back for the cholera vaccination (needles sterilised on a Bunsen flame under the hot sun)... my early schooldays specialised in draining my confidence. Despite the persistent belittling and ignominy, I harboured a fierce hope my deep connection to sports would someday lift me out of the doom.

Unsurprisingly, my happiest early school memories come from outside the classroom. Excelling in sports, top in Cub Scout activities, chowing down tuck shop *nasi lemak* or *curry mee*, loitering at Kajang's satay stalls, playing the jukebox, going on *rambutan* or *mangosteen* hunts after school, sitting next to the bus driver, enthralled by his expert controlling of his vehicle during monsoon (no gravel on estate roads so tyres caked with mud after rains) or watching him navigate flooded roads when the rivers Kajang and Langat burst their banks and the whole town turned into a sinister grey pool…

I wasn't short of friends. There were the estate boys and Chinese boys from Jalan Sulaiman, Kajang's main street. There was also Cyril Rosario, a Eurasian off-the-wall pupil like me who often fought my corner against Aziz and gang in particular. One unforgettable time, when we were around ten or eleven, Cyril literally became my corner man.

Sports master Mr Balachandran had brought two pairs of boxing gloves to the class, one black, the other red. He handed a pair to one of his favourite boys, Aziz, then asked the class who wanted to box against him.

Cyril and my Chinese friends shouted my name. I did not hesitate.

I'd heard about Cassius Clay aka Muhammad Ali aka the Louisiana Lip winning the heavyweight boxing gold medal at the 1960 Rome Olympics and him throwing his medal into a river. My early general knowledge came foremost from being in Papa's company, and also from a good supply of *Life* and *London Illustrated* magazines belonging to my cousin Rajan Mathew of Sedgley Estate, five miles from Prang Besar. Rajan was three years older and we had a much more close-knit brotherly bond than I could ever establish with my three younger brothers. His father, Uncle Mathew, was my godfather.

I still recall the sensation of putting on the pair of red gloves Mr Balachandran handed me, invoking the spirit of Cassius Clay as I did so. Tables and chairs were pushed to one side of the classroom to create a ring, the sports master proceeded to give some novice instructions and the fight began right in the middle of the class.

With quite some showmanship, Aziz started to taunt me, raising the tension of the match up. Not buying into his gimmick, I looked Aziz straight in the eye – this was in the open, not behind the bicycle shed or the toilets. Realising it to be as much psychological warfare, I was bent on imitating the Cassius Clay shuffle of jabbing, moving and jabbing, and throwing the big punch when the time was right, hopefully, to leave my opponent with no chance for counters.

After about a minute, I landed a fight-stopping blow. Aziz lay on the floor with a swollen face and a deflated ego. My gang erupted in cheers and claps. Mr Balachandran rushed to check on Aziz, who was shouting in Malay about reporting the matter to his father to sort me out. Such was Aziz's fury that even Mr Balachandran struggled to quieten him. To placate the situation, the sports master then set us all out on a cross-country run around our gloriously green town, where once again I triumphed.

From that momentous day, I became even more hooked on sports. The love continues. I maintain an active, sporty lifestyle. From my mountain dwelling in Italy, I'm able to attend the F1 races in Monza, Monte Carlo and the Spa, and watch on screen boxing, cricket, rugby union, athletics, the tennis grand slams, the winter and summer Olympics, the Tour de France and Giro Italia Cycling and, of course, badminton and international football.

Primary school, however, became truly traumatic when my voice broke; not into a booming baritone like my father's, but a husky, gravelly one. When I opened my mouth, words came out sounding raspy; some called it croaking. It was all the ammunition my aggressors needed.

If the boys dished out liberal put-downs, even teachers openly ridiculed me. The home situation was no better as my parents too often commented on my "peculiar" voice. For a year or two, left with no choice but to brazen it out, I would walk off, leave rooms, or spirit myself away to the undiscriminating arms of Limau Manis. As Robert Frost put it befittingly, "The woods are indeed lovely, dark and deep."

I've read that Margaret Thatcher decided to add power to her soft, gentle voice when she realised it was causing people to underestimate her position as a political leader, but in my case, the belief that one's voice is an important tool one has to project their personality and confidence was something I'd imbibed from watching my effortlessly voluble father since I was little.

Thinking I did not possess a good speaking voice affected me long into the future. It was a paranoia I took with me to England – to all my occupations from nursing to law and also as a trustee in various charitable organisations in the UK and other parts.

When I did court advocacy, gave a lecture or spoke at public events, I'd hear my audience clearing their throats for whatever reason, which would immediately erode my confidence and I'd have to summon my inner strength to keep going. I was unable to free flow as the monkey on my back kept saying *you are going to sound odd*. Even when I was already a fairly successful lawyer in my thirties, I remember Papa asking me how I managed to get any results in court with such a voice!

Growing up, if only people who mattered had given me some leeway and understanding, perhaps I wouldn't have acted stiff and uncomfortable when asking a girl out, wouldn't have thrown frequent glances at my audience, looking for reactions, or spent hours devising mental preparations before a speaking event.

I feel it was my spirit of fortitude and submission that carried me through early forks and junctions. I operated from the gut, often to my detriment, but with colourful scar tissues I bear proudly. Time helped heal. Also, meeting many non-judgemental people in later life.

I had badminton in my cerebrum. The racket and goose feathers provided the few confidence moments of my formative time in Malaya, always kind to me, like Charlton Heston's four horses in *Ben Hur*. I told the actor as much when I had the privilege of speaking with him on my travels, albeit in the gents' toilets of the Grosvenor Hotel, London!

For two weeks every year of primary school, I had a respite from being the waste of space with a strange voice. It was a Cub Scout requirement for each member to raise funds by doing any job asked by the person approached. We were given an official itemised four-column spreadsheet book with date, narrative of task, amount paid and signature.

I had this easily sewn up as I approached all the estate clerks and managers, and because they all knew me from badminton, they were generally kind with the tasks and generous with their cash. I washed cars, motorcycles and bicycles, did grocery shopping, swept compounds, climbed trees to pluck fruits, cut firewood, ground spices on stone grinders and sometimes read a passage from a book. Once, someone even gave me $5 for smiling!

It was one of the few times I was allowed to go into the white section of the estate. Here too my reputation as a badminton player preceded me. The English were also generous with their cash, but only after extracting the most out of my labour. It was in English homes I did bathroom and toilet cleaning and washed their cars or Land Rovers.

While cleaning manager Mr Mackintosh's house, I befriended his son, about my age, ten or eleven. William went to a school in Port Dickson, chauffeur driven. We struck up a friendship and played whenever opportunity permitted, and he once loaned me a yearly compilation of the *Dandy* and *Beano* in one thick hardback.

Whenever I took him to my house, William was spared the patronising smiles and outright aversion I received at his home. Imagine the horror if fancy Mrs Mackintosh in her Laura Ashley-type dresses and Alice band on well-coiffed hair found out I also took her precious son to the labourer quarters... she who did not bother to hide her scorn whenever I visited William. On William's insistence, I had a free pass to their property.

The pioneering plantation owners of Malaya were Englishmen of means, including their assistant managers, also known as creepers. They were the "sons of gentlemen", educated in Britain's elite institutions; men that shaped British colonialism and now the Brexit dilemma.

One of Mr Mackintosh's assistants was Mr Simm, who once asked me to wash his Ford car. Ford cleaned to my satisfaction, I knocked on the kitchen door only to hear Mr Simm shout, 'Come through the lounge, will you!'

I sauntered in to find him on a floral print English Liberty print sofa, with company who was not Mrs Simm. Mr Simm was performing an Ealing film scene, kissing an English lady, carrying on despite knowing full well I was there, stunned and somewhat thrilled by the free show. When their lips and hands were unlocked, both went about as if nothing had happened, her to the back of the house, him to the front to inspect the car. *Good job* Mr Simm signed in my little book, handing out $10 – my biggest Cub job payment ever!

During the annual school jamboree, it was customary to be awarded for the Job Week effort, and thanks to Mr Simm, that year I won a dagger to the sound of Chubby

Checker and *Limbo Rock* while attempting a 24-inch backbend.

The following year, I won a chess set, which I learnt to play expertly within hours of practice, much to the annoyance of Papa.

'What good is it for you? Not going to get you a good job...' My father's irritation still rings in my memory.

There simply wasn't anything I could do besides getting good grades in school to please my father.

THREE

# EDUCATION NEARLY COMPLETE

'You're *only* fit for climbing coconut trees!'

Papa's stinging admonishment ended the academic year of 1961 when I came home with yet another sorry report card. However, the pain from the sores on my buttocks was forgotten when a few days later my father announced he was taking the family on a trip to India.

The prospect of running wild on each deck of the huge *State of Madras* steamer – even wilder once we hit terra firma – was too much not to share.

'*State of Madras*? Not as good as *SS Rajula*,' scoffed the front row.

But she would do for me! Even if a little smelly, the *State of Madras* would give my demanding curiosity enough fun. For fourteen days, seven days each way, I was set to adventure on the same ship that launched the dreams and futures of my parents when they set sail from Kerala to Malaya.

This was not like the trips to Morib Beach, Penang or Singapore, or to watch *The Sound of Music*, *Sangam* or *Ben Hur* after church on Sundays. This was a real expedition, much bigger than my maiden journey to India at four when I'd been too small to remember much.

I could not share my enthusiasm with my sister, Shanta, who was keener on selecting dresses for the journey. My brothers Prasad and Viji were only three and one. Tom, was not yet born.

It was a long trip and I'd be missing several weeks of the start of school term beginning the new year of my fourth standard in 1962.

'Don't know how Mohan's going to cope.' Papa raised his concern over the dinner table.

Ever my cheerleader, Mummy, replied I'd be fine.

'Kunjamma, you talk as if you haven't seen your son's report cards.' Although the jibe was directed at Mummy, my father's eyes were on me, hoping perhaps that wounding my pride might perk up my school performance. I licked my fingers imperviously; the fish curry was just too good. Little did I know the heavy cost of journeying I would have to pay upon my return from that most incredible voyage.

Papa was in the best of moods each time we went to Kajang town or KL for pre-departure purchases: clocks, shoes, eau de cologne, Nacet razor blades, Jacob's cream crackers, Huntley & Palmers Marie biscuits, Wingo watches...

'Presents for relatives and friends. They'll be expecting, you know,' beamed my father, catching me staring at the forty or so watches! He also carpentered five large wooden crate boxes reinforced with aluminium steel protectors that had our names and destination address printed in large block letters.

With a week to go, Papa's "goodies" were loaded into the crates and stacked in our lounge. As I was messing about with the crates, my right knee caught a section of the protruding aluminium steel, ripping an ugly gash requiring dressing, stitches and injections, which conflicted with the travel vaccinations we had all received the week earlier. It was touch and go whether I could travel, causing great consternation to my parents, not to mention a severe scolding for the mightily remorseful offender.

Thankfully, it was all systems go and excitement resumed. On the morning of the big day, a big lorry with a Chinese driver arrived to upload the five trunks and other luggage for the journey to Port Swettenham (now Port Klang), about a two-hour drive from Prang Besar. Papa had earlier contemplated taking his beloved Austin Cambridge on the ship – with two little Malaysian flags mounted on both front flanks! The outlandish idea, underpinned by his desire to flaunt his Malayan success, was only aborted due to logistics... or maybe someone made him see sense.

We followed the lorry to the port, where the trunks were loaded by crane onto the berthed *State of Madras*.

Once our health checks and papers were stamped, we boarded the grand ship, up a steep rope-type ladder.

I was brand new from top to toe. White tee-shirt tucked into navy shorts, shiny black Bata shoes with white socks, all purchased from Robinson's in KL, feeling so happy and privileged strutting towards our cabin in the second-class middle deck.

The lower deck was close to the engine area, occupied mainly by estate labourers travelling to Tamil Nadu for a lengthy break following painstaking negotiations with the estate management. The same applied to my father when requesting three months' leave from Mackintosh – not without some heated confrontations.

We settled into a disinfectant-smelling cabin with four bunk beds and circular windows overlooking the Malacca Strait. After a long wait, the ship unanchored and slowly cast off from the dockyard of Malaysia's vital artery of commerce to hundreds of people waving and cheering from both sides; many in tears of joy, some with heartache.

We sailed via Penang on the strait then the Indian Ocean's Andaman Sea to reach Nagapattinam, a stop before a slow two-hour sail to its final destination, Madras Port in Tamil Nadu.

My parents had their hands full with my siblings, leaving me free to snoop around the ship, right up to the captain's impressive quarters. I was envious of the comfort and luxuries of the upper deck, dominated by English planters en route for Bombay for their transit to England. A games room, a television lounge, en-suites, nice linen and towels… in stark contrast to the smell of sick, latrine and hardship wafting from the lower deck's straight-into-the-sea type common toilets.

Wedged between the two decks stirred something within me. There was only one direction for my life, and it was not to remain middle class. Papa's obsession with good education for a good standard of living "to match if not surpass the colonial masters" began to make sense. His carriage, ability to converse in English despite not being very highly educated, passion for English literature, songs and movies, choice of vehicles, smart western suits, taking Mummy to fashion shows and dances in KL's hotels and clubs…

The *State of Madras* was instrumental in making me appreciate my privileged background. It was because I spoke English confidently that I could make friends without effort with the English children on the first-class deck, play with them or watch a movie on the television, as I did with William Mackintosh back on the estate.

Once in Nagapattinam, the ship was berthed well away from the shore. The early- morning sun was just about peeking when Papa woke me up to a curious scene. There were little makeshift canoes all around our ship from which skinny topless boys in short pants were jumping into the sea to collect coins being thrown by passengers. It was a dangerous manoeuvre to swim right under the giant ship, but they made it look so easy. I could've stood there all day, marvelling at their aquatic agility as well as their comradeship of looking out for each other.

At Madras Port, we alighted to join a clamorous party of barefooted *lungi*-clad lean porters rippling in muscles with rolled-up cloths on their heads to cushion a heavy load. My father expertly set about his task of clearing red tape, beginning by picking two from scores of porters jostling for his attention.

A brief authoritative conversation followed and the two led us to the "right" immigration officer and customs clearance manager, with whom Papa struck up friendly dialogue. Mr Pillai fast-tracked everything and we were soon out of the dock area. My concern was only for our five-member faithful crates, at that moment nowhere to be seen.

'You'll see them in Egmore.' Papa meant the Egmore Central railway station where we were to catch the 11 pm narrow-gauge Madras mail train to Quilon (old name for Kollam, Kerala).

After a half-day's rest in a lodge I remember for its dangerously noisy fan and family of black pigs scavenging by its detached foul-smelling bathroom, we arrived at Egmore Station in plenty of time.

It was noisier than the morning's seaport, with honking autos and lumbering bullock carts in the mix, people pushing and shoving for their own needs. There was so much shouting and talking that it seemed like the whole station might be travelling together, and, despite my mother being dressed in a sari, she was stopped by women wanting to know, 'Madam, you are from Singapore or Malaya?'

To my utter joy, I spotted our boxes being loaded onto the goods section of our train under the guidance of important-looking Mr Pillai, shouting instructions to porters.

What a grand feeling it was to see our names printed on a sheet and attached to our bogey (berth), where finally my parents could ease their grip on us children. The train set off on time and I went to sleep on the top bunk of the wooden bench bed, using a pillow Mummy had brought with her.

I woke up the next morning to a crescendo of clanging metals and human activity. The train had stopped at one of the many stations for refreshments. A travelling catering party comprising three very small children hopped on and began serving us *idli, dosa, vada* and *sambar* on aluminium tiffin plates with admirable efficiency. In a matter of minutes, a shrill whistle rang out, the children took the generous rupees Papa gave them, flashed toothy grins and scuttled back to the busy platform.

At the base of the Western Ghats, a further engine was attached to the rear of the train to add power for the uphill journey, and we arrived at the Sengottai-Punalar station at noon. From there, we made the three-hour journey through dense jungle roads, first in a lorry, then a Jeep to get to my Uncle Ourrachen's house in Ayroor.

An emotional entourage of uncles, aunties, grand-aunts, grand-uncles and all kinds of cousins greeted us at my father's youngest brother's house, a typical one-floor Kerala house set in the midst of nature, with a large verandah, courtyard and bedrooms on both wings.

Commotion settled, we were allocated the right wing of the house from where, for the next two and a half months, Papa would gleefully dip into the crates to dish out his presents.

After a week, I was sent to stay with Mummy's maternal uncle, Kochupan, in Vadasserikkara, her birthplace. It was a glorious two months of shadowing Kochupan, an eco-conscious, nurturing person with a remarkable knowledge of local plants and trees, *everything has a purpose* being his motto.

Kochupan took me everywhere he went, including to his grocery shop, where he would proudly introduce me to all and sundry as his Malayan nephew. We caught fish in his ponds, plucked coconuts and mangoes, harvested cashews, pulled out tapioca from the ground and went on spontaneous bus trips, most memorably to an elephant sanctuary where he hoisted me onto his sturdy shoulders so I could rub a mother elephant's belly. I was also fortunate enough to witness the elaborate arranged Malayali marriage of his daughter Rosama to Ravi from another village.

The trip wasn't without storms and stress. Once, my parents fetched me from Kochupan's on the way to Papa's elder brother's house for a family "dispute resolution summit". I picked up enough on the way to know Uncle had double-crossed my father. Assuming Papa was on a gravy train in Malaya, the Kerala clan had decided he did not need his land and entitlement.

From the get-go, it was all sparks: fist-pointing, shouting, cursing, threatening, name-calling to the point where I felt for the safety of my family. There was, unfortunately, not a single upholder of reticence among the fired-up clan. In the absolute absence of equanimity and good grace, my tribe let out colourful vitriol enough to convert Kerala's lush green into a sick purple. I was alarmed and deeply embarrassed. If that big feud soured our India trip, it was nothing compared to what was in store for me back in Kajang Primary School.

Standard four onwards was the upper primary level when serious learning began, and I had missed almost eight weeks of lessons. The forfeiture meant I fell behind on new subjects as well as all continuation subjects from standard three. It was an absolute nightmare rejoining a class already chapters ahead and gearing up for the term exams. The disruption to my education also caused me to miss out on mastering the fine motor skill of cursive writing, as the class was already accomplished in it by the time I returned. It was an impairment that would impact my transcription tasks in school, university and with legal manuscripts.

Familiar frostiness from teachers and bullies assailed me incessantly, causing all my fabulous Kerala holiday memories to drift off one by one. From being the celebrated boy from Malaya, I became once again the waste of space fit only for climbing coconut trees, although by that time I had become quite a skilled tree climber, thanks to Kochupan.

Papa was beside himself. I not only lagged behind my classmates but was also skin and bones and had breathing issues. That I was otherwise in perfectly good health notwithstanding, and because forking out money for tuition had already proven unhelpful, he decided instead to invest in the new miracle soup advertising itself as "Brand's Essence of Chicken – instrumental in saving many lives in Malaya"!

I finally had a reprieve the following year of my primary education – a major green shoots growth towards confidence building.

Loitering in town after *rojak* and *ice kacang*, I found myself at the Kajang Badminton Hall, a modest building with parquet flooring and a high ceiling, great for indoor badminton. It was a lively scene of the best young badminton players in Ulu Langat and Kajang, being coached by a middle-aged pot-bellied Chinese man, arms flapping, shouting instructions.

Pot-bellied man kept shouting orders in broken English, and as he backed towards me, he said something to his charges to take me by complete surprise. 'It's like playing chess, you understand or not?'

The man turned and caught sight of me by the corridor. I could tell he was sizing me up, as I was in my white singlet, shorts and sports shoes – as always, my school shirt was stuffed in my bag.

Flushed from all the shouting, he was brusque in manner with me, yet not quite dismissive.

'Which school you go?'

I answered.

'How old?'

Eleven.

'Where your house?'

I told him.

'You got play badminton?' It was a statement rather than a question, because he was holding out the racket in his hand. 'Take. Show me how you stroke.'

We'd see about that!

I accepted the racket, picked up a stray shuttlecock from the floor and put on my show for pot-belly, who scrutinised my every hyper reflex; the way I moved, the way I stroked the shuttlecock.

'Come.' He beckoned me to join the court, where he halted training and ordered me to play singles against a taller, bigger Chinese boy. I will not forget the score: 15-3. I did it at a canter and the feat earned me applause from pot-belly. And an introduction.

'My name is Mr Chan. I'm coach here.' That chance encounter was to be my ticket to eventual attainments.

Coach Chan signed me up for the Shell Badminton Youth Project under the Selangor state, and my school and parents were informed. Having heard Coach Chan say the school had produced a "potential national champion", sports master Mr Balachandran, for the first time, displayed a glint of hope in his eyes for me.

There were nine of us for coaching every Wednesday afternoon after school, and Coach Chan made us train very seriously. Stroke, hit, return, smash, drop, he'd say, adding without fail, 'Must do with correct timing and must do with *style*.'

It was all about good economical movements and anticipation. And flair. Flair and style were paramount to Coach Chan.

In England, I would find out how the western style of play was a far cry from the east. The naturally nimble Asian is conditioned to stroke the shuttlecock in the spirit of *kalah takpa asalkan main dengan gaya* (play with style, doesn't matter if you lose). The punctilious English coach, on the other hand, would bellow, 'Fuck the style! Get stuck in. Bloody win!' Very much trench warfare attitude.

I was given a Shell report card and every section was filled out by Coach Chan, signed by him and sent to the Selangor State Badminton selectors. It was a strict weekly routine: train for three hours, shower, change, get into individual cubicles for "concentration training", a light-gazing focus session where under candlelight we had to concentrate on one small object, like a pen or pencil, for fifteen minutes to prepare us to "get into the zone" before a big match. The technique has stayed with me, guiding me through anxious periods; to silence vexatious mental chatter.

Coach Chan entered me for tournaments around Selangor and I won regularly, yet Papa remained indifferent, hoping I would gradually lose interest and begin focusing on my studies. In his eyes, badminton, or any sport for that matter, did not make for an honourable pastime, let alone a profession.

He never realised the pain his inveighing caused me every time he dismissed my passion for badminton as "simply a waste of time". Neither could he understand my dejection when I was not allowed to enter or play a tournament if it fell on a Sunday. In his book, church, followed by visits to relatives in KL or to a film, could not be compromised. Each time the issue came to battle, the outcome was predictable: *you stupid boy*. In my time, boys believed in and did what fathers told them to. I was no exception.

Regardless, I remained committed to badminton. School was vague and incoherent. I was going to be the world badminton champion, and it wasn't a mere dream or ambition. I knew I had the talent to deliver.

Looking back now, I still believe I could have achieved it if only I'd had a father like Anthony Hamilton (father of Lewis Hamilton), brave enough to wager on his son, to appreciate and respect his son's passion, to hold down three jobs just to pay for Lewis's motor-racing education. It is no wonder now that the seven-time Formula One champion, following in his father's footsteps, is using the power of his voice on a global platform for a lot of good causes.

The irony is that my father had a great attitude when it came to his friends, and he had many through his forays into KL with my godfather, Uncle Mathew, at the Coliseum Café or the Kairali Theatre.

It was not unusual for groups of people to drop by our house without notice. Their rapturous jaunts contributed greatly to my peripheral learning. I called them the Lucky Strike Brigade, for they puffed away through dissecting charismatic American president JFK, by far the most popular name to crop up, always mentioned with his elegant wife, Jacqueline; JFK's tussles with the Soviet Union's Nikita Khrushchev; Russia's space flight, its economic and arms assistance to Castro's Cuba; the way "our man" U Thant, the first non-European Secretary-General of the United Nations, weathered storms during the Cold War with his peacekeeping efforts...

One memorable Saturday, two Malay and two Chinese young men in gleaming red and blue roadster cars came hooting up, and Papa welcomed them with enthusiasm.

Mummy immediately busied herself. She was experienced in feeding unannounced relatives and friends, so the day's task was not bothersome.

In no time, lunch was served in her best Wedgwood china, brought out from their pride of place in our living-hall glass cupboard. Conversations were abrasive and centred on cinema, music, cricket and rugger. The Johnnie Walker Black Label and Martell VSOP cognac rounds brought out in-the-moment politics, activism and social criticism to the sound of Buddy Holly, Cliff Richard, the Drifters, the Shadows, Elvis, Chuck Berry – it was post-war British culture entering Malaya with panache and optimism!

The future was bright and the world was there for the taking; that's what the yuppie boys represented. With stars in my eyes, I took in their wild self-expression, stylish long chinos trousers, Lacoste long-sleeved shirts and Ray-Ban sunglasses. Before they left, the boys took me for a drive. The roaring sound of their engines as we sped along the estate road made me want a piece of that action, but, *it's all pie in the sky* whispered my darker side.

While my father enjoyed carousing with such company, he made it clear that was not what he wanted for his son. Passion got you nowhere. Good grades. *That* was the path to a brighter future, not wayward thoughts of adventure and badminton. That was for the boys of Hollywood. Not for an eastern boy stuck among rubber trees.

Nearing the end of primary school, a new subject called Civics was introduced for standard five and six pupils to take place once a week on the badminton courts.

# EDUCATION NEARLY COMPLETE

The combined pupils sat on the hard floor, knocking knees, with the clever ones in front positions, outcasts like me on the back heap.

Headmistress Mrs Richards would often take the class, with several teachers assisting her, to conduct a lesson on "how to be a good Malaysian", ending with general knowledge questions. This was the moment when I stood a fair chance at shining, thanks to cousin Rajan, his stories and his magazines.

I once caused the momentary subjugation of Mrs Richards when I was the only one who knew the tallest building in the world was the Empire State Building and that it had one hundred and two floors. Teachers and boys alike gaped, and Mrs Richards, only used to reprimanding me, grudgingly acknowledged my moment. I floated home.

That very afternoon, I cycled the five miles to Sedgley Estate to share my Empire State triumph with Rajan. Incidentally, it was information obtained from an article in his archive of *Playboys*. The Chinese shop owner in Kajang town would nip to the darkroom behind his curtain counter to bring out his precious goods and I'd often be allowed to join the "centrefold discussions" with Rajan and the older boys. Our education was going places!

My Uncle Mathew, I called him Sedgley Papa, was the Chief Clerk of Sedgley Estate, and they lived in a large two-storey house. After saying hello to Uncle and Aunty, I ran upstairs to Rajan's room, our hidey-hole's walls crowded by the Beatles, and where only Rajan and I knew where his *Playboys* were stashed. My cousin was a good student at the Kajang High School and harboured big plans to further his education in England.

The usual enthusiasm at seeing me was missing. 'Close the door. I want to tell you something.' My cousin's tone was weak. I did as I was told rather anxiously, because confident, friendly Rajan had never spoken in that way before.

It all came out in one spurt. Poor cousin Rajan had been spread on that very same bed, eyes fixed on a particularly alluring unclothed Playboy bunny when snap!, the door opened and his mother – my aunt really ought to have known better – instead of scooting, had stood there demanding to know what her son was doing!

All I could do was continue staring at the downcast face looking past me to John Lennon, as if seeking solace. I imagined Mummy catching me in a similar act and had immediate visions of jumping into Limau Manis's deep, dark pool, to never be found again.

I stayed on for what turned out to be a highly awkward dinner. Rajan might not even have been there. The spotlight was on me… how was school, how was I doing…? I led Aunty and Uncle to think I was a good pupil, feeling the heat behind my ears, knowing I was telling them porkies not to let the side down.

A few weeks later, during a heavy thunderstorm, the Civics lesson was moved to the school hall. This time, the lesson was conducted by Miss Vijaya, looking graceful in a slinky sari and sleeveless blouse.

'Can anyone tell me who Brigitte Bardot is?' She threw us the question.

My sessions with Rajan once again paid dividends. Up went my hand and I stood up without being asked.

'Yes, Philip. Do you know who she is?'

'Yes, Miss. She is a French sex goddess living in St Tropez, married to the film director Roger Vadim.'

Miss Vijaya showed no shock like Mrs Richards had, and remarked, 'Well done!' then, with a knowing smile, 'your education is nearly complete, Philip!'

I did not want the bell to end school. There was something in the wet air... In Miss Vijaya's loosely hanging nylon sari, I fancied Brigitte Bardot smiling seductively at me.

As a result of my prowess in Civics lessons, I was chosen for the school debating and quiz teams and, to my surprise, was even made a prefect in my final year of primary school. Who would've thought, as my academic performance remained dismal! Decades on, in England, when I brought up my "Bridget Bardot incident" in a very important speech, it elicited great laughter from an esteemed set of audience, and I received plentiful plaudits, with several commenting on Malaysia's quality of education during my time.

My last year in primary school ought to have ended on a high note. The National Schools Football Tournament was a prestigious annual event, with the final played in KL's historic Merdeka Stadium. It was a matter of great pride to be selected to represent the school, and naturally, I was on my school's team, playing centre forward. The team also included Bryan, Cyril and Aziz. Mr Balachandran was the coach, and the selection team included Mrs Richards and two other Ceylonese teachers, including Mr Nathan, whose brother was in the team and whose other relative was in the reserve team.

Right from the knockout stages, we were classed as the underdogs; yet, within three months, we had beaten all the major teams including the top seeds in the semi-finals. There were big celebrations in school and the whole team was feted. This lifted my confidence no end, and it was easily one of the happiest periods of my school life.

One week before the final, Masters Balachandran and Nathan called me up to drop a bombshell. It was a brief, blunt and brutal meeting where the dead-set duo told me I'd been dropped from the team to make way for Nathan's relative from the reserve team since "he was the better choice for the final".

I knew my worth on the team and my contribution towards making the final, but my convictions were not worth a thing to the unconcerned teachers. The fire imploding in me wanted to do a Muhammad Ali on the two right there and then. Instead, I walked away with a lifetime's scar. When I reported my devastation to Papa, hoping he'd be my hero and confront the two teachers on their unfair treatment of his son, I received a matter-of-fact 'Never mind, get on with your studies.'

From being a revered star player, I'd become the target of Bryan and Aziz's merciless taunts. I should have known better, but I was a spurned twelve-year-old sports-mad boy looking for desperate recourse. I complained to Mrs Richards and her assistant. Aghast at my temerity, they retained the decision of their comrades and I remained ostracised. The entire episode meant I would develop a dystopian view of the future and society as bereft of equality and fairness.

My school lost the final at Merdeka Stadium (I was a spectator!), but sweet revenge it was not, because, in my heart of hearts, I knew I could have prevented that defeat.

FOUR

# OUT OF REACH

The year I ended primary school coincided with the stylish 1964 Tokyo Olympics making history when all proceedings were shown live on television for the first time. It was an era when BBC commentators could get away with "a very pretty little girl" description of female athletes!

The first Asian country to host the historic games drove Malaysians to invest in televisions and devour sports pages of newspapers. My father had already invested in a black and white RCA television set.

The celebratory mood escalated when our man, the *Flying Doctor* and Asian Games gold medallist, began his heats. The stage was ready for Dr Mani Jegathesan to make

Malaysians rejoice. No Internet and WhatsApp to transmit the collective tensions of the nation, Jega ran his heart out ever so elegantly in the 200-metre race to become the first Malaysian to reach the semi-finals of an Olympic event. He did it in a national record time of 20.09 seconds.

That timing would stick in my head and reappear decades later while watching Michael Johnson live in Sydney and Usain Bolt in Rio doing miraculous timings in the same event.

For Malaysians of that generation, 20.09 remains an iconic run. Jega ran with style, lah!

How we clapped and roared, me and the Tamil boys from the labour lines, freshly bathed, shining side-parted hair pasted with coconut oil, wearing singlets, shorts, simple plastic shoes. Papa had moved his car out of the porch for the boys' backsides, where they sat cross-legged, leaning their necks to catch a glimpse of Jega's magical run, the same way we watched *Robin Hood, The Saint, Fugitive, Mission Impossible, Outer Limits*. The value of this early start to Indian postural methods – sitting cross-legged on hard ground for regular periods, the crossing of the legs with intertwined ankles – cannot be trivialised as I believe it helped my agility during badminton.

Academia continued to elude me, causing Papa ceaseless irritation. Progressing to the "right higher institution" mattered very much to him, and after six years of sports trophies and medals and Scout certificates not impressing him in the least, I was in no position to fulfil his ambition of graduating to the Ivy League of Malaysian secondary education.

To shore up my chances, it had been arranged for Mummy and me to take the train to Singapore to look into my breathing difficulties... our southern neighbour possessed the X-ray machine which would correctly diagnose my problem. So felt Papa.

We were to stay with my mother's Kumbanad family, so the prospect was all the more daunting for me because of my cousin Sunny Thomas. The trip was ostensibly to improve my health, but I knew my father was hoping my getting to know Sunny Thomas would motivate me to turn sports medallions into academic scrolls.

I found this connivance confusing because Papa was all about giving me exposure, taking me to watch badminton at Kampung Attap, wrestling at Chin Woo Stadium, Holiday on Ice at Stadium Negara or Asian Cup football at Merdeka Stadium. Yet, he would not hear of me wanting to be a professional badminton player.

Sunny Thomas and I were of the same age and he was also an expert badminton player, but there stopped our similarities.

'Top scholar at the *Raffles Institution*. Doubtless, he's going to be *somebody* in society.' Papa drilled the message over frosty meal lectures. *Be like the brilliant Sunny Thomas* was the insane goal to pursue. With that frightful order, I began the evening berth train journey from Jalan Reko in Kajang to Singapore, thankfully, with my more accommodating parent.

Singapore turned out to be a strangely pleasant outing. The X-ray cleared me of ill health and I abandoned all reason to hold my *Raffles Institution* cousin in awe. Big and tall, Sunny must've thought me easy pickings, for he, fortunately, chose to challenge not my academic prowess but my badminton!

He might have misjudged this book by its cover, but he was magnanimous in defeat, and the upshot of that trip was that both of us bonded over badminton and long runs on the stretch of Changi Beach that would one day be reclaimed for the building of Singapore's Changi International Airport.

In a way, the Sunny Thomas episode taught me to stand up for myself – the only game in town for one who avoids the low-hanging fruits.

Back in Prang Besar, Papa was too deep in his own troubles to grind me down, having crashed his Morris Minor into a rubber tree at the edge of the road along Serdang, following frolics with Sedgley Papa at KL's then-notorious Coliseum Café.

The accident was serious enough to damage Papa's body somewhat; his car and image rather more, and I suspect, quite irreparably, Mummy's heart. This family "mess" gave me unexpected respite from Papa's scrutiny, which I spent visiting my Chinese friends in Kajang town, checking out the convent girls, and cycling between estates to Sedgley, although relations between our family elders had turned sour.

On days when the sky was intensely luminous, I'd cruise to Limau Manis to bask in its magic – my favourite memory of free and optimistic Malaya. Never could I have imagined Limau Manis's miles of unbroken jungle, wild boar-trodden hills and gullies, landmark rivers and peculiarly contorted trees to be traded for haze-veiled skies.

The way I handled studies and with my spirit of living on the edge, if I was starting again in present-day Malaysia, I would not have been able to escape the cage Papa, my teachers, the church and my Malayali clan were erecting around me.

Liberal Malaya was kind and forgiving and afforded me that freedom with her egalitarian provision of recognising my badminton talent on merit, irrespective of my perceived pigmentation problem or my god's validity. I've watched the erosion of Malaysia's charm: drifting from Tunku's assimilationist policies to the framing of institutionalised norms and policies aimed at segregation and subjugation, not unlike our colonial masters' racial discrimination, favouring rule of law facilitating the empire's survival.

My school is now a totally different construction. It looks utterly befuddling, like one is in deep Iran or Saudi Arabia. I no longer recognise it, let alone feel any of its founding ethos. Like the rotted log over a rushing river that makes you wonder if it can take your weight, the Malaysian dilemma leaves me wondering how long before the log crumbles… hopefully for a stronger bridge to emerge.

My memories and sense of attachment to Malaysia still hold up more than half a century after leaving the country. I can still smell Kajang so clearly and with great fondness, and for better or for worse, I remain faithful to the Limau Manis spirit that I most associate with my Malayan experiences.

In the wake of my tumultuous primary education and the "stupid boy" bogey conjured up by Papa lurking in my head, it was time to face my father again. Healed from the accident, he was determined to get me into only *the best of institutions*. Kajang High School was well below par in his eyes. It was Victoria Institution or the Royal Military College; all others did not meet his mark. It didn't help my cause that several of the front-row boys had already made it.

Being the shrewd operator, he got his contacts to do their bit and arranged for me to be seen by the principals of both Ivy League schools. I failed miserably to impress either man.

The drive back home after each failed interview felt never-ending, the atmosphere a thousand shades of grief, the doom on my father's face making me wish I could set up permanent camp in Limau Manis.

I was so alive to my anxieties, knowing my father was tortured by the gap between his ideals of a firstborn son and my reality. The pariah treatment meted out to me in the weeks following was not of the ruining-your-mood kind; it was of a type that damaged my self-esteem, causing me to be intensely self-critical, and would have serious drawbacks when I was studying law or appearing in court.

I entered Kajang High School hoping the large building on the soft hill, with its smart-looking big boys, impeccable grounds and, hopefully, kinder teachers, would assuage my resentment of school. The excitement of getting into high-school gear, a white shirt over white shorts, carrying my new 1964 Tokyo Olympics white holdall bag, and the thought of exploring all of my new school's sports facilities raised my spirits.

Papa might not have had a big impression of Kajang High School, but I walked into its hallowed grounds a proud boy, fired up to do justice to the school's motto on my red metal badge: *Labor Omnia Vincit* (Work Conquers All). I felt ready to scale a mountain!

The school's main building fronted the compound where morning assembly took place, and its supporting structures spread across beautiful patches of greenery, including the sports field, with football posts, rugger posts and hockey goals, encircled by a 400-metre grass running track. At the edge of the field stood a tree looking taller than our town's tallest building, the Shaw picture house. With its meandering branches and luxuriant foliage, it faced the main road leading southwards to Singapore via the causeway.

My classroom was on a separate hill, sloping down to an unbarricaded jungle. Connecting the hill was a steep covered corridor with steps flanked by smooth cement surfaces providing daredevil bobsleigh tracks for delinquents like me, much to the annoyance of Mummy, who had to clean or do remedial work to my white uniform, not to mention deal with the occasional broken bone or friction burns to one's backside.

I was placed in Form 1D, the last class. A nice change from primary school was that we had different teachers for each subject, providing me with some breathing space as I was no longer under one hawk-eyed class teacher tormenting me the whole year.

I immediately took to Mr Kuan, the Physical Education teacher, whose enthusiasm and knowledge of sports bowled me over. He knew of my involvement with Shell and encouraged me to carry on playing on the school courts, even with the senior badminton team consisting of sixteen- and seventeen-year-old boys, although I was only thirteen.

The only exception among the faculty of generally kind teachers was Maths teacher Mr Shiva, who was also the hockey coach. Tall and fit, a stern expression plastered on his Lee Van Cleef face, Mr Shiva had a go at me at the outset for some minor transgression. It would not be our only clash.

Childhood bullies faded away. I became close friends with classmates Chong See Lin, who'd progressed from a Chinese primary, and the boy with the James Dean haircut and a drum kit he played à la Ringo Starr, Tan Toh Aik, with whom I did not have a great friendship in primary school, but Kajang High School changed that. Both boys were kings of Jalan Sulaiman and knew Kajang town inside out, so it was good for me to know the local politics and how the land lay. The Malay boys too became friendly, as I was a badminton star.

Aided and abetted by badminton and the company of my Jalan Sulaiman Chinese friends, I started to develop a bugger-the-consequences attitude. During this time, I had an added freedom card: I no longer took the estate school bus.

Papa allowed me to travel in the Chinese-owned Sum public bus from Prang Besar to the Kajang main bus station. Unlike the school bus, the Sum stopped at various spots along the town, estates and *kampungs*, collecting Indian, Malay and Chinese schoolchildren on its way, making each journey a polyglot chaos of chatting and swearing in Malay, English, Cantonese, Mandarin and Tamil.

It was thrilling to visit new friends in their *kampung* houses; the Malay girls were particularly elegant and certainly knew their effect on teenage boys! It wasn't long before Papa got wind of my wide friendship circle and I was immediately subjected to the *stay away from Malay/Muslim girls unless you're looking forward to circumcision and a life of not being allowed to bury your infidel parents* table talk! Delivered in dead seriousness in that hypothetical context, Papa's message has stayed with me.

In the 1960s, there was only one place for the Chinese, Indians and Malays alike to go to in Kajang. Mui Suan Kopitiam was a very special place in my growth.

The aroma of Mui Suan's Hainanese coffee strained through stocking-like bags, golden-brown *kaya* spread over crispy buttered toast, thick tails of green *chendol* on shaved ice, onion-filled *sambal* on steam-releasing coconut *pandan* rice for the most delicious *nasi lemak* – all doing fierce combat with the smell of dirty open drains and night-soil bucket toilets wafting around the town – epitomise the Kajang of my story.

As I arrived on the seven o'clock morning bus, I would often scramble to buy *nasi lemak* from Mui Suan before walking the fifteen minutes to school, enjoying the fragrance emanating from the warm packets wrapped in banana leaf and old newspaper. Once at school, I'd sell them to my classmates for a tidy profit to fund my naughty activities.

Mui Suan was the only shop in town with a jukebox – with speakers fastened to its ceiling and an adjoining tree – where ten cents got you the Shadows or a soothing Teresa Teng track. After-school escapades at Mui Suan were like the movie *Grease* as the girls from the convent school became part of the scene. Sandy Olsson for me was Evelyn Chan.

I was easily the best at English song selection because of my exposure to all things west through Rajan, the school library, Radio Malaysia's English network and my parents, who never missed any major movie release. Papa started allowing me to go on cinema trips to KL with my friends, and I particularly enjoyed trips with Rajeevan. We'd go in his elder brother Krishnan's car to watch big boy movies like *The Graduate, To Sir with Love, Dr No*. Ursula Andress! My initiation into semi-manhood was through the French black-and-white film *A Man and a Woman*, a classy film, and an even classier soundtrack, which planted in me the dream of adventuring in Europe.

On Saturdays, I was never home until dinner time. Before the roosters could alert the estate, I'd be cycling to town to compete in various "*mahjong* badminton" competitions (challenges with money at stake). It was not unusual for the whole of Kajang's Chinese youth to turn up at the Kajang Badminton Hall for a betting match. I was always the only Indian.

I cannot forget the time my senior Joseph Liu challenged another Chinese player from St John's KL to a duel. My guy wagered on beating his opponent in under five in both sets – a brag I too emulated. Both boys put $10 each into a hat handed over to me for safe custody, and I was also asked to call out the score, placing immediate pressure on me. It felt like a Clint Eastwood vs Lee Van Cleef Colt .45 duel!

Joseph, unfortunately, could not handle the pressure and only won 15-8, 15-4, and the St John's boy collected the $20 I begrudgingly handed out. The very next year, I was ranked with Joseph and another senior as the top three in the senior squad and began feeling a form of security from my primary school demons.

My parents weren't aware of my trysts with *mahjong* badminton, and I was careful not to show off my fighter's loot. It did not, however, stop me from splashing my winnings on my friends at Mui Suan.

Sadly, Mui Suan has not survived the ravages of development.

*Everything here now shopping complexes. All your photos memories of our schooldays dating convent school girls. At the ABC stall. School holidays at your house after 10.00 pm the generator stopped. Off to bed, I miss your mother's breakfast. Variety. Before bed 1 glass of milk remember!* Chong Si Lin, 2021, WhatsApp message.

From the start, it was made clear my class belonged to the underachiever's list – not future doctors, engineers, lawyers, accountants, earmarked to become pillars of Malaysian society. As a direct result, the education dished out to us "weaker" boys was relayed in a more relaxed manner, which worked out very well for me.

I became more conversational with my teachers and started to ask questions without fear of being ridiculed. Conversation of the day with my gang and even with amenable teachers of the science labs was trivia-ridden:

Which is the best TV in the world? RCA! I broke out impulsively to Mr Gomez.

Who held the world land speed record? Donald Campbell in his Bluebird went my answer to Mr Gomez again.

Who was the motor car Grand Prix champion? Jim Clark.

Which car won the Monte Carlo rally? Mini 1275 GT.

One other reason I could hold court with teachers and the front row was the Low Ti Kok library, named after the rich Chinese tin miner and rubber planter recognised for his benevolent funds to Kajang High School. Being on the top floor of the main building, the library offered the best view of the school's sprawling green landscape, making it a thoroughly enjoyable place to be. It became my sanctuary, where I could allow my brain and inner self to wander at their own pace, accumulating what Papa labelled "unwanted knowledge".

I certainly did not go to the library to improve my academic record, because I did not know how to use it for that purpose. That would happen much later in England when a law professor cajoled a shot of enthusiasm in me: 'My dear Philip, you are here not to purely gain a degree but to learn how to learn.'

I wish someone had said that to me back in Kajang High School! But that is not to say I value my bond with the Low Ti Kok library any less. It was well stocked with serious worldly magazines such as *Pathé News*, *Life*, *London Weekly Illustrated* and *World Atlas*, which covered people, cinema, music, travel, sports, politics and world leaders and personalities, even Che Guevara. Can't imagine that in today's Malaysia!

Nevertheless, such peripheral information was lost on teachers rigidly handcuffed to academic excellence… teachers only interested in producing *men to be held in reverence*, not one like me who would go on to track down Che Guevara's *Motorcycle Diaries* trail in Argentina.

In a big moment for me, Coach Chan entered me for a tournament at the purpose-built Kampung Attap SBA (Selangor Badminton Hall), with its impressive trophy cabinet in the foyer, high ceiling, solid wood parquet flooring and wooden spectator benches.

As I entered the main hall, the Selangor Senior Championship final was just ending, and national shuttler candidate James Selvaraj was playing Richard Samuels. The swish of rackets and the squish of sports shoes as they stroked and smashed the shuttle is a permanently stored memory in my head – more so because both players came over to wish me good luck, saying they'd heard about me through the Shell sponsorship programme.

Imagine then my frustration when I couldn't make my father see it was badminton that made my heart beat the fastest, and all I longed for was the opportunity to go all out and give it a shot – something I'd talk about at length in the future with the iconic All England champion Prakash Padukone of India. Being Indian, he understood.

Papa would not hear of me missing church, no matter how important a tournament was, and I won't forget one particularly bitter Sunday. After standing for three hours of service, we proceeded to the adjoining hall where an auction was to take place. It was all orderly and subdued until the final item went on offer. *The Last Supper* of Christ print picture came on display to stir the congregation of around seventy because it sparked a bidding war between Papa and PM Cherian. Both the Prang Besar Estate stalwarts were unflinching and primed for a cock fight.

Having witnessed it before with my relatives during my India trip, I became agitated and embarrassed. Mummy too. The bids far outreached the reserve price. Both men's masks of civility were all but gone. Voices boomed and fingers were pointing, punctuated by gasps from the congregation. There was no hero, no villain, just two petulant egos fighting to establish dominance.

Salvation came in the raised voice of the visiting bishop from Kottayam, Kerala. Crowds huddled in groups watched as the man in the white gown brought the two proud characters to heel, confiscated the picture for the church hall and made both pay the sums of their substantial bids. On the drive home, I could not help thinking it served my father right for what he was doing to my badminton. I was also determined to get far, far away from that typical Malayali avarice.

I remain grateful that sport was a fundamental part of education at Kajang High School. Other than badminton,

I excelled in hockey, cross-country running, sprinting and middle-distance running.

My reputation as a Shell-sponsored shuttler wasn't missed, and I became part of the inner sanctum of the older boys who looked out for me. The whole school, especially the big boys, used to watch me from the corridors and verandahs when I played on the centre court below... it felt like being on the floor of the Coliseum in Rome!

My fortunes, however, would oscillate. The Maths and hockey master Mr Shiva, who'd long decided I wasn't one of his type of boys, was waiting for the right provocation to "put me in my place". He had only grudgingly selected me for his hockey team because I was good at right wing and a natural goal poacher. It wasn't hard to see Mr Lee Van Cleef was just waiting to pull the trigger on me.

In preparation for the annual sports day, Mr Shiva was giving us march-past practice in typical regiment style every morning to the music of *Colonel Bogey* (wildly famous after its outing in the film *Bridge on the River Kwai*). To fine tune it to a higher level, he ordered all five sports houses to meet at three o'clock on the school field, two hours after the end of school.

My position in the yellow house march team was like the pawn on a chessboard, of little importance. After school one day, since I had two hours to kill, I went to the Kajang Badminton Hall where my school seniors were playing St John's Institution's seniors. The moment Mr Kuan saw me, he asked me to play second singles in place of a boy suffering from nerves. I agreed with no second thought thinking I could get back to school in time for the march-past practice, although I did make mention of it to Mr Kuan.

I still remember his cool response: 'Badminton match is more important. Forget the march-past. I'll speak to Shiva.'

I won the important singles and set my school on the train to beat St John's, a great win over the KL school and one of prestige. It was too big a win not to stay back for the post-tournament celebration, in the course of which Mr Shiva and march-past did not feature.

Midway through History lesson the following day Mr Shiva strode into my classroom, had words with the teacher, Mr Gill, and announced to the class, 'Philip George has let the school down.'

Mr Shiva then frogmarched me to headmaster Mr Yeoh's office and, following a haughty description of my "crime", he requested Mr Yeoh summarily expel me from school! I was not sure if I correctly understood Mr Shiva; I felt I was getting out of my depth. Expulsion for missing *one* march-past practice?

The headmaster at least gave me the chance to explain, and when he'd heard me out, he summoned for Mr Kuan. Mr Kuan flew to my aid, explaining my part in winning a tournament for the school.

Seeing that Mr Kuan was succeeding in convincing the headmaster, Shiva interfered with 'Boys must be taught your word is your bond. This one let his side down,' at which point the two sports masters worked themselves into a fury. The vituperative outburst trailed on, and as if sensing a fistfight around the corner, Mr Yeoh stepped in.

The headmaster's verdict was a compromise. He declined the expulsion request and instead ordered a public caning. Ten times with a rattan cane in front of the whole school at assembly the following day. And, a week of detention class to write two thousand lines of *I will attend the march-past practice.*

Expulsion would have been the end of my world. I couldn't even imagine its effect on my family or my future. I limped out of the headmaster's office demented and fragile at the prospect of the news reaching my father and the colossal embarrassment I was going to be subjected to. I didn't care about the form one and two boys. They were used to seeing me receiving the cane. It was being humiliated in front of my adored senior mentors that caused me to sleep on a damp pillow that night.

I have now lived long enough to have known many sorrows – have done foolish things in my personal and professional life, made stupid decisions and lost loved ones, all of which have contributed to my disposition. I think I have built a healthy relationship with failure.

That public caning – meted out with vengeance by Shiva – was certainly a defining moment. More than the pain from the caning, the weeks of cowering and floundering in a panic left me broken. By surviving its emotional impact, I guaranteed myself a chance to fight another round. There was one other consolation: the news did not reach my father. Papa was having his own battles with the establishment. Mackintosh in particular.

FIVE

# STILL I RISE

'd wolf down my rice, head to my bedroom, place a candle and matchbox on standby near my transistor radio and catch enough shut-eye before BBC Radio's live coverage began. It was the 1966 Jules Rimet FIFA World Cup, hosted by England. I was rooting for Pelé and Brazil to create history.

It would be around midnight. The estate and jungles weren't as still as my house and I was thankful for nature's soundtrack. Radio in one arm, free hand slapping mosquitoes following me into the lacy net cascading over my double-decker bed, I'd clamber to the top bunk to make doubly sure my radio's gurgles did not reach my parents.

Nestled in the corner against the bedpost, radio angled to one shoulder, I heard how poor Pelé was kicked and brutally tackled... preventing the great man and Brazil from becoming three times in a row World Cup champions.

It was collective devastation for me and everyone I knew – how could Brazil miss another chance? We moped, me especially. I took Brazil's defeat personally enough to contemplate skipping further live coverage!

Rajan's magazines attributed Brazil's 1966 loss to the *complexo de vira-lata* (street dog/inferiority complex) – it wasn't a topic I could discuss with my Kajang friends but cousin Rajan for sure. Rajan, whose excitement was growing by the month as he prepared to leave for his dream England to further his education. His "calling" was getting louder, he kept saying, making me wonder when mine was going to leave the port.

Brazil's departure made the rest of the tournament sterile, but the attraction was still too much, and it wasn't just the power of the World Cup. I had become sensitive to the masterclass commentaries that took me right there to Wembley, letting me hear the roars, see Willie the cartoon lion mascot and feel the energies, much the same way I consumed music or dramas from my little transistor friend.

I continued my pursuit in the dark right up to the England vs West Germany final, until the BBC's Kenneth Wolstenholme, upon Geoff Hurst's response to the home crowd's *we want three* chants, came up with the famous refrain: 'Some people are on the pitch. They think it's all over... *IT IS NOW!*' to the background chorus of *we've won the cup*!

The Jules Rimet trophy was presented by the Queen and received by the King (of stoicism) – young, beautiful Elizabeth II to England's captain marvel, Bobby Moore, who remembered to wipe his hands before accepting his destiny.

To mark England's victory, there were big celebrations in the closed quarters of Prang Besar Estate, and all of a sudden, Bobby Moore's West Ham Football Club gained tremendous popularity in Malaysia.

All over the country, even more boys took to the *padang* with the same fervour they picked up badminton rackets – a few months before that 1966 World Cup, my badminton idol Tan Aik Huang had won the prestigious All England badminton championship at Wembley Arena. A match I watched live on television with Papa. Tall, lean Tan Aik Huang was a very stylish, elegant player with every part of his body in perfect alignment when stroking the shuttle or jump smashing. What a halcyon period it was for Malaysian badminton!

I began form three on a shifty note. Cheerful and free in the company of friends or when playing competitive sports; firewood beatings and *rotan* marks running across my face also a common occurrence.

I learnt it was pointless to complain whenever I was unfairly or unkindly treated, like not getting a chance to play cricket for school, as it was a Ceylonese fortress under Shiva's and Nathan's grip. I used to think my character and behaviour must be the explanation for the parental and authority disapproval I constantly faced… it had to be my fault.

Like the way I wanted Pele to rise again after the unfair attacks crushed his chances in the 1966 World Cup, I put my energy into ensuring my body was ever ready for peak performance, especially with that year's Sports Day approaching. I was entered in several events and was desperate for a good pair of running spikes. Although I had money saved up from my badminton "gambles", I couldn't very well reveal that to my parents.

As luck would have it, I was to benefit from our large extended Malayali clan stretching from the north of the peninsula in Penang Island to right past the causeway in Singapore. My Uncle Komatt in Penang was taken ill and since Papa couldn't go, he arranged a driver for our car to take Mummy and me to visit him.

Be it Penang or Singapore, there were always family members I adored or loathed in equal measure. Suffice to say, I was glad we were visiting cool Uncle Komatt, who'd studied in England and done parachute jumping and whose wife was ostracised by the rest of our church for being an Anglican!

I also had the secret motive of coaxing my mother into buying me a pair of spikes since I knew this nice sports shop in Ipoh town, our regular midway lunch stop when northward bound.

On that trip, Ipoh's very famous steamed chicken rice could not compete with my brand-new running spikes, which I clung to right up to the journey's end. Uncle Komatt wasn't doing too badly, which meant I could excuse myself for a run in my new shoes along Penang Hill where his house stood. *My mind took over; it raced well ahead of my body. I felt that a moment of a lifetime had come*, said Roger Bannister!

Back in school, I would go on practice runs around the running track in my new shoes, to scoffs from the front-row boys in no position to understand that the spikes and my rackets were my slow burners, instilling gradual confidence in me.

On Sports Day, I woke up feeling queasy, having only partially recovered from undiagnosed pain in my left pelvic area. On that all-important morning, I would learn that physical strength and endurance are only part of the story.

Tee-shirt damp in sweat, I arrived at school to a buzz of activity. The general consensus was approval: large temporary open-plan tent with an aluminium roof to accommodate dignitaries and guests, cold Milo refreshment for manic boys representing the five sports houses, solid wooden podium marked 1,2,3 next to a medal-laden table, band music, immaculately laid green turf, smartly turned-out teachers, anxious PE teachers and athletes and, most importantly, amicable sports weather, with not a cloud to blemish the intensely blue sky.

Dignitaries from the State of Selangor included the Chief Guest of Honour, the Sultanah of Selangor. Seated with them were the faculty and invited parents, including, to my embarrassment, Papa and Mummy, as it felt like an invasion of my privacy.

Sports masters on high alert, PE staff congregated around the circumference of the field, speeches over, march-past boys ready, it was finally the "let the games begin" moment.

The loudspeakers went silent, as did the guests and noisy stampeding boys. The *Colonel Bogey March* broke out to loud cheers and we marched smartly past adoring crowds under Shiva's *This is war! This is not a game of cricket!* scrutiny.

The first event was the 800 metres track race, my favourite event. The tense mood at the starting line was shared by ten nervous faces, me included, in my unbranded Ipoh spikes, and, niggling pain. Shiva was the start judge. After the customary *get set, ready* followed by two seconds' delay, he fired the start pistol.

From the smell of the gunpowder, Johari, Abu Bakar and Elangovan elbowed me to gain space and set off at pace. Tactically inept, I found myself in the middle of the pack and off position. At 600 metres, I fell further behind and was sixth, well out of a medal position. At that moment, I went for broke and summoned my third wind – thank you, Coach Chan! To the roars and whistles of the crowd, I started overtaking one by one and suddenly the pain completely vanished. With fifty metres to go, I was in third place with enough in the tank to summon that elusive fourth wind. I kicked away and edged Johari and Elangovan to chest the tape in first place... with exhilaration normally reserved for winning badminton matches or reaching the top of a very tall tree!

I might have been overwhelmed with exhaustion and emotion, yet, through watery eyes, I searched. It wasn't parental approval I looked for. The one face I wanted to see was that of the man who sliced my buttocks and dignity so publicly, so cruelly. To show him we all have our struggles and strengths, and really don't need any judging or fault-finding as we travel our individual journeys. That, of course, applied to my father and my clan too, who'd even rather resort to burdening poor Jesus unnecessarily than accepting their children for what they are. Much for them to learn from Mrs Moore, the England captain Bobby Moore's mother, known to iron her son's bootlaces before football games.

The Sultanah of Selangor, in a stylish Jackie Kennedy-type sleeveless dress and bouffant, shook my hand and placed the gold medal around my neck. The royal was accompanied by the headmaster – and Mr Shiva. The school clapped and cheered. Papa and Mummy watched with lukewarm pride. Shiva and I locked eyes for what I believe was a moment of truth.

That Sunday, following service and a good dose of gossip at the St Mary Syrian Orthodox Church, Papa drove us to the famous Gobi's South Indian Tamil restaurant in Brickfields, an experience I always looked forward to. It served the best banana leaf meal in town and I still hanker over it, despite having tried the same in many star-studded Indian restaurants in the west.

Papa parked his Austin Cambridge right outside the restaurant and Mr Gobi himself came out from his busy schedule. '*Vanakkam*, please come,' he greeted us, palms pressed together, walking us to a wooden table with plastic chairs.

Within seconds, large fresh banana leaves, tapered ends on the left side, were placed in front of each of us, along with ever-silver tumblers for boiled water. This was followed by a contingent of four-member staff serving us dishes in order: rice from a bucket using a plate as a scoop, a *thali* tray with an assortment of Indian vegetables and yoghurt, another bucket with *sambar* (pouring utensil devised from coconut shell), followed by another chapter on a tray with fried masala fish and mutton. The combined aroma made my stomach growl, but I knew the etiquette of traditional Indian dining.

As the waiters hustled piping hot food onto our leaves, we went in pairs to wash our hands in a communal washbasin next to an odorous Indian-style toilet adjoining it. Back with wet fingers, I tucked in straight away, making a serious sensual connection with my lunch, licking the dripping gravy to avoid it flowing onto my long-sleeved shirt. It was all washed down with vermicelli and gram dhal *payasam*, the hot liquid dessert poured onto the same leaf for some deft slurping. When we finished, the banana leaf "plates" were rolled top-down (the opposite way for sombre occasions) into a cylinder for the staff to clear and deposit in the backyard for the compost heap.

Another memorable eatery Papa would take me to was this Sikh-owned ramshackle tin shed chapati place by the railway sidings, a stone's throw from KL's landmark Moorish Central railway station. The no-name joint only had four medium-sized tables with two chairs per table and was always filled with proud Sikh warrior types in colourful turbans and with long majestic beards.

The food, like Gobi's, was incomparable, and they

would surface every time I tried artisanal Indian fare in the west. It was exactly the case the time I was in Greenwich Village, Manhattan, sitting next to the actors Diane Keaton and Goldie Hawn raving about an artichoke speciality on offer at MIMI. If they only knew where my mind was at the time – golden *sambar* atop piping hot rice, pure ghee-infused soft chapatis, Sikh warriors...

Saturday remained big on my social roster. After badminton, it was off to meet Chong See Lin then Tan Toh Aik, who lived above a shop and entertained us with his extensive drum kit. Unannounced, we would call on Evelyn Chan's house and persuade her to join us at the jukebox bar. That I was sweet on Evelyn was common knowledge. It was a respectful relationship, reflective of the period. I worshipped the ground she walked on, madly in love in that boyish way, not wanting to drop my guard, playing James Dean, yet at the same time very attentive, on listening mode to catch small moments. I enjoyed her company at the doorstep of her father's shop in Jalan Sulaiman, outside the convent school, or when I walked her home or met her outside the cinema before catching a Saturday matinee when no badminton.

It was all a mental experience and requesting *Sugar Sugar* on the South Pacific Radio station (so teachers found out too!) and listening to John Lennon spout his Jesus Christ moment with Yoko Ono, staging their bed-in for peace in Amsterdam. The stir I caused among the boys when I brought my very pretty girlfriend to the school for a film I'd organised through the school's cinema club! I remember it all like it was yesterday... the same way I can never forget how one incident changed the lives of an entire family so very dear to me.

A severe rift had developed between Papa and Sedgley Papa, and from being extremely close, ties were broken just like that. It made not any difference to me. I continued to visit them despite strict warnings not to and remained on the same terms with the Sedgley family, especially with cousin Rajan.

I was getting ready for school one day when I overheard Papa telling Mummy in a concerned tone there'd been a serious robbery at Rajan's house. It caused havoc in my mind and I made the easy decision to play truant. On the bus, I kept seeing Rajan's two-storey colonial house guarded by a rifled security guard on watch each night.

There were policemen and detectives tramping the vast property when I arrived. Scattered locals were peering through fence holes. Pushing past a thick crowd at the front gate, I explained to the policeman on guard that I was a relative, and was thankful to be allowed in.

The relief was mutual when I met the family huddled in the living room. Between grief and tears, I heard it all. Sometime after midnight, four masked men had broken into the bungalow, having poisoned their Alsatian and muffled and gagged the guard. The family was hustled and tied up and in under an hour, the robbers had vanished, after making a clean sweep of cash, gold, jewellery and other valuables.

I couldn't offer any words of consolation to my traumatised relatives, all bearing bruises on their wrists and legs, with Sedgley Papa sporting sore marks on his face too.

As news of the robbery spread, the story grew, and set off a chain of events to bring down the mightily proud Sedgley family that had at one time rejected the Syrian Orthodox Church Sedgley Papa had helped build with Papa and the others. It was all some of the church congregation needed to start the uncharitable "God's way of bringing them to heel" rhetoric, piling even more misery on the family.

Our families patched up soon after, but Sedgley Papa died of a sudden heart attack in the early part of the following year. Much to the anger of Papa and the others, I decided to miss the funeral as I had an important badminton tournament in Penang. On my own, I prayed for the Sedgley family's pain to be lessened, and asked for forgiveness for deciding to let my heart speak its own religion. After all, hadn't I also on occasion hated the institution for forcing me to be in the pews instead of the badminton court?

Rajan's Senior Cambridge result was not up to par; that combined with a lack of funds due to the robbery and his father passing away forced him to abandon his England dream. It was decided India was the only option for him, a country he did not like, being terribly anglicised in his ways. I was there at Subang International Airport to bid him farewell, to be cut off from him for years, leaving a deep vacuum in my life.

In 1967, I sat for and passed the mandatory LCE (Lower Certificate Examination), a feat many saw as against the odds. It was my good fortune the education board introduced multiple-choice questions that year.

With my improving peripheral knowledge, I was able, through a process of shrewd elimination, to arrive roughly at the correct answers!

Papa was not bothered if it was due to strategy or pure luck that I cleared the LCE; he was that pleased. The same day I received my results, a salesman from the Universal Library Company arrived at our doorstep and succeeded in sweet-talking Papa, normally a shrewd buyer, into purchasing a whole volume of the expensive Universal Library Encyclopaedia set, including two comprehensive volumes of the *Oxford Universal Dictionary*. By the next morning, all Prang Besar knew of his purchase and by afternoon, all my friends in school.

'No match for the *Encyclopaedia Britannica*,' teased the front row. The teasing did not bother me. Nonetheless, my father's gift to me for passing the LCE did come at a great cost.

The long-running animosity between Papa and Mackintosh was in essence a competition based on pride, with my father refusing to cow to his colonial master. KP George wore his pedigree on his proud face and had the valour to support it. There was much about Britain and the west he admired and incorporated into his life, but there was also much about the English's divide-and-rule scheme he would not condone. Papa would not decry the east and exalt the west, for he was fully aware of his worth and genuinely believed in a balanced social system.

He must also have known of its pitfalls, yet chose to live his life on his terms, always the leading actor. Once, he booked seven premium tickets for our family for the touring *Holiday on Ice* show at the Stadium Negara. When we got there, the organisers deliberately "misallocated" our original seats close to the Royal Box, to some insignificant area of the stadium to accommodate a Malay family that had walked in without making reservations. There was quite a rumpus when Papa refused to give an inch, resulting in an uproar, in the presence of royalty!

The situation was only placated with the intervention of the King's aides. The Malay family were moved to another part of the stadium and we sat in our rightful seats, with state-of-the-art air conditioning on each handle. I was embarrassed at the time with all the unwanted attention we were attracting. Yet today, I draw sustenance from my father's courage and élan in facing injustice with so much self-assurance.

Papa's defiant and cavalier approach did not go unnoticed – not with my father doing things like hiring a Cessna plane upon the launch of Subang International Airport in 1965 so he could take his family on an hour's circumnavigation over Prang Besar Estate!

Another of Papa's traits was his distinct sartorial choices, normally the preface of the Home Counties. It was like a red rag to a bull all the way: Mackintosh had a Ford Prefect, no match for Papa's Austin Cambridge. Papa rode out in his AJS and Norton motorcycles, seizing the imagination of the labourer classes. He bought the RCA television before Mackintosh, he owned Omega and Rolex watches, spent holidays in India, Singapore and Penang, was a regular at the Coliseum Café, took Mummy to catwalk fashion shows and the Miss Malaysia pageant, shopped at Robinson's... These weren't things the non-English classes were expected to do, and my father was none too discreet at that!

The camel's back broke around the time Papa made the outrageous purchase (Universal Library Encyclopaedia set), paying a lump sum for it at that. After watching and waiting for his moment, Mackintosh demoted Papa. KP George was made to understand he wasn't just deserving of punishment but also responsible for it, and was to be transferred to Galloway Estate, a backwater in comparison to Prang Besar Estate.

## SIX

# RUMBLE IN THE JUNGLE

'I'm sorry about that caning…' The words whispered into my ear made my day – and year!

I was sixteen and ending my academic year in form four, that grand high school year when boys who got through the LCE earned their stripes to wear long white trousers to school. Receiving confirmation that the headmaster had been on my side made me all the more proud that I was part of the social committee organising Mr Yeoh Teng Khoo's farewell. He was ending his service to Kajang High School, in 1968.

Mr Yeoh added a final sweet hurrah with another confession: 'I know Shiva was not fair; he'll receive his due.'

Sydney Poitier, he was perhaps not, but it was that era and we cheerfully performed a very upbeat *To Sir with Love* for Mr Yeoh. And in keeping with the script, we gave him a leaving present and requested a parting speech. For me, he'd already delivered it in my ear and to my heart for posterity.

To speeches, fun, laughter, a tinge of sadness, music, and even more singing, Kajang High's main hall celebrated the great headmaster… in due course swelling with Paul McCartney's fade-out of all fade-outs *na na na na na na naaa…*

All very different to how I'd begun form four!

At the start of the year, I thought Mackintosh and the burglars at Rajan's had robbed me of 1968. After my father was given the letter, Mackintosh's diplomatic posturing did nothing to ease the gloom felt by the George household. Having been dislodged, KP George was told he would be "on par of manager level to the respect of a hundred and fifty labour lines" in his new posting at the Galloway Estate. But we knew what everyone knew. It was no secret that Galloway offered little prestige or privilege. Nothing to be gained by its association. Not the same glory as declaring one worked in vast, visible, thriving Prang Besar Estate.

We packed our belongings and bid our farewells with anger, disappointment, sadness and anxiety… feelings that still burn in me when I operate in the west. Like my father during the Stadium Negara incident, I will give no quarter if right is with me. With my constant dwelling on history, knowledge of the law and holding the freedom of speech with the Human Rights Act as my anchor, I will take anyone on. This is the parody of KP George.

Galloway Estate lay in the sleepy Dengkil district, a proper rural backwater, too tranquil and altogether too depressing for my family, especially for Papa. It was clear to see the downgrade was sinking his flamboyance and vitality; there was not the same girth he possessed bossing about Prang Besar. It also didn't take long for Papa to find out his assistant Ismail was a Mackintosh stooge, ensuring a mutinous work environment that would have a ripple effect on my family.

The overall disillusionment began to impact my parents. Their hopes, dreams and lives in a liberal, progressive Malaysia were diminishing before them, and talk of resettling in Kerala was occasionally discussed in the open, especially when we had family members visiting. Mummy's knight in shining armour story would then come out – how in 1963, a year after our big family trip to Kerala, she had flown alone out of the then Sungei Besi International Airport into Madras, catching the night train from Madras Egmore to Chenganur (Kerala State) and a bus to Vadasserikkara, her hometown. From there, she had set about investigating investments and the result was she returned with the purchase of two houses, one in Thekkemala and the other in Kowdiar, a salubrious part of Trivandrum, in addition to two acres of paddy fields surrounded by coconut trees in Venikulam, adjoining the district of Ayroor.

Instead of absorbing my parents' discontent, I made the best of Galloway Estate and its surrounding jungles, to me an extension of Limau Manis. I explored my new habitat on my gleaming Raleigh bicycle, another gift from Papa for clearing my LCE. A timely one, considering school was now twice the distance from our new home.

I begged to be allowed to cycle and bus my way to school. My parents' main concern was the jungle stretch across two secluded *kampungs* and a looming Chinese graveyard our new neighbours warned was "best avoided in the dark". Within days of settling in, we'd heard much about the graveyard – of various supernatural beings, particularly beautiful long-haired, jasmine-scented apparitions preying on unsuspecting males, and Bermuda Triangle-type strange, unexplained occurrences of lorries and cars veering off the single unlit road or crashing into mysterious objects.

Seeing how quickly I was settling into my new environment, Papa began relenting about the idea of me making my own way to school. I spent the long year-end holidays roaming all over Galloway and nearby riverside *kampungs*, making many new Malay friends. Once I had learnt to ride Papa's smaller Honda motorcycle, I went on secret bike trips to as far as Dengkil, and even Banting and Morib Beach. Sometimes I'd plonk my littlest brother, Tom, on the back for a long jolly. It's an amazing feeling when a young child is holding on to you for dear life… a special bond was forged over those trips and I'd carry Tom's small photo cut-out in my wallet on the day I flew out of Malaysia. On one trip to Dengkil, I introduced Tom to John Wayne, Claudia Cardinale and Rita Hayworth as we watched *The Magnificent Showman* in a Shaw picture house with a leaky roof!

It was this way too I made friends with a Chinese medicine shop owner in Dengkil who doubled up as a *sinseh* (traditional Chinese medicine practitioner), administering treatment and dispensing herbs, oils or dried condiments from large glass jars of exotic cordyceps, roots and animal products. There was no way Papa could deny me my freedom of travel when I explained I'd already arranged with the *sinseh* to park my Raleigh in his shop for safekeeping when taking the bus to school. I thought I caught admiration in KP George's eyes at that moment! A realisation perhaps that his firstborn might just do all right in life… at least that the boy knew how to build contacts through rapport.

I would leave home before five-thirty in the morning, with my bicycle lamp the only guiding light, to cycle the five miles to Dengkil, where I'd holler a *selamat pagi* and park my bicycle at the *sinseh*'s shop to catch the six o'clock bus to Kajang.

My siblings went in the estate taxi belonging to a Sikh man, and they of course reached Kajang much quicker and not at all sweaty and puffing. If I did not stay back at school for extramural activities, I would be back at 2.30 pm to collect my bicycle. If I did, I would only reach Dengkil at 8 pm in pitch darkness to unsettling jungle noises.

It was the scariest half-hour… I knew the road well, my Raleigh was in mint condition and my legs were in good shape to muscle enough ground to charge up its dynamo light. Even then, there was not one time I could make that graveyard stretch without my heart pounding, my legs turning bionic and my mind fixed on thirty: to reach home in thirty minutes or under!

I entered form 4C, became more interested in school subjects and started to get better reports. That's not to say I was anywhere near the front row, but certainly more assertive and positive, in part due to confidence builders like Keats, E M Forster, Byron and company, as well as supportive teachers. Shiva, fortunately, had no cover to my class. When Forster's *Where Angels Fear to Tread* was introduced for English Literature, I was quite in demand with the Chinese boys – we'd swap English homework for Maths.

I carried on playing badminton at a higher level and on a Saturday would still do *mahjong* badminton. In Galloway Estate, there was only one cement badminton court in the centre of the labour lines where I practised under the curious eyes of half-naked children of labourers who held me with reverence because I was the boss's son. For hours on end, I'd practice my Tan Aik Huang stroke and style, also high jump using my own makeshift pole and bar. When I broke the school's high jump record, Mr Kuan saw in me the potential to be a decathlete since I also had the long jump under my belt. Decathlon, however, was not for me, seeing how my father was already on my case: SENIOR CAMBRIDGE!

Long after Rajan's sudden departure to India, I continued to feel a massive void of emptiness. In that void crept a desire to aim for what my poor cousin could not have. After all, Papa had already assisted my other cousin Philip Cherian (PC) to further his ambition in England. PC, around ten years my senior, was the son of my Uncle KP Cherian in Singapore, my father's elder brother who was a storekeeper at the RAF (Royal Air Force), located at Changi. Uncle Cherian was not an admirer of the English and had only agreed to his son going to England because of Papa's advice and financial support. I'd be in total awe of PC each time he visited us from England, often with little gifts for me, babbling and taking in every word, enraptured by his England stories. Then, in 1968, PC's sister Susan also left Singapore to study nursing in England under her now well-settled brother's sponsorship.

Why couldn't Philip George too join them in England?

The thought made me worry about my red identity card dilemma. I suspect permanent residency in Malaya was not in Papa's initial plan, the reason he never considered the blue identification card for me despite being born in Malaya, and despite my numerous complaints to him each time schoolboys taunted me for being the *red IC immigrant*.

On many Saturdays after badminton, I drifted from my Chinese friends, catching the bus from Kajang to KL to wander around the Bukit Bintang and Chinatown areas. I'd get off at the Main Market, a late 1880s wet market built by Yap Ah Loy, the father of modern KL. Today, it has been transformed and rebranded as Central Market, a tourist mainstay for getting to know Malaysia's culture, arts and heritage.

I easily recall the chaotically atmospheric Main Market right by the decaying River Klang. The frantic cacophony of bargains at its seafood stalls where the biggest action took place, with live slaughtering and butchering and where it reeked the most, the gush of water over wet, soiled cement floors flushing away blood, guts, scales, the state of that finished water entering the poor river...

I'd walk past the market to make my way to my favourite destination, the British Consulate, towards its library and reading room to catch up on England updates, given Rajan's absence.

It was easy to get lost in magazines, newspapers and journals. That year, the biggest news-making headlines were very close to home: America's long-running Vietnam War. Vietnam's liberation fighters had launched the surprise TET holiday attack against warring South Vietnam, breaching the walls of America-controlled Saigon to achieve a strategic shock victory, forcing President Lyndon B Johnson to announce he would not seek re-election. It was only two years earlier, in 1966, that President Johnson became the first American president to visit Malaysia, after taking over from the slain John F Kennedy.

The more I discovered about the Vietnam War, and especially after watching the 1968 Mexico Olympics' black power salutes of Tommy Smith and John Carlos during the 200 metres awards ceremony, the more prepared I was for reconciliation with my one-time hero I'd had a "fall-out" with. Cassius Clay, alias Muhammad Ali.

Young, brash, loud-mouthed rank outsider Cassius Clay made a huge impression on me with the way he beat defending champion Sonny Liston to the World Heavyweight Boxing Championship in 1965, but I couldn't understand his subsequent radicalisation and change of name and religion. But with the way the Vietnamese showed the world the real situation was very different to what was being portrayed by American politicians and media, Ali's refusal to be inducted into the army to fight in Vietnam and his saying, *'I ain't got no quarrel with them. My conscience won't let me go shoot my brother, or some darker people or some poor hungry people in the mud for big powerful America,'* began to mean something.

Another big highlight of 1968 was when His Imperial Majesty Haile Selassie, the Emperor of Ethiopia, became the first head of state of Africa to visit Malaysia. It was a landmark trip and a significant forerunner to closer ties, not only between Malaysia and Ethiopia but also between Malaysia and other African countries.

The emperor was a very important figure in our Syrian Christian Orthodox Church, so when it was announced the state visit included our church in Brickfields, there was enormous excitement among the congregation. On the morning of the big day, my siblings and I dressed in our very best and had to listen to Papa and Mummy's lecture on decorum and protocol, mainly about being on our best behaviour, before we took off for KL to meet the *Lion of Judah whose lineage went back to Solomon… the next coming of Jesus.* A very big occasion indeed for a boy properly and fully hanging around the Chinese, Malays and Tamils and their faiths, gods and mystics!

There was much pomp and ceremony where self-appointed church authorities unilaterally took charge of the proceedings – while ensuring their children got the coveted front seats. My siblings and I were assigned to the rear crowd. I was game to praise the emperor's name from anywhere since for me it was more a jolly to grab the occasion when I saw television cameras and journalists present.

They were not going to keep me in the back row, so to the horror of the disciplined congregation, I went for my "get up, stand up" moment – lunged to the front as the emperor was walking to the pulpit and shook his extended hand! The only adults not to show consternation were my parents… Mummy's smile conveyed pride. I would only realise the weight of that moment years later after discovering the dreadlocked Rasta from Kingston.

Moments like that served me the courage to sail with the waves, to take on the wild, rugged ones with the calm, gentle ones, knowing full well it's not possible to always win. No mistake has sunk me yet.

I floated through form four. My cycling, badminton and playing other sports kept me extremely fit, and with my explorations into KL, I began to see life with colour and enthusiasm. The initial gloom of moving to Galloway Estate turned into positivity, and I developed a degree of optimism and some sense of ambition. With newfound determination, I studied late into the night under a small kerosene lamp with either Papa or Mummy staying up with me in the lounge to look out for burglars, trespassers… or ghosts!

In 1969, I entered the final year of high school in form 5 C. Rightfully, all three form five classes were on the top floor of the main building facing the school's imposing grounds. It was a fairly smooth transition from form four, with the same teachers, who encouraged me to find my own level without shoutings and beatings.

My badminton progressed rapidly and I was entered for the Senior Selangor Novice Open featuring the best youngsters from Malaysia, like Moo Foot Lian, who ended up playing for Malaysia. Coach Chan nominated me for the Selangor state team and I was also on standby for the national squad, which meant training in KL under national coaches. It forced me to part ways with Chan, who continues to have a special place in my heart.

Football, badminton, athletics and hockey tournaments for school meant on weekdays I did not reach home until around 9 pm, after which it was burning the midnight oil to catch up with school work. Curiously, I did not mind, as I'd started to appreciate academia and had become adept at time management, having to multi-task between sports, studies and socialising – awfully important for a seventeen-year-old boy with a girlfriend, and other female friends besides.

On our porch on Saturday evenings, Papa and friends lit up, drank up and plunged into deep discourse about growing political tensions. In the immediate aftermath of the May 1969 elections, riots broke out in KL leading to incidents of mayhem and massacre. Suddenly a curfew was imposed in KL and parts of Selangor.

A military truck trudged past our Galloway house, its loudspeakers blaring in Malay, *24-hour curfew imposed apart from 5 pm to 6 pm. Anyone seen outside during curfew hours will be shot.* It was a seminal moment in Malaysian history leading to the resignation of Prime Minister Tunku Abdul Rahman, the birth of the pro-Malay affirmative action policy and the search for the yet elusive Malaysian identity.

By the time Apollo 11 made its historic landing on the moon on 20th July 1969, the tension in Kuala Lumpur, where the riots were confined, had been brought under control and the curfew lifted. The curtains were brought down very heavily on the race riots, and 13th May became a taboo subject. Yet, generations on, its "us vs them" impact continues to tenant in Malaysia's psyche.

Galloway Estate was too remote to be touched by the riots, but I found out from conversations with my Chinese friends with first-hand experience how frightened and tormented they were following the harrowing few days. In school, the topic was completely ignored; not at all brought up at any time, not by boys, not by teachers, who continued with their bigger task at hand – preparing school leavers for the all-important Senior Cambridge examination that year-end.

For my siblings Shanta, Prasad and Viji, it was to be their last academic year in the Malaysian school system. Tom hadn't started school yet. The 13th May incident was the last straw. My parents decided it was time to make the move back to Kerala in early November, just before my exams.

There was no clear plan for my future, except that Papa wanted me to stay on and do well in my Senior Cambridge. Mummy's shrewd investments in her hometown ended up saving our bacon and all they needed to do was pack and leave. Papa was to travel with the family and return to continue in his position, so only I needed sorting out for the duration my father would be away in Kerala. Arrangements were made for me to stay with the Kunjamboo family, with my friends Rajeevan and Krishnan, who by then had also moved out of Prang Besar Estate, to Cheras, in KL.

Departure day came – and went – just like that. A large lorry rolled up the hill to our Galloway house, everyone supervised the loading, the house was locked up, goodbyes were said with short hugs and my family were off in Papa's car to Port Swettenham to board the *State of Madras*. I was left with my Raleigh and some personal belongings watching them go. No song and dance and with little sense of loss. I would not see my mother and siblings for the next six years.

I hung around to give away some surplus stuff to the estate children then cycled to Dengkil with my kit bag, where I gifted my bicycle to Sundramurthy, a Tamil boy from a neighbouring estate I used to play kites with. After a goodbye to the *sinseh*, I got onto a near-empty Kajang bus, sat on the corner of the back seat, alone, fiddling with my steel bracelet and Tissot watch, wishing the bus would take off immediately from my familiar station, overcome by a peculiar blend of sadness and exhilaration.

At Rajeevan's house, a room was kindly made available for me, my abode to sit my Senior Cambridge exam and until Papa's return. I got down to serious revision and sat for my papers the following week, travelling daily to school with Rajeevan and returning together. By the second week of November, my tenure at the Kajang High School ended without any celebration and everyone went their separate ways. Being on my own without my family, I felt a pervasive sense of loss and knew a huge transition awaited… after all that Kajang High School had done to "educate" this wanderer.

Relieved of the examination burden, my stay at Rajeevan's became a lot more fun as we had all the time for boy pursuits, which we did not waste. The week after ending high school, I entered the Senior Indo-Ceylonese Badminton Championship at the Kajang Badminton Hall, conducted to great fanfare and prestige, and heavy rhetoric among the Ceylonese community.

Being an outsider, I was intrigued to see the names of my primary and secondary school Ceylonese teachers, particularly Shiva and Nathan. There lay my *float like a butterfly, sting like a bee* opportunity! I immediately rounded up my Jalan Sulaiman boys for the three-day communal festivity.

On the night of the finals, I walked away a triple champion, bagging the singles, doubles and mixed doubles to the blare of *In the Ghetto, Bad Moon Rising, The Ballad of John and Yoko* and the aroma of Jaffna cuisine. As if thrashing my former tormentors wasn't enough, following the trophy presentation, I was asked to raise three cheers in front of them! Hoisting the trophies for all to see, the Chinese boys and I made a roaring exit before hitting the town on the razzle.

Catching the moment remains the mainstay of my energy, and that day was an unforgettably satisfying moment. Impressionable in age and unsophisticated in thought, my only concern at the time was to make use of the chance to deal a rebuff to the men who had aggrieved me with their bias. I'd been pushed to revolt and possibly pushed to become a political thinker.

1969 being such a trailblazer year, it was only right to end it with a bang. I thought up a plan to go on a hitch-hike with Rajeevan and another friend, Lim Cheong, beginning at our high school, all the way across the southern border to Singapore, covering the four states of Selangor, Negeri Sembilan, Melaka and Johor.

I arranged for us to stay with my family, the Oommens. Using my previous travel memories, I drew a road map using the old road to Singapore, with the main towns as coordinates and reference points.

Rajeevan and I met Lim Cheong by the landmark tree near the running track of our high school, a poignant location for me, a sort of good luck charm I'd respectfully acknowledge before a match or race.

From right outside our school gate, I stood with my left arm out, thumb pointing south. A car stopped to give us a lift to Seremban from where we walked further south and carried on hitching. Within an hour, we were conveyed by another car to Tampin, arriving in time for a quick street fare lunch. Tummies filled, hearts pumped up, we got a lift in another car to Segamat, reaching there at around five to threatening weather.

Under a rapidly darkening sky, we slow marched into monsoon territory in the direction of the Segamat River road bridge. About a mile on, we came to a brand-new BP petrol station not yet in use as construction was ongoing. A lone, dim street lamp our only source of comfort, we performed a quick reconnaissance of the site... no one in sight to bother us, perfect for a halt.

With the South China Sea blowing cold breezes warning of bad weather, our plan to sleep under the stars was foiled and we needed to come up with some form of bedding on the dusty cement floor. The silhouetted petrol pumps dressed up in sturdy cardboard gave us an idea. Using the cardboard, we erected three 'A' huts, with one layer for the base to double up as our makeshift beds. Satisfied with our camps, we cleaned ourselves at an outside tap and propped our wet towels to dry on the pump heads.

Twelve hours had passed since we began our day and we were hungry boys. Taking our rucksacks, we set about looking for food, knowing it wouldn't be hard to find something in our food-friendly country. Not three hundred metres away we spotted a small hawker area, filled up on chicken rice, *pau* and *ice kacang* and raced back to our campsite in time before the rain. Grateful for the roof over the petrol station, we quickly fell asleep on our rucksack pillows, I in seventh heaven because my road map had worked like clockwork.

Hours later, I woke up in pitch darkness to feel dampness seeping through my cardboard mattress and immediately sensed a change in the air. I switched on my torch to see a pool of water all over the forecourt, reaching up to our huts. The Segamat River must have burst its banks, and I figured the situation must be worse down the road as our petrol station was on raised ground. The boys too were up.

We left under a relentless drizzle, quietly aware of our predicament. Before long, we found out the whole of

Segamat was rendered helpless – north and southbound trains had stopped running and many lorries en route to Johor Bahru and Singapore were stranded on various flooded roads. A decision had to be made.

*My* mind was made up and I was not going to waver, but Rajeevan and Lim Cheong voted to return to Kajang, or at least wait a day or two for the water to subside. After a brief exchange, the boys reluctantly followed me in the direction of the Segamat River, where an alarming sight awaited – the road bridge was submerged in about three feet of water!

Within eyeshot, running parallel to the road bridge but on slightly higher ground, stood an imposing steel railway bridge, avoiding the swelled river by a whisker. Water was just about touching the underside of its sleepers. It was our only way to get to the other side. I proceeded to lead the way.

There were no side walkways, just sleepers fixed inches apart with gaps revealing the grey river's rage. With utmost caution, I stepped over each sleeper in my rubber Bata school shoes, the boys following, knowing full well if we slipped we'd fall straight into the deep river to the pleasure of crocodiles. Betraying no outward fear, I kept my concentration, wrapped in indescribable stillness, and safely covered the forty metres or so.

Seeing me reach shore, the boys moved more confidently and soon we were together. Looking pale and stricken, it would take the two a while to become chatty again. Still, we rolled up our pants and waded through the inundated road, passing a long stretch of lorries with cargoes and other vehicles on both sides, most abandoned, some with bewildered drivers pondering their next move.

About a mile on, I noticed a cargoless lorry on the road shoulder with a Chinese driver struggling to start his engine. It was not firing up and he opened the boot to dry the spark plugs. I knew because the sight took me to my form two vocational skills class taught by a visiting American teacher – the Volunteer Service Overseas (VSO) was a popular programme back then for youngsters from the west to gain work experience in the east.

We stopped to give the lorry driver a hand, who, when he found out about our mission, offered to take us right across the causeway into Singapore where he too was headed – if he could restart his engine. Finally, something to uplift the mood of my fellow hitch-hikers!

I immediately got down to assisting Sung Tan, for that was the driver's name as I remember it, and we managed to get the vehicle going. Rajeevan and Lim Cheong got to the back of the lorry and Sung and I got into the driver's section. I had a whale of a time watching my hero expertly manoeuvre his straining lorry back to the flooded road. Water gushed in and out of the footwell of the cabin as we chugged along, while other drivers sat staring. With me egging him on, Sung very slowly and skilfully treaded the flood water for about 400 metres before reaching dry road, at which point I and the two boys in the back shrieked our lungs out! Sung stopped the engine and got down to check his vehicle. When he felt the mud-caked wheels needed cleaning, all three of us helped.

Following a late lunch at a nearby coffee shop, I joined the other two in the back of the lorry for a grand ride into Lion City. We encountered further road flooding at Ayer Hitam and also Muar, but after the Segamat stint, Sung was in his element; nothing could stop him reaching Singapore. We went full steam ahead to Johor Bharu and the causeway, cleared Singapore immigration and customs and reached our final destination in darkness. Sung dropped us off at the RAF Selatar airbase, where we bade a sad farewell to my shining knight of the road. I was so proud when the boys admitted they were glad I had taken the dangerous risk over the Segamat River. Fortune favours the brave, they say, and I know we emerged from that amazing experience changed youth.

It was past dinner time when we reached the Oommens' house. Aunty Oommen greeted us and told us the four Oommen boys were at the Christmas Christian Festival close by, so we quickly tidied ourselves up and walked to the lively auditorium. We were greeted with joy and enthusiasm by my cousins as groups of young people from as far as Christmas Island and Australia were singing *Kumbaya* and *Jasmine*. Word quickly got around about the boys from Malaysia who had braved the Johor floods to reach Singapore and before we knew it, there was an announcement about our incredible journey and we were being called to the stage!

On that explosive note, we began our Singapore holiday, making many new friends on the first night itself, one of them a nice girl called Mercy. Rajeevan and Lim stayed for a week before returning to Kajang by train. I stayed on until early January to coincide with Papa's return from India.

I returned by car with our KL church priest and stopped overnight in Batu Pahat at his congregation house, where I was surprised and pleased to see Mercy once again. We chatted through the night and just before I left, she wrote in my autograph book, *When will I see you again, in thunder, lightning or in rain?*

## SEVEN

# RULE THE WAVES

January 1970. Kajang High School's foyer was a rush of front-row candidates knocking shoulders, standing on tiptoes, straining necks to catch a glimpse of the paper all felt carried their future fortunes.

Throat dry, palms sweating, I was surprised to see my own eight O-levels, albeit far from distinctions or strong credits. What might it have been, had I given just as much attention to studies as I did to badminton? Form six? Path to Universiti Malaya?

My grades did not impress my father, no surprise there.

Papa's unsettling silence was as good as letting me know I was now a burden: no longer in school, not eligible to enter form six. Being a seasoned hand at dealing with setbacks, I knew it was time to take matters into my own hands. Putting on my Segamat River resolve, I set about to remedy my dilemma, my peripheral knowledge darting ahead of me to help chart my options and road map to put in place an out-of-reach plan. Treating it as a stealth mission, I kept my own counsel.

After my return from the hitchhiking trip to Singapore, I moved out of Rajeevan's house into Papa's next demotion. My father was transferred from Galloway Estate to Sg Buaya Estate in Banting, where he would spend the rest of his years in Malaysia, until retirement. Ironically, Sg Buaya brightened up Papa somewhat. He had many Chinese friends in Banting, a lively little town close to the sea. It also helped his cause that he got along very well with his new assistant, Ahmed, ex-army personnel trained in Sandhurst. Ahmed would often let me borrow his smart Vespa for long drives around Banting and Morib Beach, and for secret rendezvous in Malay *kampungs.*

It was a period when the price of rubber was dropping in the world markets and Harrisons & Crosfield had made a policy decision to convert half of their huge Prang Besar Estate from rubber to oil palm. Knowing this might create new openings, also unwilling to be idle, I rode to Prang Besar hoping to land a part-time job.

I caught a moment with the assistant manager Mr Simm, who remembered me and my *diligence* (he taught me that word) from cleaning his car during Scouts' Job Weeks. Hiding my nervousness, I presented a brazen front and told Simm I was prepared for any legwork if he needed someone. I got more than a reasonable bargain when Simm offered me a census clerk position for three months, with accommodation and a new Honda motorcycle thrown in! The bike was needed as my job entailed going around the swathes of new oil palm sections now substituting rubber trees, to calculate the number of young palm plants required and draw contour maps of the new sections.

Papa was happy to have me out of his hair and earn my keep. He'd done the training with me for as long as I could remember – be it assisting him to chop and clear a fallen branch on the Prang Besar road in slanting rain at midnight during the Malayan occupation period, knowing Chin Peng's communist comrades could be lying in wait, or putting me in the witness box to conduct a seventh-degree cross-examination of the movie *Spartacus* to confirm I had indeed watched the movie as per his instruction and not spent his money frivolously!

I had no need to worry about Papa being alone. He had his Chinese buddies from Banting, and there was never a weekend when they weren't having a good time in popular seafood haunts by the Banting/Morib coast. Beneath the surface, I suspect there must have been some deft wheeling and dealing going on as Papa was an admirer of the Chinaman's entrepreneurial zeal, his natural ability to see everything from a business perspective; quite simply his love of making money. It's a trajectory not unfamiliar to the Malayali. My parents shared similar attributes when it came to hard work, accumulating money and being shrewd with their acquisitions and financial investments.

Papa additionally shared his Chinese friends' fondness for spending, another quality that made him a hit with the cloistered *taukey* club, which must've led to mutually beneficial "deals" considering they were all involved in the wider agricultural and plantation industries. Having kept a watching brief of sorts on Papa's operations with the Malaysian Chinese and witnessed how they functioned, seeing China's current economic revolution, particularly its path of international acquisitions and mergers, comes as no surprise at all to me.

I started work immediately and moved to my staff quarters in a bungalow with PM Cherian (Papa's nemesis in the *Last Supper* auction) with the use of a Nambiar cook from Calicut to guarantee great Malayali cuisine in place of my mother's cooking. Nothing compares to an aromatic fish curry with thick coconut milk and hot rice after a hard day's toil!

It was with the spirited excitement of an emerging star that I began my first proper job. No way was I going to pass the opportunity for a sartorial display. Out came the purchases I made on my Singapore trip: Lee Wrangler jeans, Oxford and Lacoste shirts, duster boots and a red floppy corduroy hat, not to forget my throw-me-a-curveball attitude.

Of all my choices, though, it was my red corduroy hat that caught the fancy of the *kampung* Malay girls making up the bulk of the workers on the oil palm sections. They were mostly young school dropouts, eager to please the new rough-boy-trying-to-be-posh clerk, and soon began calling me *Kerani Topi Merah* (Red Hat Clerk).

During this time, I made many trips to KL in my Honda, with the British Consulate being my regular haunt on Saturdays. It was, after all, the hand that was going to deliver my BOAC ticket to England!

I already knew my magazines quite well: sections of articles, current events, sports *and* jobs in England. I detected a demand for nursing, which seemed the ideal way to kill three birds with one stone since it provided visa, lodging and salary... no need for any outlay of funds from Papa. My grades not being good enough for general nursing, I only qualified for psychiatric nursing. They were both the same to me. It was still a posting in a mental asylum, and I knew the type of reaction I was going to get from Papa.

A map check revealed my two best options to be Queen's Park and Whittingham, both psychiatric hospitals within reasonable travelling distance of cousin PC's house in Lancaster. PC had already agreed to act as my sponsor for the student visa application.

I was absolutely gobsmacked to obtain offers from both hospitals within three weeks of applying! Notwithstanding the dilemma of informing my father, I made my way to Kajang's quaint gable-roofed post office (it still retains its charming old Malay compound-house architecture) and posted my acceptance to Whittingham Psychiatric Hospital, Lancashire, the largest mental hospital in Britain. The hospital provided weekly wage, accommodation with catering and laundry facilities and the annual renewable student permit.

My next course of action was to secure a UK visa.

My working relationship with Simm, Mackintosh and their company of people in the higher ranks of the estate pyramid was a roaring success as I was adept at code-switching. For the most part, people change their language style and mannerisms to identify with a particular social group, sometimes without even realising it. At that time, my blind obsequiousness and deferential attitude felt like a natural reaction to being around a very different set of people. It certainly felt good to be appreciated by the higher-ups *as one of them*. That is to say, without my realising it, I had begun playing Uncle Tom, something my father had refused to do.

To my benefit, Simm obliged me with an impressive letter of reference, mentioning the words diligent and reliable, fundamental values of the west, as I'd find out. That was all done oblivious to Papa. I knew he would not approve of me doing nursing, never mind mental nursing. Imagine the chatter at our church and among the clan!

It was no longer possible to avoid the subject with Papa as there was the crucial matter of my citizenship status hanging in the air because of my red identity card, which meant I was only a permanent resident in my country of birth. And so on the weekend after receiving my first salary package, I made a visit to Papa in Sg Buaya Estate.

As per Indian custom, I offered the envelope to him. KP George's handsome square face paused in thought; his eyes glistened as he mumbled, 'Thank you. You keep it.'

To my surprise, Papa took my news with far less disdain than anticipated. He even appeared pleased to shove me off to England at minimal cost!

My father next used his contacts to pull strings and I soon obtained a blue identity card and Malaysian citizenship, and thereafter, attaching Simm's reference to PC's letter of sponsorship, I managed to get the UK visa stamp on my passport.

Time for Papa to trumpet and, boy, was I relieved I was no longer a regular churchgoer! He served the congregation a suitably palatable follow-up to his *my son is going to England* boast. Without telling porkies, he told them I was going to do "Medicine". As lawyers will tell you, the definition of a word depends on one's take on the Literal, Mischief or Golden rules of interpretation, which means technically part of nursing would fall under the science umbrella. KP George would've made an excellent lawyer for his guileful rhetoric.

Before the end of my employment as a census clerk, I completed the two-hundred-page census and at the bottom of my assignment signed it off not as Philip George but as *The Drifters*, after the group. Although meant for Simm, it reached PM Cherian's desk first, who pounced on it for lacking correctitude. Cherian gave me a nasty telling-off, letting my "improper behaviour" be known to the entire office, which even Simm and Mackintosh could have heard from their big offices separated from the rest by a glass door.

Bumped back to *you stupid boy* by Cherian's unnecessarily harsh reaction, I sat down to retype the last page and put my proper signature before handing my project to Simm. Simm accepted my neatly bound bundle and to my horror asked what all the commotion was about. Feeling downright silly, I told him about *The Drifters*, convinced I'd hit the buffers.

'Was that all it was?' Simm remarked. 'I like *The Drifters*, but, you should take the credit, and your name now has its rightful place.' The assistant manager also expressed his delight at my "splendid work", leaving me quite speechless.

I was left further stupefied by what he said in passing as I was leaving his office: 'England will be the making of that boy.'

That incident with PM Cherian and my father's word manipulation with our churchgoers shone the spotlight yet again on the propriety of such false pride and obsessive focus on discipline and conformity achieved through abusive behaviour. I was just being a little adventurous, maybe even self-assertive. Cherian could have explained to me why he felt my action was inappropriate, or at least given me a private scolding instead of bringing down the office.

It left me feeling all the more desperate to flee my community for the liberal world of Simm, who with his easy handling of the situation instantly lifted my spirit. I was not going to allow my lot to take the wildness out of my system and make me into an ordinary gravy human. *England was going to be my making*!

The day ended on an even higher note, once again owing to Simm. He called me to his office before I clocked off with an offer to extend my work term a further three months until July, this time as a weeder's clerk. I accepted without a second thought.

April 1970 produced a spectacularly memorable FA Cup final between two leading English football teams of the time, Leeds United and Chelsea, noted for their north-south divide. Chelsea striker Ian Hutchinson said it quite plainly in a later interview: 'We hated them and they hated us.' The teams had played to an exciting stalemate in the first round, forcing a replay at Old Trafford, Manchester. The replay was another brutal competition in an era of ferocious footballing on a mud-bath of a pitch, and it was won by Chelsea, much to my disappointment since I fancied the gritty northerners over their flashy London opponents.

Immediately after that match, or because of it, I gathered all the Sg Buaya Malay and Indian estate boys to form our own Sg Buaya Leeds United Football Club! Included in the bargain were Malay boys from neighbouring villages. With the same spirit, I also rallied the boys to convert an abandoned house into an indoor badminton court. During the weekend, we would start in the evening and work through the night clearing the pulled-down old house, repairing its cement floor, fixing the net, hanging Petromax lamps on poles...

There was never a dull moment for the boys in the next few months, with football and night badminton matches with other estates attracting large crowds coming to watch us.

In my new position as weeder's clerk, I oversaw the oil palm nursery on the road to Galloway bordering the wild Prang Besar River, an abundant, climate-driven tropical river that caused floods and hardship, where I'd had close shaves with drowning and water snakes.

The weeders were all Malay girls who worked hard to ensure the palm saplings were well protected from quick-growing weeds. They were also very chatty, so it didn't take me long to find out their problems, which I took upon myself to address using my direct link to Simm. The girls walked miles to work from remote villages, were exposed to insect and snake attacks and were hourly staff with no guaranteed minimum salary to compensate for the loss of working hours during rainy seasons.

As proud as I was to have completed an exhaustive census for Prang Besar Estate, I was equally happy to arrange for transport, dispensary cover and minimum wages for its oil palm weeders.

When the girls found out their *Kerani Topi Merah* was leaving for England, I was invited over to their homes for simple, delicious Malay food and lovely notes, gifts and a few photographs of themselves with beautiful handwritten messages which I treasure to this day. I hold those memories with great fondness, and that true multicultural Malaysia of my day is what I hang on to.

When I bade farewell to Prang Besar after the end of my tenure in July, Simm shook my hand, wished me well and said what at the time caused me confusion but would later turn out to be so true, 'Your honesty when expressing yourself, Philip, will, unfortunately, reveal your many flaws. But, no matter, go for it.'

Preparations began in full swing for my departure once Papa had booked my air flight ticket using his regular travel agent. I went along, recalling the time we sent Mummy off at Sungei Besi Airport and I caught a glimpse of a flying BOAC's tail with its iconic Speedbird emblem, thinking *out of reach*.

At the travel agent's that day, BOAC remained out of reach for me as it was almost double the £365 KL to London Heathrow via Moscow on the Aeroflot Ilyushin my father bought for me.

From there, we headed to KL's go-to shopping attractions, Globe Silk Store and Robinsons, for suits, shirts, trousers, socks and shoes. It was to some speciality shops next, and Papa got me a Yashica camera, a gold chain, a Timex watch, a BOAC holdall bag (to make up for not being able to fly BOAC!) and, most importantly, half a dozen Grays of Cambridge badminton rackets and a pair of Bata badminton shoes. I had every intention of taking my Racket Boy adventures to England!

A telegram was sent to PC: *Philip George leaving 6 September.*

Reply telegram from PC: *Postpone trip.*

Papa to me: 'Ignore him. Take the chance.'

Papa's reply telegram to PC: *Philip George arriving as arranged.*

Papa further sent an express delivery letter to PC with my flight details.

The 6th of September 1970 turned out to be a dramatic date. Four jet planes bound for New York – two from Amsterdam, one from Frankfurt and one from Zurich – were hijacked by the Palestine Liberation Organisation. Two of the planes, along with a BOAC Super VC-10 hijacked three days later, would be blown up minus their passengers and crew. As my departure to England coincided with the hijackings, and because of the time difference, the major headline news would only reach me much later.

It was a Sunday. In my new Globe Silk Store stitched suit, I arrived to find Subang Airport bubbling with excitement raised by student types like me and their families. My team included Papa, Ahmed and around forty friends from school, badminton and even the *kampungs*. None from my church.

It was a largely jovial atmosphere untinged by sadness, to be honest. I was overcome by glorious expectation – of going in search of John Lennon in England! There was no room in my heart for unhappiness. The cage lay open.

I walked up the tarmac with my rackets, hand luggage and Yashica camera over my neck, turning frequently to wave at my Malaysia, which I would not see again for sixteen years. Inside the single-aisle plane, I had a window seat with a Chinese student next to me. He told me he was going to study accountancy at Manchester University, and I concealed the fact I was on my way to pursuing mental nursing. He settled with the impression I was going to study to be a doctor – Papa's use of "medicine" coming to my first aid!

Doors closed, engine roared, the Aeroflot took off.

Four hours later, our plane landed at Colombo Airport, allowing us to disembark at the transit lounge. Transiting passengers were mainly Caucasians and there was strangely not the familiarity of the Simms or the Mackintoshes… this felt like another world.

I remember admiring a young white boy travelling on his own, wearing shorts with long socks and brown leather shoes, looking comfortable, confident and very natural. The spell was broken. I immediately felt all frumpy and uneasy in my ill-fitting "special" suit. It hit me like lightning. I wanted to be that boy.

The next stop after another two hours of flying was at Karachi, but this time we stayed on the plane. I caught my first sightings of women in black burkas – a different type of Islam was looking at me through peeping holes. I was thankful to all my Malay Muslim *kampung* girlfriends who happily revealed their beautiful hair and beautiful manners in elegant *baju kebayas*.

There were two more refuelling stops in Teheran and Ankara before we landed at Moscow International Airport at around midnight. All twenty-seven Malaysian students on transit to Heathrow alighted, with two other French girls. That was the moment I discovered I was not just the only non-Chinese Malaysian student on that flight but also the only one not doing Medicine, Accountancy, Law or Engineering!

After clearance, we were handed some propaganda books in the Russian language (the Cold War was in full flow) and bussed to our transit hotel close to the Kremlin. We were all confined to the eighth floor of the hotel and I shared a room with a boy going to study Law. Interestingly, without even asking about my choice of study, he assumed I was going to study Medicine. I did not correct him.

I woke up the following morning, the heating on full blast in our room, eager to see how Russia looked. A cloudy, drab, wet autumnal scene showed itself when

I parted the heavy curtains. Nothing too exciting so we joined the rest for my first meal on European soil.

It was cornflakes with cold milk and a continental fare of bread and cheese with jam and coffee. In a Proustian moment, my nose reeled from the fragrance of Hainanese coffee and a warm packet of coconut rice wrapped in banana leaf…

We were supposed to catch the connection from Moscow at 8 pm on that day but soon after breakfast, an Aeroflot official came to tell us in broken English that the flight to London Heathrow had been cancelled and that we would be travelling on the 9th of September at 8 pm.

There were murmurs of discontent in English and Chinese and brisk eye contact between the Malaysian students, but no one protested. Everyone listened quietly as the official went on to add that we weren't allowed to leave the eighth floor of the hotel as we were transit passengers who did not possess a Russian entry visa. That elicited a round of *awws, not fairs* and one or two *aiyos* from the Malaysians, which the official dismissed, but the two French girls would have none of it. They took up the lead roles to express their disappointment in accented English but with an ease and confidence I could only admire.

Their persistent arguing earned us a bus tour of Moscow the following day (without being allowed to alight), and we managed to see the Russian capital's main attractions, especially the Kremlin and Moscow University, which we were told was the largest university in the world.

After returning from the day tour, we were back on the eighth floor to be cooped up for another day in the strange capital. On the afternoon of the 9th, our supposed departure date to Heathrow, the same official came once again to tell us that only four of the twenty-eight of us could fly out that night!

I was not on the list of four; neither were the French girls. This time, the girls went berserk, and I too summoned my Segamat moment all over again to create an international scene. We kept up the pressure until the official asked for some time to "recheck" the list. He then arbitrarily moved our three names to the front of the list and just like that we managed to get what we wanted.

I struck up an instant friendship with Michelle and Collete. We exchanged addresses and to this day when I drive through Aix-en-Provence and Arles in the South of France, we catch up and often reminisce that Moscow madness when the girls showed me the value of having your voice heard when it matters. It was to become my lifebuoy in the future and has not let me down in any tight situation.

We boarded the packed Aeroflot flight for London via Paris, where the two girls disembarked. An hour after take-off from Paris, I still could not get any shut-eye, like the rest of the plane was doing. Must have been the excitement of finally gliding towards my dream destination three days after leaving Malaysia. Home was already morphing into memories.

At around 11.30 pm, I had a smooth landing at Terminal 3 of London Heathrow. After clearing immigration and customs and collecting my luggage, with £20 and Tom's cut-out photo in my pocket, I walked out of the exit gate.

In spite of the late hour, there was a large gathering of people at Arrivals, people spotting familiar faces, waving, embracing, exiting. In the predominantly white crowd, my cousin should have stood out. No such luck for me as PC was nowhere to be seen. It wasn't panic that swept over me. Just the familiar sinking feeling telling Racket Boy to dig deep and switch on the Segamat mode.

EIGHT

# 'YOU CAN SAY THAT AGAIN'

I'd arrived on a one-way ticket in the land of the Beatles, swamped by white faces, holding out for Cousin PC to emerge with a frantic wave and sincere apology for his delay.

The only familiar face from my plane whizzed past me waving a floppy hand. The Malaysian Chinese Law student, who'd also fought for his name to be added to the Moscow list with me and the French girls, seemed confident about where he was headed. A *towkay*'s son by the look of him.

It was already in the early hours of the following morning and I made my way to a public phone booth.

My spirit lifted when once again I saw the Malaysian boy, getting into the red cubicle. Clutching my racket bag in one hand and a telephone number to a Lancaster public phone booth in my other, I peered to see a black dial-up showing A and B. Being the irrational optimist, I thought there was a chance Cousin PC might be awaiting my call at that hour in the public phone booth at his end, which he'd told me he used sometimes!

When the boy finished, I approached him for assistance and he showed me using his 2p copper coin. No one answered, 2p was returned and boy disappeared into London.

There was nothing to do except make Terminal 3 my campground. As I was organising myself on a metal seat, I saw two nuns opposite me with the same intention. They agreed to look after my belongings while I took my faithful Malaysian memory – the *Good Morning* hand towel Mummy always insisted I had with me – to brush my teeth and freshen up.

Early the next morning, I went to the airport post office to ask for directions to PC's address. Aside from the shock of being served by a white person, I also struggled with the counter staff's heavy cockney accent. Understanding my plight, the man adopted a theatrical style, enunciating each word a little too loudly for my liking. 'Catch a London red bus outside the main arrival area, go to Hounslow and, from there, catch a tube to Central London. Then change at Victoria and catch another tube to Euston. From Euston, catch an overland train to Lancaster.'

'A tube?' I wondered what pipes had to do with transportation. The man chuckled, as did the two white ladies behind me, and explained a tube meant the underground train... the start of my many ground-gobble-me-up moments. I scurried back to my bench wishing I could rip off my Globe Silk Store suit for a jacket or a polo neck and be belted, buckled and scarfed like these stylish people.

'Would you like some coffee?' one of the nuns offered from their thermos flask cup. Between sips of coffee that calmed my frayed nerves, I explained my predicament, and they said since they were headed to Euston why not share a taxi with them? Then all I needed to do from there was catch the train to Lancaster to locate PC's house. A godsend proposal!

Once again, it felt strange to have an English driver sorting out my luggage next to his open-fronted Austin FX4, because hitherto the only white people who served me were the doctors who came from KL once a week to the estate dispensary when folks made a beeline and nodded earnestly to everything the doctor ordered.

It was just as well the driver wasn't one for conversation, and his few exchanges were limited to the habits sat facing me in London's proverbial black cab. An icy draught came through the front of the moving taxi as we entered Greater London, causing me to shiver, but inside I was warm with good cheer and a sense of adventure at finally being in the city so synonymous with the country that people back home simply said *study well in London* or *enjoy London* when really it should've been England! A country I'd dreamed of visiting, latching onto PC's thrilling accounts and Rajan's ambition.

Low-hanging brooding clouds, shrouded streets, buildings looming dull and dismal and rows and rows of tight houses bore little trace of joy, yet I soaked in London's grey gloom. 'We're not in the heart of the city yet,' one of the nuns beamed, then both launched into satisfying their curiosity about the strength of my abidance to my faith, with a name like Philip George.

Approaching Central London, the buildings got bigger and murkier, certainly dripping in history and not without an old-world charm. My cabin mates made a timely diversion from matters of the theological strain, allowing me to look out for revelations from my main teen bibles, *Titbits* (UK) and *Fanfare* (Malaysian magazine billed as *The Weekly for Swingers*), which had stocked me with Brigitte Bardot, Alain Delon, James Bond, the Rat Packers, Soho and Carnaby Street, the Mod movement, Sgt Pepper's Lonely Hearts Club Band, Woodstock...

The driver suddenly found his voice and began pointing out one landmark after the other, and, just like that, London began to swing! Pedestrian walks were filled with girls and boys championing psychedelic meanderings of the era in fearless fashion, colours, geometric patterns (Mary Quant's minis still going strong), tights, platform shoes, go-go boots, tousled hair, smoking as they walked.

When we arrived at Euston, I carefully parted with a one-pound note, the nuns returned some change and I made my way into the busy station. On a big timetable board dangling from the ceiling of Euston railway station, newly opened by young Queen Elizabeth II, I found my train. It was an Edinburgh train, stopping in Lancaster after a four-hour ride. *Same distance from Kajang to Singapore or Kajang to Penang*, I worked out in my head, and that would become a distance-and travel time-gauging mechanism for my future world travels.

Hungry, and also thinking of the long journey ahead, I purchased my first big bar of Cadbury's Whole Nut chocolate – highly desirable but out of reach for me in Malaysia due to its high price. Thus began my lifelong love affair with this heavenly bar.

My carriage compartment was a thrilling sight straight out of Sherlock Holmes or Agatha Christie with its two long bench seats facing each other to accommodate three people on each side. I had a seat to myself. Across from me sat a young blonde girl and an old lady, their eyes boring into me as I sorted my luggage, holdall and racket bag with exaggerated dexterity. It was my turn to stare when the lady sprang up, sought out a guard, gave blurry orders and sped off like lightning without turning back. She never returned.

The train set off on time and I broke into my wonderful Cadbury Whole Nut chocolate, offering a small piece to the girl heading to Edinburgh. We chatted for a while, me struggling with her Scottish lilt and her with my Malaysian expressions before I drifted off, dashing my earlier determination to marvel at the English landscape.

It was Rachel who woke me from my deep sleep to say Lancaster was approaching. I walked out of the station at about three in the afternoon with the feeling that grim weather was stalking me. To a driver at the taxicab rank, I showed Cousin PC's address. He was up to the task. I bundled into the back and soon the taxi careered up a hill onto the main road and down towards the city. We passed Lancaster Castle peeking out of tall trees. 'Roman fort it was,' said driver, eager to be my tour guide, 'then became a prison. It's a court now.' The castle was followed by the Royal King's Arms Hotel and snap came the trivia: 'Charles Dickens has stayed there. The writer, you know…'

Never in my life would I have thought I'd one day walk down Court Two in Lancaster Castle for my first case to face a judge looking at me testily through gown and wig as I worried about whether my voice would stand up; that I'd be visiting prisoner clients in the castle's dungeons; or that I'd be inaugurated as President of the Law Society of Lancaster and Morecambe at the Royal King's Arms; *and* put up in the room where *Charles Dickens* had stayed!

My driver was happy to let me unwind my window to take in the autumn views. For a city lined with buildings of brick and stone, steeped in tales they looked, Lancaster had its proportionate share of scattered parklands and hedgerows. We continued through the high street flanked by offices and specialist shops, none open-fronted like back home. At Dalton Square Town Hall, the taxi slowed down.

'You see there… that one in the middle is Buck Ruxton's house.' The driver pointed to a big square block of buildings. 'He was a doctor… rich he was. Murdered his wife and servant years ago. They hanged him for it. No one lives there no more.' Before I could react, he pointed in the opposite direction to the back of a Queen Victoria statue, therefore sparing me the gory details. In a fit of jealous rage, Dr Buck Ruxton had killed his wife and the maid who had witnessed the act, before dismembering both bodies in the bathtub. My man also spared me a pertinent detail: the doctor was of Indian origin.

We continued on the A6 main road and up the hill to Bowerham. Traffic became scarce as the taxi drew up in a quiet street at PC's double-storey terraced house with a chimney. While my luggage was being unloaded, I knocked at its front door. No answer.

'Have you got another address?' The driver's blue eyes flashed concern. I replied no, how much, please?

'One shilling two pence.'

Not knowing how to use my new currency I held out my palm with some monies, asking him to help himself.

As the hours progressed, I waited on the front steps, the sky stretching out above me grey and stark, turning expectantly each time someone came by. It was getting colder and I was bored of the rows of uniform houses, walls grimy, windows dewy… no zinc or *attap* roofs or houses leaning higgledy-piggledy under an orange Kajang sky; no sight of endlessly comforting tropical canopies over dirt roads.

When PC finally arrived, it was with Judith, his English wife. I instantly backtracked to the time his three sisters came crying to my parents over the news of their only brother going out with a white girl. My cousin bridled upon seeing me, foreshadowing what was to come. His wife looked a little less horrified. The dreary atmosphere and even chillier reception I was getting made me worry about England. John Lennon looked better in magazines and the television!

The chill on the street extended to inside the house. I was hastily allocated the back room upstairs and shown how to use the bath and how to clean it after use. 'We only take a proper bath once a week. That's when we wash our hair,' I was told. And that they used the washbasin to wipe themselves down daily, using two lots of water! Central heating was only for the rich, and PC's house, like most, had an open coal fire. Next, I was introduced to toilet paper as a "hygienic" necessity (Izal toilet roll was coarse and smelt of disinfectant). I was being robbed of the joy of a bucket bath… of pouring, splashing a limitless flow of running water all over my body. For someone habituated to bathing twice if not thrice a day, with that many changes of clothes too, how I received the toilet orientation without displaying alarm remains a wonder. Setting aside my bathing sentiments, I had my first bath then skipped downstairs, stomach in edacity after only that bar of Cadbury's Whole Nut chocolate since morning. Dinner was Heinz baked beans on toast and tea (using teabags!), with cutlery and linen napkins wasted on me.

Ignoring my protesting taste buds, I focused on the exchange of news with my cousin, then handed him the presents from Papa, including the costly latest model Yashica-D twin-lens reflex camera PC had specially requested. We ended the day watching BBC on a black and white television and I went to sleep, hoping the next day might be better.

The next morning began as a trial by ordeal over breakfast of toast, marmalade and a mug of tea. *You are not suited to make it here, nursing is not the path for a male* was the one-sided narrative… it sort of ended with a prickly 'but you are here, we have to do the best. First thing is to obtain your National Insurance number.'

There was nothing I could say without giving offence to the couple and I had no intention of doing that hardly twenty-four hours after meeting them, so between flushing and blushing, I learnt what a precious commodity silence was.

After breakfast, PC drove me in his white VW Beetle to the Employment Office in town. There were long queues; we stood out as the only non-white people. When my turn came, I withstood the searching questions asked of me and obtained my National Insurance number, allowing me to start employment restricted to the conditions attached to my annual student visa. In another part of the building, we found a vacancy for a factory process labourer with Nairn Williamson, a linoleum/wallpaper factory and Lancaster's major employer. I applied over the counter and was told there'd be an interview the following Monday morning.

The local BHS department store was next, where PC bought me some cut-price white badminton tee-shirts, trousers and a blue plastic foldable mackintosh. Creased and too large, it made me look and feel like a vagrant, but I soon realised it was the standard raincoat of most. My frumpy mackintosh caused me to miss shopping with Papa, his indulgence, his eye for quality… For the first time, I thought about having lived at Papa's expense all along, wondering how my father could have raised so much money for all that pre-departure shopping we did, not to mention the £365 for my one-way Aeroflot ticket to London, which incidentally was more than half the £625 PC had paid for his brand-new VW Beetle! Papa could've loaned some money from his Chinese friends or cleaned up his savings; I'd never know. My father was too proud to tell me, and I never asked.

Lunch was a tuna and cucumber sandwich with crisps from Spar. I ate my first English takeaway on a park bench in Dalton Square by the statue of Queen Victoria on a pedestal, holding a sceptre, scowling at her subjects in Lancashire's administrative capital. The memorial overlooked the magnificent Lancaster town hall standing not far from the canals that serviced its industrial revolution, and the River Lune which had played a major role in the city's dark slave-trading past. I would gather information like this throughout my decades exploring every nook and cranny of Lancashire, a county of charming contrasts, responsible for shaping much of my life – from the finest countryside in the north and the east, the Irish Sea on the west, fringing Morecambe, my eventual playground, to the mill towns of Liverpool, Manchester and Leeds in the south. I devoured my sandwich with no inkling of how devoted I was going to be to every aspect of Lancashire life.

After an early tea at home, PC and I went out again, this time to Brookhouse Badminton Club at Victoria Institute to check out the place, and perhaps play. Knowing of my badminton prowess, PC felt the Brookhouse Club would be ideal for me; besides, his wife Judith's relative Arthur was there. We arrived to find out it was club night – only for members to practise and socialise. Heads turned when we walked through the heavy oak door. PC left me by the door to greet Arthur. My attention drifted straight to that afternoon in Kajang town hall for my first meeting with Coach Chan. The difference was, Kajang did not intimidate me.

Having heard of my standard of play, the punditry began a deliberation to decide whether as a non-member I should be allowed to play. They approved and my name as a visitor was identified in the club draw box with the others. They only played doubles and mixed doubles. When it came to my turn, my opponents happened to be Arthur and partner, with my partner being a slow-moving elderly guy. I picked up my racket and *Good Morning* towel – my consistent source of transcendent inspiration for years – and summoned my Kajang spirit before stepping onto the court. Within fifteen minutes, we had breezed to victory to loud clapping and appreciation. No wild cheering or whistling like my Kajang boys, but no matter. I was in my element and enjoying myself.

Club box policy was again set aside and I was next asked to play singles against their best player. What more could Racket Boy ask for on his first badminton outing in England? With Brookhouse's top man thrashed, the going got better. They put up four guys to take me on! I kept winning and it went on like that until the close of play at ten o'clock, whereupon I was given star treatment over tea and biscuits as was the custom. PC shared my joy and was especially proud when the committee asked me to join their club to play as their top player in the upcoming Lancaster and Morecambe District Inter-Club competition.

'We'll let you know,' shot my cousin before I had time to respond. Just as well because Brookhouse's low ceiling did not impress me. Good height was paramount for my style of expansive stroke play. My obsession was also the result of being used to whipping the shuttlecock high into the air while playing in the open or under the high ceilings of the Kajang and Kampung Attap halls.

PC and Judith had the weekend off from their jobs as clerical staff in the civil service; good jobs, I was made to understand. Pensionable and respectable. They took me on a tour of the seaside town of Morecambe, the Trough of Bowland, an area of remarkable countryside beauty, and then to Dalton Square's ABC cinema for Richard Harris's *A Man Called Horse*, which made for a fun outing; yet, my biggest thrill was my first experience of watching *BBC Grandstand* and *Match of the Day* on the same day, on English soil. Leeds, Liverpool, Manchester United, Chelsea were all already familiar to me, including the fifth Beatle. I made up my mind to take in some stadium matches at the soonest opportunity.

At the Nairn Williamson factory downstream from the St George's quayside warehouses, I was told I could start work the following Monday on £7 a week, paid each Thursday. After the interview, I explored the city centre and found Ear Ere Records, where I purchased *Band of Gold*, the first of my vast vinyl collection. From that moment,

I began to seriously engage with the great pleasure of all things music related, to the point I would summon a song for each mood or phase I was experiencing.

It was time for my first great British favourite: fish and chips with mushy peas, smothered in salt and vinegar, wrapped in greaseproof paper over old newspaper. It cost one shilling and five pence. After years of curiosity stoked by *The Gambols* comic (*Straits Times,* Malaysia) – Friday was fish and chips night in the Gambols household – I was finally in possession of the hot, sour-smelling package. But then another drizzle began without notice and I ran to a bus shelter to see it out. English rain was so different to the buckets back home that I never bothered to take cover from. One other shelter seeker was standing at the far end, a tall woman looking in the opposite direction, her short powder-white hair just visible inside a nylon scarf knotted at her chin.

Unwrapping my bundle from my corner, I stuffed two very hot, sodden chips into my mouth, causing the vinegar to shoot up my nose, making me splutter down my lunch. In a flash, I turned to look at my shelter mate and, sure enough, her attention was on me. I quickly turned away but not before catching her *how uncouth* expression. I wasn't bothered. I was that hungry. Had I known then it would be sixteen years before I would taste my next proper Malaysian food, I might have cried!

Sorely missing my *Kerani Topi Merah* swag in my soggy, sloppy plastic raincoat, I then went searching for accommodation, wanting to move out of PC's house, where I knew I was surplus to requirements. Three bedsits flashed *Room for Rent* signs... all 'already taken up, sorry love' once the landlord or lady caught sight of me on their doorstep.

Smothered in my mackintosh, I walked back to PC's, feeling every look I got along the three miles, resigned to turning a blind eye and ear to my cousins' hushed whispers as they cast the occasional chilly eye on me... until November, when I was due to begin my nursing career at Whittingham Hospital.

That evening, PC and I went to check out the next badminton club, the Phoenix Club, set in a drill hall of the British Army, among tanks and a rifle range. It had two badminton courts with a slightly higher ceiling. Again, it was practice night, and the upshot was I received the same adulation from very nice English people. PC played this time, only for me to discover sports talent did not run in the family, making for a rather frosty late drive home.

Three more clubs in the next three days, and we departed unimpressed each time. Then came the Wesley Badminton Club in Sulyard Street, Dalton Square, a one-court hall with a high ceiling. I also found irresistible the colourful Middle-England English who would become my lifelong friends: Geoffrey Knowles, Joan Knowles, David Ashcroft, Jean Ashcroft, John Lamoury, Janet Knowles, Mason Whitaker, Bob Collins, Ron Gardner, Steve Clarkson, Jean Oakes, Trish Ashcroft, John Keats, Marion Keats, Elizabeth Metcalfe, Helen Metcalfe, Martin Jackson.

That night had a Kajang feel to it, and I decided I could have tea and biscuits in Wesley Club without too much worry, which was just what I was invited to do with the lot of them after the matches. I had the honour of my first handshake with the man who would shape much of my life in England: Geoffrey Knowles. In his fifties then, Geoffrey was senior partner of the law firm Whiteside and Knowles in Morecambe and the president of Lancaster and Morecambe District Badminton League, among other decorations. Geoffrey went out of his way to put me at ease.

'Came to say hello to the boy from Malaya,' I recall his first banter. I felt like a spinning shuttlecock, nervous and worried foremost about my gravelly voice! But with the big man himself so jovial and warm, my awkwardness thawed and I became quite excited when someone asked who my favourite sportsman was. Seeing it as my chance to up my game, I rattled on about Muhammad Ali beating Sonny Liston, winning the Rome Olympics, throwing his medal into the river... ending my recital with 'He was a confident rebel.'

Pleased with my little performance, I paused, just as Bob Collins exclaimed, 'You can say *that* again!'

I stared in bewilderment. What? The whole story!? Thinking my little moment of glory was lost on them, I repeated for Bob and the others: *Muhammad Ali beat Sonny Liston, won the Rome Olympics, threw his medal into the river... what a confident rebel he was.* This time, the Wesley gang stood at attention, simply letting me carry on. Then they rolled... taking their laughter all the way to the top of Wesley's high ceiling! It was hilariously contagious and despite me not getting that the joke was actually *on* me, I joined them. It was no wonder I felt a connection to this bunch, whose ebullient outburst made me realise they were laughing with me and not at me. That moment remains a standing joke as the gang has never let me live it down.

Without letting PC act as my mouthpiece yet again, I straightaway informed the captain, David Ashcroft, that I was joining Wesley, safe in the knowledge the gang were unmindful of my shortcomings. Their gracious manner, confusing humour and cheerful self-deprecation most appealed to me, none of which, I realised there and then, I could have picked up from merely reading the *London Illustrated* from KL's British Consulate! I went to sleep late that night reflecting on the contrasting playing etiquettes and styles of the English to back home... how easily I had run circles around the elite clubs of Lancaster, something I most definitely couldn't have achieved in Malaysia. Somewhat getting ahead of myself, I smelled opportunity. To become a big fish in a small pond.

One other high point of my early initiation into Lancaster life was a visit to its prestigious university, where I couldn't get enough of its mouth-watering sports facilities, and got hooked on the Great Hall's concerts and gigs. Lancaster University's Badminton Club had five courts, where I began hanging out with my age-group student players. They introduced me to the university's Sports and Indoor Recreation Centre Director, Joe Medhurst, who encouraged me to practise with his charges. The boys were intrigued by my "Eastern" tactics in that my footwork and cross-court speed were a lot faster, and my overhead strokes, reflexes and racket movements reflected flair and superior physical fitness. I remember one time when I played Coach Chan's trick shot from an impossible angle, flat-footing a desperate opponent into imploding, 'Come on, Phil! Can you just play the white man!'

On my first day of work, I arrived at the huge Nairn Williamson factory emitting a pungent odour of linseed oil and was told they'd rotate me between three shifts. I stuck out as the only coloured person, but that was no deterrent. I joined its trade union and made several friends, including Andy, who that very evening introduced me to my first pub visit and my first pint of English beer: Tartan, for five pence.

On each payday, I was given a small brown envelope with my name on it containing cash. I gave £5 to PC for my accommodation with food and kept £2 for myself. I could tide myself over with the sum even after doing my washing at a public laundry – a fish-out-of- water experience, making me appreciate Mummy all the more.

Back in the day, Lancaster had a reputation for "lunatics and linoleum". I'd completed my linoleum journey. The other loomed.

In November 1970, after two months of working, I left Nairn Williamson and PC's house to join the Whittingham Hospital in Preston, further south of Lancaster. On a drizzly, misty Sunday evening, PC drove me to the nurses' home where I had to report to the chief nursing officer for induction and placement the following morning.

Dark clouds shadowing us throughout the thirty-mile journey had merged into the night by the time we turned into the long, tree-lined driveway, past silhouetted lawns and flowerbeds leading up to Whittingham's main building. Like a lot of Lancashire's architecture, it was an imposing red-brick structure. Except, this one conjured up horrible images in my mind of frail people being strangled with towels, dragged by their hair, locked in cupboards, wailing, weeping, making tremulous pleas. I was not prey to my imagination or to the notion that we were entering a mental asylum. It *was* that bleak.

It was about eight o'clock when PC and I passed the main building to reach the St John's accommodation block. We got out of the car to profound silence brooding over the building and the dark acres surrounding it. As we entered the open front door, there was a curiously strong smell of curry and indistinct murmurs coming from somewhere underground. No one came to greet us. PC and I carried my luggage up the stairs where it was indicated the rooms were. My key hung on its latch, a lonely, despondent sight, a warning against any great expectations.

I did not mind the dim lighting and low bed, but I minded very much the cobwebs and lingering smell of not cigarettes but tobacco, neither of which I took a fancy to. PC did not stay long and I could not blame him. He'd done his bit for me. As I watched my cousin's back, a pang of desperation hit me. Is this what I'd left Malaysia for? Perhaps the coconut tree was designed for me.

## NINE

# THE VEIL DROPS

A veil of fog curtained my window, preventing me from finding out what my view offered. Trees and fields, no doubt, for that was what Whittingham's grounds had looked like on arrival the night before – a huge parkland hosting blocks of ghostly buildings in its suggestive midst.

I worked the rope by one side of my window and the single pane opened upwards, letting in a gust of wintery air to let escape some of my room's dank and must.

I'd been having bouts of dread since my arrival in England, but on that first morning at the hospital where I'd chosen to be trained for my future career, it was engulfing me. It didn't help my cause to see the faintly emerging view from my window: two grim red buildings. The children's unit and the hospital's factory. Leaving the window ajar, I made my way down the long corridor to a small queue at the communal bathrooms. Three brown faces ahead of me turned my way. They looked like Indians and they thought I was Indian. The reality was we were all foreign student nurses of Indian origin, me from Malaysia and the rest from Mauritius.

'St John's is for *our* people, see... other two hostels are for white boys and girls,' said one of them, referring to the St Luke's and St Margaret's students' quarters. Bathroom chat continued with the excitable brotherhood throwing questions at me in pleasing French-laced English.

There were thirty rooms in all, twenty-nine occupied by curry- and tobacco-loving Mauritians. I was also told the main St Luke's building was the hub for most activities, including meals and official matters, and where I was due to have my first meeting with Mr Murphy, the chief nursing officer. When I finally emerged from the Mauritian inquisition, it was to a feeling of being an intruder in their pile. They jokingly declared me a *foreigner*. I seriously felt like one – and was secretly pleased they thought I was more like the English.

What a relief it was to see large ceramic baths, albeit stained, with pipes for hot and cold water... and a bucket and cup. I had my first proper shower in three months, felt so good to start the day completely fresh. Free from Izal rolls at last!

For breakfast, I made the short walk from St John's to St Luke's, dressed in dark woollen trousers, a shirt and a Globe Silk Store tie bearing Malaysian motifs; a black jacket and black shoes, purchased with my earnings at Nairn Williamson completed my get-up. Long over Bata shoes and Globe Silk Store suits, I was already aiming for Fred Perry and Riley and Braithwaite gear.

I entered a lively, warm dining room bathed in a mild aroma of English breakfast and active conversation from around fifty people, largely white male and female nurses in immaculate hospital suits and well-starched frocks. Huddled at two corner tables were more Mauritians. I joined the queue to be served each item of food on a hot plate placed on a wooden tray. Quite a monster breakfast, I was pleased to see: cornflakes, bacon, eggs, sausages, black pudding, baked beans, mushrooms, tomatoes, fried bread, toast with jam/marmalade, orange squash, fresh cold milk from a jar and copious amounts of tea and coffee – all for just ten pence!

Balancing my laden tray precariously (my manual dexterity score in every school report card was never impressive!), I made baby steps towards the tables wondering where to sit. The decision was made for me by Bernard Pennington getting up from a nearby table to invite me to join his group. All fresh-faced and white. A few Mauritian heads turned in our direction.

My two months in Lancaster proved to be enough training for me to partake in the introductions and greetings with Bernard and the gang to reasonable success, and I even became the centre of attraction for a short while. As would be the custom, as soon as the eating was over, cigarette packets and lighters came out. Coach Chan's stern face called on me when someone offered me a stick and before I knew it, I was shaking my head, letting out a firm, 'NO! NO! I don't smoke.' I realised straightway what a needless affront that was to my new friends. It would be some way to go before I would pick up the art of English diplomacy, let alone understand their nuances in humour, irony, sarcasm or snobbery. That morning, though, I was happy to have got away with only a couple of eye rolls and one pair of raised shapely brows. Bernard even invited me to join them in the St Luke's TV room that evening.

Buoyed by the good-natured amiability of Bernard and company, I went to meet Mr Murphy in his office, a friendly Irishman who declared he was very happy to receive Whittingham Hospital's first Malaysian student. I was elated and at the same time nervous to be carrying the unaccustomed weight of being a country representative!

As if that wasn't enough, Mr Murphy clasped his hands on the table, leant forward and asked me to give him an "overview of my life". He was supposed to ask me why I'd chosen Whittingham and psychiatric nursing in particular, and I was going to impress him with a well-rehearsed piece containing white lies about how I believed "Whittingham would be the making of me", throwing in "diligent" and "reliable" to supplement my moment. What was there about myself to talk about? Unless it was about badminton or sports in general, but Mr Murphy certainly wasn't wanting to know about my sporting interests. I was left gawping at him after 'My name is Philip George. I'm from Malaysia. I've finished my Senior Cambridge…'

Mr Murphy came to my aid by switching to questions

instead, which freed me from my anxiety, and I began to answer him as best I could, even venturing to talk about my passion for badminton in which he showed genuine interest. He then examined my certificates, passport, yearly visa and my National Insurance number. That was followed by a detailed explanation of my responsibilities (patient care, ward management, attending lessons, observing rules…), work hours (7 am until 7 pm for three and a half days, with two and a half days off) and wage: £7 per week gross. After deductions for income tax, National Insurance, accommodation and laundry, a net of four pounds five shillings five pence payable every Thursday, again, cash in a little brown envelope.

'If you understand and accept the terms of employment, you can put your signature down,' smiled Mr Murphy. Contract signed, I officially became a Registered Mental Nurse (RMN) student for the three-year course at Whittingham Mental Hospital.

At the stationery issue department, I collected four grey woollen work suits and six white cotton coats, feeling the same relish of collecting new school books at the start of an academic year. Load in hand, I headed back to my room, passing impressive St Luke's students' quarters overlooking the church, cricket ground, park, lake and the Staff Social Club.

Changing into my new uniform, I went to Ward 20 situated in the same complex as St John's, a large geriatric ward where Mr Murphy had assigned me for the next three months. Timothy, the Charge Nurse, showed me around the ward. All twenty-five male patients in Auschwitz Camp pyjamas and fluffy flannel cotton dressing gowns were draped in the ammoniac stink of urine compounded by the heat emanating from the ward's huge heating radiator pipes. Some sat on plastic-cushioned geriatric chairs with various handles, locks and footrests. Almost all were or appeared to be half-asleep, a few with tongues sticking out, one with a tablet still stuck on his.

I was instantly transported to old folks back home – lecturing grown-up children, expecting to be lodged in the centre of family portraits, *never* parked in hospitals or mental asylums, even grand Victorian-type ones. Looking around Ward 20, I could not help feeling deeply for the indignity those poor old things had been condemned to. Not one looked to have any hope of recovery from whatever mental illness was afflicting them.

Tour over, I changed into my white coat. It was noon and lunchtime for the patients. Two ward orderlies came pushing a large heated aluminium trolley on wheels and started dishing out mashed potatoes with corned beef, gravy and peas into plastic bowls handed to us student nurses to place on the attached table of each patient's chair.

I tied a plastic bib around my first patient's neck with difficulty, not because of the task at hand but because of the hovering odour making me sputter and cough into his lank, greasy hair. When I picked up the spoon for my first act of feeding, it was to a surge of memories… sitting on a hard cement floor, Mummy's hand gently shoving a ball of rice into my demanding mouth.

As gently as I could, I inserted a spoonful into my patient's ready mouth and watched him desiccating the food in a manner as languid as if it were a drill. Nothing came out of my effort to make conversation with him, but I understood when I got used to the state of his brown eyes. They were vacuous, not tranquil.

Most of Ward 20's occupants were long-term patients suffering from various psychotic disorders, including dementia and Alzheimer's, and were prone to incontinence, accounting for the mastic smell pervading the ward. But the one piece of information that sent the blood rushing to my head was that the patients were only given a bath once a week, midweek! That being Monday, the malodour made sense in a very senseless way, leaving me in utter despair on my first day of work. I also found out the hospital took in young girls unable to cope with depression following out-of-wedlock babies being given away without their consent; returning soldiers struggling with post-war traumas; and anyone requiring rehabilitation from drug abuse or the "unnatural" urge for same-gender relationships…

When I clocked off from work that day, my mind was swamped with the good going of my time in Lancaster… the pull of my Wesley gang and Lancaster University! Even the dread of fighting fierce winter winds blowing from the River Lune while making my way to clock in on time at Nairn Williamson, lest I was penalised an hour's wage for being a few minutes late, didn't seem quite as depressing as the hole I seemed to have got myself into.

I made straight for my room and changed into shorts and two woollen jumpers to seek counsel from a good long run – the start of my devotion to running. I sprinted past Whittingham's private cemetery hosting the souls of many once confined to its walls, sometimes for decades, throughout the hospital's almost one-hundred-year existence. The few heads I passed in the provincial village of Goosnargh, where Whittingham Hospital ruled the landscape, turned because running wasn't fashionable at the time (wouldn't be until marathons got popular), and certainly not in shorts in the winter.

It took about twelve miles of running for me to shake off the hopelessness and desolateness and feel ready to dress up for St Luke's TV room to meet Bernard and his friends, including pretty Susan Leadbetter from Nottingham, a trainee social worker who appeared to have taken a shine to me. We drank beer out of bottles and ate crisps and nuts till midnight. Much of the English humour soared over my head. I didn't mind. It was the only way to chip away my insecurities.

I returned to St John's to find team Mauritius in conference in the foyer and spent time with them too, realising full well I could not fit into their communal solidarity. I would gravitate to St Luke's all the time because the St John's TV lounge was not keen on *Morecambe and Wise* or *Match of the Day*.

Tuesday was lessons day at the nursing school block – theory of general medicine and nursing, types of mental disorders, types of patients housed in the various wards and so forth. Each break ended with a cigarette social and I made more friends. I couldn't wait for school to finish as I'd agreed to meet Bernard and friends in the main hall's ballroom. It was a huge imposing arena, and I only had eyes for its *five* badminton courts.

There were already about forty players around the various courts and we had to wait for our turns, whereupon I got introduced to ward orderly extraordinaire, Willie Cunningham, ex-Scottish international football player, also of Preston North End, who had captained the Scottish team on their FIFA World Cup debut in 1954 *and* played with Liverpool great Bill Shankly, among other greats! Willie was in his forties, retired and revered, yet thoroughly unassuming. I was thrilled when he asked me to play men's doubles with him against another pair. As the game got underway, my style of play got noticed and the others began gathering around our court. Willie took matters into his own hands, stopped the match and asked me to play singles instead against Whittingham's top player. As if I needed an invitation to eat Cadbury's Whole Nut chocolate! Once again, my racket took me into orbit. I crushed my opponent in under five and became the toast of the ballroom.

The night ended with me playing mixed doubles with another charming girl, Julia Collinson, who wasn't a trainee nurse and had only come to use the courts since she lived nearby. After the game, Julia's mother suggested to me and Willie that I should join the BAC (British Aircraft Corporation), one of the top clubs in the Preston area. Mrs Collinson offered to make the introductions. We agreed and that was the beginning of my long-standing friendship with Willie and the Collinsons.

By the start of my first weekend in Whittingham, I was a member of BAC, my second prestigious club after Wesley in Lancaster. I'd also landed myself an English girlfriend.

It was so different to the coy courtships in Kajang. Susan let me hold her hand when I walked her to St Margaret's. When we lingered in the hush of the night, unbothered by the fog shrouding us, I took it as a promise of things to come.

It was during this period I began hitchhiking, something everyone did without batting an eyelid those days, as I would do right up to my thirties. I would hitchhike to Lancaster all the time, where I continued playing for Wesley twice a week after work; also from county to county for badminton tournaments and later for concerts and movies in Manchester and London or the Isle of Wight Festival, Knebworth Fair, Reading or Glastonbury because I didn't have money to spare. Walking miles in freezing weather to safe thumbing spots along the motorways was no fun, but the gratification came with the chance for free education, like that which my Kajang High School library offered me. Anyone letting you into their confined space was ready for some conversation, if not adventure – a perfect opportunity for me to improve my conversation skills, understand accents, cultural norms and practices, and learn about making connections across time-space. It also set the standard for my lifelong travel culture of planning my travel routes using maps and atlases, setting off early and paying attention to road signs.

I went along with Ward 20's daily routine: cleaning the urine and defecation of patients, brushing their teeth, shaving them, washing their chairs, changing them into fresh, dry pyjamas and dressing gowns, and inserting tranquillisers into their mouths. The whole exercise felt pointless when the patients themselves continued to reek in the ward's stagnant air. By then, I'd already been exposed to the weekly bath session and was fully aware it was hard, heavy work wheeling patients to the bathroom, needing two nurses to undress and lift deadweight patients one at a time into a warm bath, then scrub them clean, wipe dry, lift, place in the wheelchair.

Fortunately, my friendship circle was there to rescue me from my work stress. I spent a lot of time with Bernard, Susan and the others, for drinks, bingo, snooker and disco evenings at the Staff Social Club. I was introduced to the glam rock musical movements of David Bowie and T Rex's Marc Bolan (men in make-up and glitter!), and various rock singers and bands from Led Zeppelin, Alvin Lee of Ten Years After, Wishbone Ash and Pink Floyd to Crosby, Stills, Nash and Young… Bernard and his friends took me to the Floral Hall, Southport, to see Peter Green and the original Fleetwood Mac perform *Oh Well* and *Albatross* live – all new to me and so different to the Beatles or Cliff Richard!

One night, Susan wasn't at the club and I was desperately missing her. The lovesick boy that I was, I decided to visit her unannounced at St Margaret's. My first proper girlfriend was not good at concealing her irritation. In a manner stiff and withdrawn, she started giving excuses. I could sense I was no longer her fancy. It hit me hard when she accused me of "being like a rash, suffocating her". It took a while to process the unexpected denigration but I got the message. That night, I sought therapy in my diary and pledged to make it a lesson for life.

At the start of my fourth week on Ward 20 – typically Monday was when the stench rose – I suggested to Charge Nurse Timothy we give the patients an additional bath a week and how about starting right away. What a triumph for me when Timothy saw my point and summoned the rest of the nurses, auxiliary staff and ward orderlies to assist me.

Contempt *is* indeed the sharpest reproof, and I witnessed it on the faces of Ward 20's staff that day. Lips tightened, jaws tensed up, eyes flashed *who does he think he is?* Two of the staff nurses immediately complained to Timothy. Thankfully, he stuck by his decision and the bathing of all twenty-five patients took place. Shutting out the nasty comments directed at me, I led the first patient to the bath. There was, however, no let-up for me.

When I entered the staffroom, I was confronted by six nurses warning me not to be "so clever". I was more confused than disturbed. It wasn't like I'd committed a crime; all I did was put in a request for *one* extra bath a week, and that certainly did not warrant such aggression and mutiny from people being paid to do just that. During lunch, I confided in Bernard, who took me to see Mr Murphy since he felt things could get out of hand if I was labelled a troublemaker. After an interval of protracted silence following my story, Mr Murphy asked me to return to the ward. Later, he appeared on the ward to hear from everyone. I should think it wasn't hard for Mr Murphy to see through some of the attempts at truth bending. What followed was a severe talking-to. Ward 20 listened in sullen silence. Silence not lost on Mr Murphy.

Mr Murphy proceeded to praise my efforts in front of the lot, doing so while scrutinising the despondence settled on my face. He ordered me to pack up my gear from the staffroom locker, take the afternoon off and start the next day on another ward, despite two months remaining of my term on Ward 20. I did as ordered, saying goodbye to the more lucid patients, and also to Timothy. He did not respond. I left, disappointed, but happy the ward stank no more. When the film *One Flew Over the Cuckoo's Nest* was released a few years later, I was no longer in nursing; yet, watching Jack Nicholson's mesmerising performance as a rebel inmate of a mental institution was a stirring experience, as it must have been for the many people even remotely associated with mental asylums.

The next day, I reported to Ward 6, a high-security ward with three padded cells to the usual ward setting. Everyone had heard about my Ward 20 "shenanigans" but thankfully made light of it. From handling geriatric patients, I was now to care for patients with serious psychotic disorders such as schizophrenia and manic depression (bipolar), including some convicted criminals. Weeks went by generally incident free. Nevertheless, there was always a small fear for personal security, knowing I was dealing with people with severe functional impairment and prone to violence. It didn't help knowing there were murderers and sex offenders in the mix.

There was one untoward incident on Ward 6 that curiously involved the only non-white patient in all of the hospital, a rather timid-looking Pakistani murder convict. I was playing snooker with a patient in the lounge and, unbeknown to me, the Pakistani man, not provoked in any way, was lunging at me with the thick end of a cue stick, aiming for my head. By the time I turned to see what the commotion was about, a ward colleague was on the floor wrestling with the patient. Stupefied, I could only watch as others joined in to subdue my assailant. They injected him with a tranquilliser, forced him into a padded jumpsuit and hurled him into the cell, an experience that left me in severe shock and embarrassment as trouble seemed to follow me!

It was all very well my parents didn't have a clue as to the exact nature of my job, for there hadn't been a single correspondence between us in the three months since I'd arrived in England. With Christmas approaching, I wrote one letter each by airmail to Papa in Malaysia and Mummy in Kerala. In all honesty, I was not terribly homesick. I had learnt to organise myself around my new living arrangement – an active social life built around films and music, sports, work and friends. Quite simply, I liked the feeling of facing life on my own terms. A feeling that has stayed with me.

I ended 1970 in England enjoying a very traditional English Christmas with the Collinsons, then rang in the New Year with all my friends in the Grapes Inn, our local pub, beginning with the likes of Bolan and Bowie and ending with singing *Auld Lang Syne* and *Your Song*, by the upcoming sensation Elton John.

I began the New Year on the epilepsy long-stay male ward, where I learnt about petit mal seizure and the more life-threatening grand mal seizure. It required working closely with the charge nurse and specialist consultant psychiatrist on cutting-edge treatment and risk assessment, only offered to select student nurses.

On a weekend in February 1971, the annual North of England (Fylde Open) took place at the Lytham Sports Club, a prestigious badminton tournament that attracted top players from the whole of England. I entered the Men's Senior singles with the help of Willie, who managed to tweak the rota to get me the elusive weekend off. What a surprise to see most of the players arriving in cars, some in expensive new models. A shiny Rolls-Royce was preening in a private section of the club.

Being an unknown in that circuit, I was unseeded and had to play four rounds on Saturday in a freezing hall. I won them without too much strain, advancing to the quarterfinals to be played the following day. In that match, I despatched a top Lancashire County player, and interest began to grow in the boy from the east as nobody there had heard about me. Through another player, I found out my next opponent was Paul Wood, the recent All-England Junior champion. 'Be prepared for a wallop,' warned my new friend.

Spectators and players congregated around the centre court, some watching from a centrally heated glass room with a bar, among them, Peter Birtwistle, a stalwart of Lancashire and England's racket sports (also a Wimbledon All-England Club official). It was his Rolls-Royce I'd spotted earlier.

Paul and I did a few minutes of practice rallies after which the loudspeaker blared, 'Whites only, please.'

I failed to understand the message until a gentleman walked over and, between explaining and gesturing, told me to remove my blue top and bottoms for the strictly white clothing dress code. Some sections of the crowd broke out into laughter as I hurriedly changed, placing my *Good Morning* towel on my bag. 'PLAY' ordered the umpire, and the match began.

Paul was cheered on by a partisan crowd that went quiet after my passionate trouncing of its star in the first set. Birtwistle was shouting out guidance to Paul to put the shuttlecock on my backhand, possibly thinking I would tire and not be able to arch my back quite as often for my favourite forehead shot. The second set was a close fight, and Paul and I were locked at 10-10 when I won the rally to gain the right to serve. Just before serving, I walked to the side of the court to wipe the sweat on my hands and racket handle. Without warning, Birtwistle sprang onto the scene, grabbed my towel and flung it onto a chair at the back of my court!

'This is cheating!' he proclaimed loudly.

Placing towels by the side court was customary – I'd seen Tan Aik Huang do the same in international tournaments – and it had never caused trouble for me before, but apparently, it was an infraction of Birtwistle's law. I plucked up the courage to pursue the man, wanting to know what rule I'd breached. 'UNGENTLEMANLY conduct,' he snapped.

With the crowd behind Birtwistle and the umpire threatening to disqualify me if I didn't continue play, I went back to lose the second set 18-16 to the hall's delight.

Hiding my face under my *Good Morning* towel, I pushed Birtwistle away and allowed Coach Chan into my head.

It took me forty minutes in the deciding third game to beat Paul 15-8. I could feel I was not popular; still, support for me was not entirely lacking. It included Paul, who would later become my sparring partner and travel with me to many tournaments, along with other England players.

Three hours later, I got on the court again for the final and completed Birtwistle's nightmare by beating another Lancashire County player, in two sets. As president, Birtwistle passed me the silver trophy. When I offered him my hand, he responded with a limp shake. I'd planned to bus back but missed the last one and ended up hitchhiking again. No matter. The silverware was in my possession and my diary was waiting.

# TEN

# MERITOCRACY

In England, the badminton season ended with winter and I was intent on winning the showpiece Lancaster and Morecambe Badminton championship at the Morecambe Central Pier, where Geoffrey Knowles was the kingpin as its owners were his friends and clients. The Wesley gang had spoken so much about the prestige of the coastal town's tournament (the local press came to cover the event), and I saw it as an opportunity to wrap up my first season in England with a bang.

Before its demolishment in 1992, after more than a century's service, the Central Pier was Morecambe Bay's most iconic landmark, with a view of the northwest coastline, the open Irish Sea that contributed to Britain's (and Lancaster's) incredible wealth growth through the transatlantic triangular slave trade. For hundreds of years, loaded vessels left British ports for slave barter in Africa, then delivered the slaves to its colonies in the Caribbean and America, and returned with luxury cargoes, namely sugar, cotton, tobacco and rum, to enrich merchants and ports, ameliorating the living standards of the British people. The inconceivable irony was that when slave trading was fully abolished, it was the slave traders and enslavers who benefitted from the bestial business when they were awarded "compensation" by the British Government for their loss of economic interests due to the take-over of their "property". Nothing for the African slaves: men, women and children captured for chattel slavery and dehumanised in gruesome ways. The British Government paid out £20m (billions in today's money) to tens of thousands of people making claims from across the country. This burden of compensation was borne by British taxpayers until 2015, and it aggrieves and infuriates me to know I had contributed to it for over fifty years!

Lancaster's many imposing halls, houses and manors were built on the shackles of black slaves, which might have included Morecambe's Central Pier, but, in 1971, due to play my first Lancaster and Morecambe Badminton championship, my thoughts did not extend beyond lifting trophies. I was entered for the men's singles and doubles. This time, the dilemma of taking time off from work at Whittingham Hospital with enough time to hitchhike from Goosnargh to Morecambe was solved by Mr Murphy, who kindly instructed the charge nurse to put me on a special early shift to finish at 4 pm.

I arrived at the pier to ripples of excitement filling the ballroom's arena stage seats used to having the Beatles, the Rolling Stones or the Who troop in for some wild performances. By then, I was a hardened competitor with a vociferous Wesley unit to lend me support, and some female groupies besides! 'They come for your bum, Phil,' Geoffrey claimed, his quirky humour never in short supply in such moments.

To the squawks of gulls and the smell of the ocean, I swung and smashed with ease, winning both my events to two honours; the trophies were presented by Geoffrey, and, both local dailies, the *Lancaster Guardian* and the *Morecambe Visitor*, carried picture stories of the event, captioning me as the year's dark horse.

After a wonderful night of celebrations in Morecambe, I dreaded returning to Preston, particularly to Whittingham's emptiness. There were only three TV channels, commencing in the afternoon, and on Sundays we couldn't even head over to the pub as shops were closed. To allay the doldrums, I went on a much longer run than usual, my stomach empty, my head loaded with thoughts of Lancaster. The way my Wesley family embraced me into their fold, my frequent visits to Lancaster University for matches and concerts, as well as seeing my pictures in the papers, propelled me to consider my next chessboard battle.

With winter ending, Whittingham's grounds and gardens under the care of long-term patients were coming into bloom, filling up lanes and verges, synchronous with the thawing mood of the hospital's staff and patients. The unfolding of spring and summer was peppered with a hospital fete, ballroom dances, local bands and cricket league matches in which I participated with gusto. My heart, nonetheless, was in Lancaster.

Lancaster was parading on me – showering me with relentless, instructive masters. None more so than Geoffrey Knowles, and I will always carry much gratitude in my heart for his unstinting efforts in giving me the kind of exposure to put me in good stead right away, even with me being away in Whittingham. I struggled to keep up, felt inadequate and was often tongue-tied, yet kept up because Geoffrey treated me with so much kindness and respect. Perhaps in my shy, wide-eyed enthusiasm, he saw my will to persevere.

If Geoffrey wasn't at our matches in the Wesley Badminton Hall in Dalton Square, he'd join us afterwards at the Boot and Shoe, Fat Scotsman, the Blue Anchor or the Golden Ball Hotel in Overton, waltzing in with Whiteside and Knowles' secretaries, all of whom adored him. His wife Joan and daughter Janet often followed, and we'd all move the party to their palatial home, Shefferlands, in Halton near Lancaster, with its enormous grounds, gardens, stables, bootroom, gunroom and Geoffrey's son Clive's barn building, holding his stock cars. Joan would whip up bacon and eggs, soft buttered bread and mugs of tea from around midnight to about 2 am on a Friday night, which meant I'd always miss the last bus and Dave and Jean Ashcroft would drive me back to Whittingham in their sporty Triumph Vitesse as I needed to be ready and sober to begin shift at 7 am.

Having Geoffrey take me under his wing, I had no choice but to hit the ground running! To watch, observe, learn and, most importantly, shed my inhibitions and open my mouth. I dare say none of the Malaysian students sharing my Aeroflot from KL to England for studies in elite British universities would have benefitted the way I did with the privileges and advantages Geoffrey's company and mentoring afforded me. He'd drive up to the hospital to take me to football matches at Blackpool, Liverpool, Old Trafford, Manchester City, Burnley or Preston North End, to watch from prime seats, which was nothing compared to the majesty of the cricket grounds he introduced me to. Imagine being suited up with the Lancashire County Cricket Club tie following in Geoffrey's style; occupying a plush seat in the Members' Pavilion at the Old Trafford Lancashire County Cricket Club or Lord's Cricket Club after an exquisite afternoon tea to take in a test match; being introduced to Clive Lloyd, Farokh Engineer or Barry Richards; or watching Geoffrey say to the England captain Tony Greig, 'Bug off to South Africa,' when I didn't know anything from anything!

It was a whole new world for the boy from a rubber estate in Kajang to partake in the splendour of cricket and its politics. And when it was not cricket or football, we'd travel to Silloth or Carnforth to watch Clive Knowles racing at stock car meets in his Ford Escort Mexico rally car. Anything to do with cars always floated my boat!

I was often dumbstruck by Geoffrey's generosity in

grooming and protecting me – once rolling up his sleeves for fisticuffs with another member trying to shove me from my seat at the Old Trafford Cricket Club – to say nothing of the pride I felt when Geoffrey began introducing me as his second son, or hearing him say, 'Thank you, son, for a lovely day and especially for your company,' every time he dropped me back at Whittingham.

With all that happening in the background, I turned nineteen feeling completely sapped of motivation to continue in Whittingham. Running, social activities and my Lancaster escapades were of no help; neither did it even occur to me to share my feelings with anyone. Then came the double whammy – watching Charlie George score Arsenal's winning goal in extra time to beat Liverpool in the FA Cup. I remember so well how close I came to an emotional breakdown as I laboured out of St Luke's tele room after that match, with only one thought in my head: get out of Whittingham.

Quick searches in newspapers showed most jobs required 'O' Level English and Maths, neither of which I had, so I immediately enrolled on a night course at nearby Longbridge, and would pass them too, which would come in very useful in later life but not for immediate rescue from Whittingham. Once again, I used badminton as a means to my end. Through badminton, I had become friends with Liz Blackow, the chief nursing officer at the Lancaster Moor Hospital, who put in a good word for me with the hospital's chief managing director. My plan was to put in a transfer request to continue my nursing course at the Moor Hospital. When I met the managing director at

Standen Park House, the hospital's grand office building, I was told a transfer would only be possible with a reference from Whittingham Hospital.

It was another period of anxiety as I prepared to face Mr Murphy. Would he construe my proposal as a defection after all his support of me? How was I even to execute my plan?

My early sense of dislocation being a foreigner settling in England was fast diminishing as I was reaping the benefits of my badminton rigour, hard work and personal virtue, and, although certain distinctions remained, I was no longer such a clear signpost of not being up to the playbook. Had I decided to grit my teeth and bear the Ward 20 conditions, I would not have gained the notice or respect of Mr Murphy, Willie Cunningham and subsequent charge nurses. When they realised how I never allowed my late hours after badminton matches, with only a few hours of sleep, to affect my performance at work, it generated mutual respect, making my tenure at Whittingham enjoyable despite the drudgery.

Growing up in a plural Malaysian society was also bearing fruit – the guile and guts of the Indian and Malay boys plunging into raging rivers and the inexhaustible curiosity of the Chinese. After a particularly irretrievable shot, the Chinese badminton player in Malaysia would not complain or find fault with my "conduct". Instead, he'd come to the net and ask, 'How did you make that shot? Who's your coach?' A strong need to know, acquire and emulate – qualities that make the Chinese dominate the economies of Malaysia, Singapore and Indonesia. Using that as my guiding spirit, I put myself in the sorting machine and let myself be shaped and influenced by my new environment in quite simply the best of decades.

And so when I relayed my memorised transfer request to Mr Murphy, he understood. As it happened, Mr Murphy also wrote a good reference, allowing me to continue the remaining two years of my training at Lancaster Moor Hospital.

I spent my last weeks at Whittingham in the Admission Unit for short-term patients, mostly professionals, even doctors, and farmers and bankers, who received counselling, drugs and the controversial ECT (electroconvulsive therapy, simply known as shock treatment) before they were discharged, often to return.

While my English friends were easily accepting of my decision, my Mauritian housemates were stunned at my perceived temerity. I think if I'd tried to make them understand that it was my racket charting my course, or that I functioned with the jungle spirit imbibed in Limau Manis, it would have been even more unfathomable to them. Instead, we bade fond farewells. Many of them would return to Mauritius after completing their course; some of the few who stayed back would become my clients in my later years as a lawyer, effusive with their praise of my success in a completely different profession.

I left Whittingham with that "I've arrived" feeling when my English friends declared *you're one of us, Phil*. I did not stop to wonder what might have been the measure of merit, just proud and happy as if I'd been accepted into an Ivy League university!

In September 1971, I moved to the Moor Hospital sprawled over Lancaster, drawing attention straightaway for being the only coloured student. It was to the Standen Park House office building once again for registration formalities. The rambling gothic structure looked more foreboding and repressive than it did on my first visit in spring. Never could I have imagined ever returning there in the future to live on its grounds as owner of the property!

Standen Park House fringed the hypnotic Trough of Bowland, which was going to be my backyard for the next forty-two years. The hospital itself adjoined Williamson Park and the iconic Ashton Memorial on a hill overlooking Morecambe Bay in the distance, my other future playground. My accommodation was on the ground floor (for males) of a four-storey building housing student nurses. Female students occupied the second and third floors. The fourth floor had a large sitting area with a black and white TV where all the nurses gathered to create a great atmosphere.

My first placement was in the Admission Unit in a building nearly a mile away from staff housing, and I walked every time I was on shift. The set-up and work shifts were similar to Whittingham, as were the work routine and politics. The difference was, Lancaster Moor felt less sinister and threatening.

Every nurse had a decent stereo system and, not to be outdone, I swapped my simple record player for a stereo with two speakers from a Currys Electrical shop on a hire purchase contract. From then on, it was buying vinyl albums weekly. In what felt like a mass cultural movement, Britain was churning out influential world-class artists, and my taste and attitude towards music and songs was very much shaped by the rising phenomena of the period's exciting, innovative creations. My transition to music with strong underpinnings of rock was quick and easy, helped to an extent by *Melody Maker*, the weekly music paper. I didn't feel out of place with the differing ethos from what I knew in Malaysia, although I grappled with the sheer creativity of titles like *Selling England by the Pound, Teaser and the Firecat, Nursery Cryme* or *The Lamb Lies Down on Broadway* – a long way from *Me and You and a Dog Named Boo*!

It was all going on on the fourth floor. Laughter, chatter, smoking, drinking, watching BBC 2's new avant-garde show Richard William's *The Old Grey Whistle Test*, sniffing soft plants with incense… hedonistic and out of control at times, but I took it in my stride, never compromising my sportsperson's self-discipline. Rain, snow or sleet, I put in an eight-mile circular run every day through the rising and falling paths of the Trough of Bowland, loving its desolate beauty as it did not attract the kind of traffic heading further north to the Lakes or the Dales. It was routine to finish at Williamson Park with twenty-three (just liked the number!) shuttle runs up and down the mossy steps of Ashton Memorial I christened the Taj Mahal of Lancaster despite its state of abandonment at the time.

One of the first things I did after returning to Lancaster was to hike to Liverpool, for a very special purpose. With the help of a badminton friend, a Liverpool native and regular match attendee, I organised my first football experience without Geoffrey to be nothing short of legendary. What a sensation it was to be standing in the Kop at Anfield, the only person of colour, watching the Merseyside giants take on Manchester United! Seeing Bill Shankly screaming instructions, Ray Clemence in goal, Ian Callaghan, Brian Hall, Bobby Graham, Georgie Best, Bobby Charlton, Denis Law all in action, I realised a boyhood dream that night, still a boy, revelling in a wild night that made plain football's larger-than-life avatar. A fair 2-2 draw, I told my diary.

I didn't work most weekends and if I wasn't spending them with Geoffrey, playing for either of my clubs or hitchhiking to some badminton tournament, I'd get to the side road leading to the M6 to hitch up north to Scotland or south to London, frequently doing a distance of 250 miles. There was never a moment's lull, except on Sundays with the Sunday trading laws in full operation, meaning the city was dead, but I was completely immersed in the repertoire of the era's popular music and would habitually blast my favourite vinyl in a loop.

On Saturdays, when Manchester City had a home game, my Wesley friend Mason Whitaker would pick me up from the hospital and we'd drive to Dave and Jean Ashcroft's house in Garstang from where the four of us would head to Maine Road to watch a home match, using our season passes. On the return drive, we'd listen to the radio for the complete football results and upon returning to Garstang, the ritual was to plonk ourselves in front of the television with a tray of whatever Jean rustled up, often pie, sausages, mushy peas, mashed potato bathed in brown sauce, and soak in BBC 1's fantastic offerings, including coverage of one of the day's football matches, which could just be the one we'd caught earlier, before ending the evening with the elegant Michael Parkinson serving a great conversation with personalities of immense merit. What a schooling that was for me, although I couldn't get my head around most of it.

I ended 1971 spending my first Christmas at Shefferlands, where Geoffrey's prized gardens were hibernating. He won numerous trophies for growing roses exhibited from Bentham to Overton and was in the habit of going home for lunch to spend time in his gardens, sometimes forgetting appointments at his Morecambe office. Not wanting me to be alone during the festive period, Geoffrey invited me to join his family for dinner, which included his elderly mother, whom I took care of for brief periods at the hospital.

By then, Geoffrey and I had forged a great bond, the more than thirty-year age gap between us easily bridged by his candour, humour and amazingly cutting wit. He was a powerhouse in the north of England as much for his legal work as for his colourful style as a raconteur in and out of the courts, be it dealing with pesky judges or higher-up clients. Our long drives to football matches or the cricket grounds were veritable classroom sessions, with Geoffrey showing me the ropes: how to drink beer, chat up girls, what the difference was between a Tyke and a Lancastrian, what the *War of the Roses* meant in cricket... I learnt he was a proud Sandgrown'un, and also that he'd been a prisoner of war in Malaya during the Japanese occupation, the painful experiences of which he would open up to me in dispatches over our long friendship.

The way Geoffrey imparted his wisdom was akin to listening to Papa and friends going on about Tunku Abdul Rahman, Chin Peng, Lee Kuan Yew, Churchill, Gandhi or Kennedy. With Geoffrey, it was Heath, Wilson, Powell, and in those early years of the Troubles, a lot of the IRA and the UVF. The environment might have been attentive to social awareness and political processes, but our interactions were dynamic, always interspersed with sumptuous doses of his man-about-town dalliances that sometimes led to capers of the kind to put Geoffrey's formidable reputation on the line!

Not caring that it was Christmas, Geoffrey gave me a lecture on what was a major headline-grabbing topic that year-end in 1971: Britain's affair with the European Union. By a vote of 356 to 244, the House of Commons had approved British membership in the European Common Market, an outcome that brought joy to Common Market leaders who had fought several abortive attempts for Britain's entry. Prime Minister Heath announced, 'Many millions of people across the world will rejoice that Britain will be taking her rightful place in the true European unity that we are going to win.' Perhaps it's a facile generalisation, but it was just as well Heath did not live to see the UK squander its "rightful place" it had fought for with true wisdom at the heart. Neither did Geoffrey. But he didn't exit this world before he had provided me with a solid foundation for my assimilation into Middle-England society. Served me well later in communication skills and managing expectations in the legal field.

Being in Lancaster certainly unleashed potential in me I never knew I had. For one thing, I became intensely curious and invested, wanting to grasp, to possess everything England had to offer. The BBC became a great friend; I'd scour the tabloids and broadsheets too, which led to noticing things like how on the heels of Britain's entry into the Common Market, continental sophistication began arriving in the UK. England's admiration of France's charm and style reached its masses when the first French hypermarket, Carrefour, opened in Caerphilly, Wales in 1972, going against the grain of Britain's quaint single checkout shops.

1972, however, did not begin well for Heath's government when it chose to pick a fight with Joe Gormley and the powerful coal miners' union. It caused mayhem, with the energy supply leading to a state of emergency and the closure of many power stations and factories. It was the peak of winter and all of Britain went into a freeze. Fortunately, my hospital had its backup generators and we largely escaped unscathed.

The '70s would continue to be gloomy and volatile for Britain, with blackouts and strikes, union troubles, a rising tide of violence and a sharp downturn in the economy, especially after the Arab-Israeli War, which led to massive oil price inflation. It's tragic how, five decades later, following the self-inflicted Brexit, domestic policy failures, the Covid-19 pandemic, successive dysfunctional leadership and the Russia-Ukraine War, England faces a return to the same age of being the sick man of Europe, with the economy in recession, all-time-high government debt and nationwide strikes in so many industries causing everything from disruptive transport services and overflowing bins to halting court cases.

My final months at the Moor Hospital were on the children's ward, a deeply disturbing period. I was treated with great intrigue and amusement when I first arrived. 'Are you from the jungle, mister?' 'Where is Malaysia?' And the most heartbreaking of all… 'You won't beat, will you?' At times, children as young as eight were sent to the hospital by parents or guardians wanting a few months of respite from the children's "behavioural issues" (ungovernable, sexually precocious St Trinian's candidates). I was still only twenty and not much older than some of the children there and my heart went out to them, not unlike how I felt with the poor old dears on Whittingham's Ward 20. I could not understand what caused so many children in a wealthy nation like England to suffer from all sorts of psychological problems to the point of needing hospital intervention. Was the system so blind as to not see that the punitive environment was more likely to exacerbate their conditions than improve them?

Looking at the state of the children, I felt a surge of helplessness – this was no Ward 20 that could be solved with an additional bath a week. I was already familiar with the pattern of malpractice and abuse in psychiatric hospitals, but this was raising a much more sinister stink, the impact of which was clearly going to affect future generations, because, unlike geriatric patients, who largely lived out their lives in the mental hospitals, these children were to be returned to the folds of society to possibly even more devastating consequences.

The best I could do was to employ the moral treatment approach (part of training) by showing kindness. I invited the children to watch me play badminton at the hospital's Starkie Hall and taught the interested ones to play chess. On a Saturday if I was on shift, I would take them to a morning matinee at the ABC cinema, then walk around the city centre to Lancaster Castle or the museum and treat them to soft drinks and ice cream before heading back.

It wasn't long before I gained their trust. As they shared their miseries, I took notes. It bothered me how to take it forward by way of a complaint or grievance on behalf of the children. There were no templates to follow, and it was doubly difficult as higher authorities appeared to have closed their eyes to the abuse. There was also the nag of presenting such a *report* to my friend Liz, considering it was an act beyond the call of duty.

Setting aside my loyalty to Liz, I formulated a report of my findings to hand over to Liz to do with what she liked. I wrote on the thick Lancaster Moor Hospital stationery paper, a three-column spreadsheet report in chronological order of date, name of youngster and allegations. It ran into about seventeen pages, signed and dated by me, not unlike my oil palm census report for Prang Besar Estate! The report paid dividends when it ended up with the local member of parliament, resulting in an inquiry.

On the personal front, I was now peppering Brut and upping my sartorial game for dates with Lesley, the hospital's records clerk. Outside of London and the bigger cities, it was still unheard of for an Asian to walk into a local pub with a white girl, which was exactly what Lesley and I did in parochial Lancaster on our first date at the Lancastrian Pub. With gin and lime with ice for my girl and a pint of Tartan beer for me, we passed the ordeal.

It was on a high note that I celebrated my twenty-first birthday in the spring of 1973, held at the Cypress Tavern in the centre of town, attended by about a hundred friends from five different badminton clubs, Lancaster University, and nurses from both hospitals. On that significant birthday, I experienced a hard-earned epiphany from my choppy, heady three years of life in England. I was well and truly in Lancaster's inner sanctum, to the utter disbelief of Cousin PC, who was also at my party. Geoffrey, Dave, Jean and Mason were there, of course, to make my day very special, as was my girlfriend, Lesley, who in another moment of personal epiphany liberated me of my virginity.

To make my year even more memorable, I headed on a hike to Scotland on a four-day break, beginning from the north exit to the M6/A6. An elegant MGB GT open-top sports car with an attractive female driver wearing a chiffon headscarf stopped to give me a lift up to Glasgow. The Glasgow University lecturer was impressed I was doing a worthwhile occupation in psychiatric nursing. I felt otherwise.

It was evening by the time a lorry got me into Edinburgh, where Waverley railway station was my shelter for the night. I woke up early the next morning to use the toilets before the station got busy, and headed up to the castle to explore Edinburgh's famous landmark. It was a cool spring morning and in a moment of wanderlust I made up my mind to head north to Aberdeen. I left Edinburgh by the local bus to Queensferry to check out the "haunted" Hawes Inn mentioned in Robert Louis Stevenson's *Kidnapped*. Unfortunately, too many decades had passed since the time the novel was written, and all I experienced was the desperate longing to spot ghosts.

By the time I reached Aberdeen railway station, it was already out of bounds and I checked into a cheap sailors' lodge next to the harbour. I could not bring myself to sleep on the bed bearing after-sex stains, therefore settled on the floor. Lodging and a greasy breakfast cost me just four shillings, paid at checkout.

On my way back to the hospital, I got a straight ride to Edinburgh in a lorry, arriving in the evening at Waverley Station to spend my final night in Scotland. Scottish bobbies were more accommodating in looking the other way than the cockney ones at London Euston or the Lancastrian ones at Manchester Victoria! After my morning usuals the following day, I got three different lifts and reached the M6 roundabout outside Carlisle by 4 pm. As I approached the thumbing point, three other youngsters were doing the same exercise. We exchanged brief pleasantries and I found out the two girls and a fella were together.

A large white Triumph 2000 MK with a male driver stopped, saying he was London bound. The trio cried out they were going to Oxford and clambered in. The driver kindly asked whether I too wanted a ride and I got in the back seat with the girls, with the boy sitting in the front passenger seat. 'Call me Dick,' Richard introduced himself in a clipped English accent. As the journey progressed, Dick asked what we were "reading". The boy introduced himself as Robert and said he was reading Classics at Cambridge, and Emma and Louise were at Oxford reading Medicine (Louise thankfully let the cat out of the bag by using the word *studying* instead). The three were making their way back to their halls of residence after the Edinburgh Fringe – a major eye-opening moment that would set me off on an almost annual pilgrimage to the world's largest arts festival, for "the world's greatest celebration of arts and culture".

As introductions progressed, I was drowning. I should have known better since I had not encountered anyone in England who judged me on academia, yet I told them I was a student at Lancaster University *reading* Economics! Fortunately, my carmates moved to pastures new, with Robert talking classics and medicine chat from the girls, and I listened without a word to their effortless chatter, envying the group's self-assertion, up to the blue Lancaster sign where Dick dropped me.

On my four days of travel, I covered about 400 miles, seeing and doing many exciting things and feeling proud of them, yet, on the six-mile walk back to my room I had a most cathartic realisation: the confines of my eastern straitjacket thinking would have to be removed if I was to make it in the west.

ELEVEN

# FREEDOM COME, FREEDOM GO!

I graduated from Lancaster Moor Hospital as an accomplished psychiatric nurse who would be applying the extremely useful knowledge and experiences acquired there in my personal journey. *Not* as a professional nurse.

Twenty-one years of age, completely unanchored from Papa's control, I was raring to design a new life for myself. Feeling I wasn't cut out for nursing, I made the decision to walk away from a secure future.

Solidarity with my instincts has guided me well throughout my life... admittedly, there have been impetuous decisions I've come to rue. Sports, my hospital life, tapping into Middle-England society, my willingness to upset the apple cart and my zeal for learning something from each experience coming my way have been useful at different points in my life. Like in badminton when I needed to summon my second or third wind to overcome difficult patches to notch a victory, I feel it is important in life to keep adding plenty of strings to one's bow.

I searched the local papers for employment vacancies and spotted a position for a bank clerk with the National Westminster Bank (Nat West) in the Morecambe branch. Within a week came a reply to attend an interview with Mr Shorrock, the area manager of the northwest, in his Lancaster office. I went in my dark single-breasted suit with a white shirt and my standout Malaysian tie to meet Mr Shorrock in his plush office dominated by a mahogany table and deep leather chairs. Mr Shorrock surprised me when he said he'd seen my pictures and read about my badminton prowess in the local rags, leading to a really good chat that ended with a firm handshake. I was offered the position to begin in four weeks.

Looking for my own accommodation at long last was an incredibly liberating experience, even if I had to do it in the company of my English girlfriend for "credibility". I was fresh off being stopped for questioning by two police officers late one night on the A6 for lugging home a large silver trophy wrapped in a towel, as usual, hitching my way back after missing the last bus. During the unnerving interrogation, I had to convince the authorities I wasn't a robber escaping with my loot! If only centuries prior the Crown's servants had been as vigilant with their colonialist brothers returning with ship after ship after ship of their loot from all over the world… in Papa's words, "plundering India of her immeasurable wealth and dignity to feed the greed of an empire at the expense of millions of our people dying torturous deaths".

After three years of nurses' home accommodation, I transported my few belongings in Mason's Ford Cortina GT to my first private digs, a self-contained apartment on the third and topmost floor of a stone-terraced property overlooking Chatsworth Road in Morecambe. With my own address, a rented black and white TV from a local shop and a little kitchen to cook what I liked, I began living on my own terms for the first time. For my first dinner, I made myself a Fray Bentos steak and kidney pie with chips, green peas and gravy to go with sliced bread and margarine, washed down with the BBC on my tele to feelings of blissful domestication despite the autumnal chill making me miss the hospital accommodation's centrally heated rooms.

Mrs Jones, the landlady, lived with her family on the ground floor, while the middle floor was occupied by a female tenant with whom I shared a toilet, bathroom and frivolous conversations, mainly lending an ear to her confessions about her "unattractive husband", grounds enough, she hoped, to claim the union had irretrievably broken down as per the new Matrimonial Causes Act 1973. The law made divorce far easier, exciting many couples, in particular those who'd married young or entered into shotgun marriages, creating a big demand for lawyers. A continuation of the sexual and social revolutions stemming from the psychedelic '60s, including political reforms such as the decriminalisation of homosexuality and abortion, kept changing and opening up British society.

On my first day of work, I went on my usual morning run on Morecambe's seafront promenade to the sweet, thrilling taste of freedom. Showered and shaved, I put on my blue Lord John single-breasted suit, a plain cornflour double cuff shirt with Papa's silver cufflinks, black leather shoes with pink socks and my Timex watch. I arrived in good time, to be let in by a security guard, and was greeted by Mr Lucas, the assistant bank manager, a six-footer with a strong voice and friendly smile. When the rest of the staff of around fifteen arrived, Mr Lucas introduced me to all-round smiles and greetings.

How smartly dressed my new colleagues were to match the bank's corporate image, and how they all seemed to look forward to their daily grind in an atmosphere exuding warmth and security. Everyone was friendly and openly curious about my Eastern origin, being the only non-white employee. Not for the first time, I was very happy to have made the switch from psychiatric nursing. I was assigned to the machine room to learn basic banking procedures. Handling cheques, balancing the daily post-franking machine and so forth was a cinch compared to the hospitals. At the end of my first week, Mr Lucas sent me over the moon when he informed me of Mr Shorrock's instruction that I be allocated time off to play badminton, plus monthly trips to the Continent with an unlimited expense account to represent the United Banks team.

Work did not affect my other commitments, especially considering I was only a short distance from Lancaster University and its Great Hall. After badminton practice with the university boys, it was common to head to the sauna; five or six naked men discussing everything under the sun. No embarrassment, no shame, unlike my Kajang High days of running behind bushes or the tuck shop to get changed for sports! It was daunting as I lacked self-confidence and was severely conflicted – didn't feel attractive and was often tongue-tied for my lack of English wit or sense of humour. I wasn't diplomatic and spoke from the heart, yet the boys found me intriguing, if not entertaining, which was comforting. Many of my inhibitions dropped away and I began speaking with more colour and passion, all stemming from the sauna and showering naked!

Our sauna conversations, when not talking sports, were dominated by the Great Hall concerts. The haloed venue played host every Saturday during the winter months to some of the world's greatest rock artists. Such a boon it was for Lancaster and, in particular, its restless youth. Each concert was the real deal. The Who, Pink Floyd, U2, Black Sabbath, Queen, Eric Clapton, Wishbone Ash, Van Morrison or Dire Straits, you got to experience them up close; you felt their spit and smelt them. No overzealous security guards or agents back then to manage bands or footballers. Celebrity was non-existent; neither was prejudice. It was all rhapsodies of bohemia and I was having the time of my life. Very liberal, laissez-faire, anarchic, colourful… I was completely inside the 1970s zeitgeist enraptured by Marvin Gaye's *What's Going On* or Led Zeppelin's *Stairway to Heaven*, just as I was with the Jackson 5 or Janis Joplin; watching *Star Wars, Superman, Jaws* or *Grease* with the same fervor, I explored the remarkable diversity of themes the era's movies offered… counterculture, anti-war, black comedies… *The Godfather, Clockwork Orange, Straw Dogs, Blue Velvet, The Deer Hunter*… What memories to take to my grave!

Within weeks of starting work, on Mr Shorrock's instruction, I was sent on a one-week induction course at Heythrop Park in Banbury, Oxford, the bank's stately home training venue. Upon arrival, I was assigned a double room with two single beds. The other delegate's belongings were on one bed but he was not in. With still a few hours to go before the official dinner, I managed to take in a long run in the estate's vast grounds. When I returned, I once again missed my roommate.

The magnificent dining hall was packed with delegates being served six-course traditional English fare followed by speeches from the bank's bigwigs. By the time I went to bed at around midnight, my roommate was still not back and I was too tired to wait up to say hello. It turned out he had no qualms about wrecking *my* sleep.

Sometime in the early hours, I was startled from a deep sleep by the weight of a bare body thrusting itself on me. Grappling with my assailant, I fastened a chokehold around his neck and had him off me and on the floor from where he begged me to stop, seeing that my leg was directed at his now flaccid undercarriage. My first brawl with a white man ended with me letting him go with a warning to not try it again on me or face an official complaint of indecent behaviour. Raunchy roommate meekly crept into his bed as I straggled to the bathroom to wash off the violation. I was free of further unwanted advances for the remaining days as we kept our distance and silence. The experience, though, would return whenever my future clients/survivors of abuse confessed their enormous shame, guilt or self-blame, which caused them anxiety and depression among many other psycho-social consequences.

In the middle of the week, we were asked to project our minds into the future and work on an essay titled *Banking in the 1990s*. I hadn't known it then, possibly because of the emotional raw spot ('fit only for tree climbing') developed in my childhood, but I had the natural ability to pick up concepts and process information quite accurately.

I immediately plugged into my peripheral knowledge and since the task involved finance and business, my thoughts settled on Papa's Chinese friends, who were unquestionably ahead of the others in Malaysia when it came to commerce. It was beyond the thrift, hard work and focus on good education Indians are renowned for. Papa always said, 'If you want to make money, learn from the Chinese.' On that premise, I submitted my thesis based on the world economy of the future being under the control of China and the tiger economies of Southeast Asia.

On the last day, the results were announced from the faraway stage of a huge conference room. The third and second prizes went to representatives from Middlesex and Sussex respectively, after which the emcee read out, 'We've had an unusual report that wins the first prize this year from Philip George of Morecambe Branch, Lancaster.' As I stood transfixed, the emcee went on to highlight the importance of China and the Far East and something about my vision to see this. With the loudspeakers blaring out Deep Purple, I went onstage to accept the certificate, where I was asked to give a speech!

Conjuring up the spirits of Papa and Geoffrey, I blurted out from my assignment: Chairman Mao, the vision of the SWIRE Group, Cathay Pacific, the role of Hong Kong, HSBC... Watching the audience's applause from the stage was a big thrill, but not bigger than the urge in my heart wishing my Kajang High School detractors had been there to witness my triumph, in particular the teachers who took joy in calling out my tendency to "go off track" or to be "too wild with imagination". All of a sudden, nothing felt out of reach for Philip George, the "waste of space".

To my great delight, my office colleagues greeted me with felicitations, and coffee and cakes were the order of the day. Both Mr Lucas and even the elusive branch manager, Mr Brian Heller, were there to congratulate me, after which I was sent to see Mr Shorrock, using the bank's taxi hire company. Over lunch with Mr Shorrock at the Portofino restaurant on Castle Hill, a novelty in itself, I found out a copy of my Heythrop Park report had been couriered to him. Mr Shorrock was most bemused to hear me relate how I got the data for the assignment from years of eavesdropping on Papa and Co's inexhaustible discussions on anything and everything, as well as making libraries my haven. He in turn said he had big plans for me for the following year – merchant banking training in

London. To prepare for that, I was to be promoted from the machine room to being the manager's assistant clerk. Life could not be better.

On the way to work the next day, I posted my passport to the Home Office for the yearly renewal of my student visa, with a forwarding letter to say I had left nursing and was now working in the bank. If only I had kept quiet...

My Nat West Morecambe branch memories are paradisal. Friendships, camaraderie, hanging out, especially after my badminton trips to the Continent, as my colleagues were eager for information. It was a luxury those days for the middle classes, whose holidays were restricted to Bournemouth, Brighton or Blackpool. Another time, the bank was quite star-struck with the arrival of the hugely popular Black and White Minstrels stage act (white performers blacking up their faces) to perform in Morecambe. Its 150-strong cast and crew came to our branch for their weekly wages and I cashed their cheques. Caught in a servile trap, I was unable to see the prejudicial tone of the show... or to be offended by it. Nor was I aware that the BBC had been petitioned to axe the television version of the show for its racial discrimination and lack of representation.

Approaching the end of 1973, the IRA was blowing up everything, there was the Middle East oil embargo to punish the West for its support of Israel, causing a massive hike in oil prices, inflation of food prices and continuing rise in unemployment. My fortune, however, was taking the opposite trend – a good job, own apartment, girlfriend and a burgeoning flirtation with females drawn to my sportsman reputation. It was hard to hold oneself back, most certainly not conducive to maintaining a steady relationship. I chose to be honest about it with Lesley, ending in tears for her and a very long run on the promenade for me.

The decadence of the era and a mischievous mentor like Geoffrey proffered licence to indulge in my share of some wild fun, and my Wesley friends would joke I was as bad as *Alfie*... Morecambe Promenade certainly holds many Philip George stories! There were also liberal moments when yours truly was entrusted to provide an alibi as my mentor took off with lady friends in his Peugeot for lunches looking down on Lake Windermere, Ambleside, with red tartan blankets, Marks and Spencer's Wensleydale cheese, ginger beer, Thornton chocolates and a flask of coffee.

It was a time when enchanting young Jane Birkin types in the shortest of miniskirts discarded their coyness for a *Je t'aime... moi non plus* moment. Like the one night after a particularly intoxicating three-hour performance of Alvin Lee and Ten Years After at the Great Hall when I ended up not in my third-floor Chatsworth Road bedsit but in a beautiful stranger's flat to wafts of incense sticks, replicating Serge Gainsbourg and Brigitte Bardot.

That's not to say I was awash with success all the time! With girls who knew me from badminton and admired my athleticism, I could *score*, but it wasn't the case when I went pub-crawling with the blokes, when my lack of social skills stuck out and I was often the only one of five or six to return to empty digs, seeking refuge in Joni Mitchell, Bob Dylan or Elton John. *Rocket Man* was a particular favourite... Hindsight and maturity may cast a different light on it all now, but we were beneficiaries of a time when relaxed sexual attitudes were sweeping through the country.

Two years after my nasty encounter with Birtwistle's *you can't place your towel here* petty prejudice, I played at the Markland Hill Lawn Tennis, Badminton and Squash Club in the upmarket Markland Hill suburb of Bolton – the home of Birtwistle – and where he was the founder member and president of the club. Nothing had changed.

Just before the final, when the tournament secretary hollered, 'Whites only, please,' I deliberately played court jester. I walked off the court and sat down, eliciting great laughter from the crowd but not from bristling Birtwistle. The man's hostility was just as palpable when he presented me with the winner's trophy!

My trips to the Continent were far more joyous. I represented the United Banks team of Great Britain with five other England national players to play against the national teams of Denmark, Sweden, the Netherlands and Germany, taking me from Amsterdam and Rotterdam to Stockholm, Copenhagen, Frankfurt and Cologne. I recall the journeys with fondness and nostalgia – travelling first class on the train from Lancaster to Euston, the tube to Liverpool Street Station, the overland British Rail train to Harwich for an overnight ferry to Hook of Holland and from there to the respective destinations by a well-connected continental train system.

On each visit to a different city, I made special friends who took great pride in introducing me to

European culture. Being insatiably curious, their cultural advancements and refinement struck me right away. If the sights exploded with amazing architecture and fantastic roads, the first time I walked into a hotel room I was smitten by the understated elegance of their duvets to England's patchwork bedspread throws and granny crochet blankets. Ambivalence began creeping into my long-standing belief that England was the beacon of liberty and sophistication.

I couldn't help noticing how exquisitely *beau monde* the continental crowds attending matches were. Chic in their dressing and manner, I discovered it applied to everything from their coffee culture to how they drank wine and ate their food to their thinking and attitude. Quite simply, scenes from *Playboy* and James Bond flashed before my eager eyes. Meanwhile, wine drinking as a habit was only just catching on among a growing section of English society.

Mr Shorrock had another surprise for me when he arranged for an interview with the senior national manager, Mr Whitty, at the London Nat West HQ about a promotion to merchant banking. For two days, I was put up in the classy Cumberland Hotel in Marble Arch, and soon after the interview was offered a position working in the Nat West London branch in collaboration with Chase Manhattan of New York, commencing January 1974.

My excitement was short-lived when on a Monday morning before setting off for work a bombshell arrived from the Home Office. It was a short, threateningly legalistic letter: I had breached my conditions of entry and the UK Government required me to immediately resign from my bank post and leave the country by 31 December 1973; otherwise, I would be arrested and deported at my own expense.

Walking into the bank that morning felt like entering the doghouse. I was asked to go to the manager's office, who then sent me straight to Lancaster. Mr Shorrock appeared unperturbed, which was somewhat comforting. He apologised for putting me in the predicament for he had not done his due diligence – missing the student visa stamped on my passport. He said the bank would challenge the Home Office decision and that Mr Whitty had instructed their legal firm to appeal the decision and thereafter if unsuccessful go for a judicial review. Mr Shorrock assured me my merchant banker position in London would be placed on hold until the immigration issue was resolved. It was all beyond me! All I knew was that I was in safe hands.

There was no Portofino lunch that time with Mr Shorrock. I was sent back to continue work and expect to "receive a letter from the Home Office stating postponement of the date to leave the UK being extended" to give the bank's lawyers nine months to put right the matter. Sure enough, the letter came confirming the same, which I carefully placed with my passport for my travels to the Continent.

After that very frightening interlude, life returned to normal and 1974 rolled out memorable episodes in succession. ABBA won the Eurovision Song Contest in Brighton with *Waterloo* to go on to become international megastars. Shortly after, I was at the Empire Pool Stadium in Wembley to witness a titanic All England final between Rudy Hartono and Malaysia's Punch Gunalan, where on the same afternoon a few streets away the attempted kidnapping of Princess Anne, just failed. The football season ended with two major shocks. Bill Shankly retired as Liverpool manager after fifteen glorious years, and Manchester United were relegated to the second division, with Denis Law, one of its Holy Trinity, switching to Manchester City and scoring the decisive goal in the closing minutes at Old Trafford of all places. I was standing in the disconsolate Stretford End to witness Denis perform his Judas act and felt the pain of United fans.

Much to Geoffrey's joy, I passed my driving test and began driving us around all the counties in England and Wales to follow Lancashire's cricket boys. He made me a full member and a season ticket holder of the Old Trafford Cricket Ground, and soon I was mixing with the England and West Indies international cricketers. How not to marvel at my good fortune when comparing it to my high-school days when certain snobby masters considered cricket their domain and only fit for their clan?

Geoffrey also introduced me to the Morecambe Golf Club, where I became a member. Most of its members knew me from badminton – Middle-England people stuck in their ways – yet I had no trouble buzzing about the club making friends, including with Vernon Eastwood, a large-built, well-travelled man who always made time to counsel me on matters of the heart! A lot of times I was the only coloured person, and it made no difference. I was invited to all sorts of functions, from birthdays and anniversaries to the president's dinner and summer dances, and was also privy to its tittle-tattle and scandals. Affairs, marriage breakdowns, divorces, family inheritance disputes... as the place abounded with middle-aged men getting up to mischief! The sort of old stalwarts, Vernon included, who had their special corner, dubbed the "departure lounge", where we enjoyed ready repartee – never mind that I was still wet behind the ears – leading to many of them becoming my future clients, mainly with requests to act as executor of their wills and attorney to their lasting power of attorney documents. Being at their age now, these memories carry endearing messages for me – as does Geoffrey's oft-repeated 'Never walk past a toilet without using it'... He'd slowed down by then and would add, 'You never know when the next flush is going to be!'

All the while, I never spoke about my immigration troubles with my friends, not even to Geoffrey, as I was embarrassed, and perhaps a little confident it would end well. In early August 1974, I received official registered mail from the Home Office stating the earlier decision stood and that unless the bank terminated my employment immediately, the Home Office would take criminal proceedings against the bank. I had to leave the UK by the end of August. In twenty-nine days!

Mr Shorrock this time explained with compunction and remorse that it was the end of the road for me. Should my immigration issues be resolved in the future, he added kindly, the bank would willingly re-employ me. In recognition of the bank's fault and in appreciation of my one year's contribution, I was terminated with six months' ex gratia salary without deduction of tax, a substantial amount in those days, along with a very favourable letter of reference.

I hitched and walked my way to Chatsworth Road, my heart sagging under the weight of misery at the prospect of returning to the eastern sky an utter failure.

The next week, I was invited by my bank friends for a farewell at Morecambe's Victoria Hotel. In attendance were around seventy-five people, including Mr Shorrock. A buffet was laid out followed by music and dancing, after which I gave a short farewell speech. Unbeknown to anyone, I still had one final badminton trip with the United Banks team to Holland, and I decided to take matters to the limit since it was already paid for – at the risk of not being allowed back into England, or being placed in an immigration cell till deportation. I did it because of the measure of carefree optimism I had gained in England, a cavalier *I'll be all right* thinking.

I made it to Holland without incident and was drawn to play a Dutch champion from Indonesia. When the spectators established our respective identities, it was billed as a monster match between Malaysia and Indonesia, giving me the joy of one last hurrah before perdition.

It was all going well until our return journey when the immigration officer at the Harwich ferry port could not resist the urge to make me feel like a fraud, announcing for all to hear that I only had another seven days to leave the country. My team started a rigorous cross-examination and for the first time I opened up. It was a silent train ride after that. Sadness aside, I was contemplating how to surrender my tenancy without revealing the real reason and causing further hurt to Mrs Jones, seeing that things had been uneasy between us since the time I'd rebuffed her Mrs Robinson desire.

It was club night at Wesley when I finally broke the news to a shocked David Ashcroft, Joan Knowles, Bob Collins and Mason Whittaker. I tried to mask the turmoil and sadness raging within me, but I think everyone could feel me.

Early next morning, there was a knock on my door and the visitor turned out to be Dave Ashcroft.

'Phil, we have no time to waste. I've spoken to the others. We've come up with a plan to take on the Home Office and make you stay. I suggest you give notice to the landlady and pack your belongings. I'll be back at one to take you with me. Is that okay?'

'Yes. Thank you, Dave.'

'Good. I'll see you later. I'll explain then.'

Off went my knight straight from the chessboard, leaving me guilty and embarrassed at troubling them all, particularly David, who was a very busy builder and successful businessman. It seemed so incredible the way my Wesley friends were rallying for me that I needed a promenade sprint to assure myself I wasn't hallucinating.

Dave arrived promptly with an estate car. We loaded my belongings into it and made our way to his Lancaster office from where he used a sophisticated loudspeaker telephone to make a call to the UKAIS (United Kingdom Advisory Information Service, a charity in Manchester).

After a long chat, a loophole was established. If I reverted to being a student, the Home Office would cancel my deportation notice and renew the student visa up to a year, ending in September 1975, by which time I would qualify for permanent residency, having stayed a full five years.

We then drove to Lancaster & Morecambe College to sign up for the A-levels programme. I chose Physical Education and three other subjects: General Principles of Law, British Constitution and Economic Geography. Being a foreign student, the fee was double and it swallowed up most of my settlement from the bank despite opting for the cheaper condensed one-year programme. By three o'clock that afternoon, I was enrolled to start the course the following Monday.

Armed with my certificate of enrolment, Dave dictated a letter to his secretary for the Home Office. We attached six letters of reference and evidence of accommodation and financial support from my Wesley friends, which I signed, placed inside a large envelope with my passport and sent off by registered post. After three stressful weeks, my passport was returned with the deportation notice rescinded and a new student visa. It was a moment I realised conventional destiny was not for me.

While I managed to extend my stay in England, I did not have enough money to sustain myself. Once again, my Wesley family came to my aid, for whose kindness and support I am forever grateful. I rotated between the Ashcrofts, the Knowles, Bob Collins and Mason Whittaker's parents.

Throughout attending college, I held down two jobs, as a stevedore at Heysham Harbour unloading cotton bales, oranges and potatoes, and as a barman at the Miami Bowl on Morecambe Pier. It is said trying times bring out the best in folk – it was amply demonstrated that year when I was moving between houses, juggling two jobs and college, and yet got through my A-levels with decent grades.

Geoffrey was very proud of my A for Law and B for British Constitution, but it was the A for Economic Geography that gave me the greatest satisfaction because of the two projects I undertook. The Tesco salt project was an experiment I devised with my teacher as a herd mentality test when faced with the perception of scarcity. I stood outside the supermarket making intermittent announcements – 'We are going to run out of salt' – to test people's reactions. Within two hours, the store ran out of salt! I was therefore not at all surprised when Covid-19 caused a collective paranoia in many communities to hoard and brawl over toilet paper!

The other was a farm project for which I stayed with my friend Julia Collinson's sister and her husband, Frank and Ruth Wrathall. For one week, I followed their daily routine, taking part in every activity for first-hand experience of managing a farm. Quite unexpectedly, I became involved with the delivery of a calf. Watching the cow go through agony at each stage of the birth was a spiritual moment. The calf's umbilical cord tearing away from its mother, the cow tendering her calf immediately after delivery, with barely any fuss – just cathartic. The phenomenal calving experience taught me the importance of getting on with it. Whinging is pointless, no matter the situation. I went to bed that night pricked by a strong pang of conscience, shock and an overwhelming desire to be in my mother's embrace.

In October 1975, five years after arriving in England, I became a permanent resident. I moved back to Morecambe to live on my own again, contacted Nat West and was offered a job. The bank agreed to my request for a later start date as I was feeling the impact of ploughing a lone furrow. I sent Mummy a telegram: *Coming Home.*

TWELVE

# CUI BONO

Upgraded to the upper deck of the biggest commercial aeroplane at the time, the Qantas Boeing 747 jumbo jet, I was off to a homecoming to be remembered for posterity. Joining me on my journey to a home I had yet to set my eyes on was my friend Julia Russell. We became involved when she came to play badminton at the college and she was excited to accompany me, displeasing her terrified mother – as if her daughter bringing home a brown boy wasn't enough, she was also insistent on travelling with him to risky, chaotic, diarrhoea-inducing India.

We almost didn't make it, because, for what I can now organise in minutes using my smartphone took me four weeks of search, labour and distress in 1975. I'd found an advertisement in the *Daily Telegraph* for a travel agent bucket shop in Croydon, London. Bucket shops were a new type of business that sold airline tickets for a fraction of the normal price; with that came unscrupulous agents ready to fleece people.

Wallet stuffed with £600 and carrying copies of our passports, I hitched to London, spent a night at Euston railway station and took the next morning's underground train to Croydon. I showed the man at the desk their advertisement: *Flights to India £250 return per person from London Heathrow to Bombay Santa Cruz International* and he booked us for 22 December (three weeks to departure), with open returns. I then enquired about a connecting flight to my home state, Kerala. Agent swung open a large global travel folio, scanned the kit and read out, 'Three daily on Indian Airlines to *Tree-van-drum* departing the following day. Forty pounds one way.'

Please book, I said. He went, umm. 'The domestic ticket will carry a pending status and you have to convert it to confirmed at the Indian Airlines counter in Santa Cruz. Just a formality.' On that basis, he gave me a receipt for £580 with a caveat: 'We're unable to issue the tickets now. Our brokers at Qantas are facing some red tape issues. They'll arrive by post next week.' There was no chance of weighing the risks and I had to accept his explanation.

I hitched back to Morecambe, a distance of KL to Singapore, frightfully worried at the thought of having to explain the situation to distrustful Mrs Russell. When the tickets did not arrive the following week, I made a frantic call to the Croydon office from a red urinal-smelling, coin-guzzling pillar-box phone booth outside Morecambe's post office. The same agent assured me the tickets would arrive shortly, which they did, *not shortly* but just three days before departure, during which time I played Santa Claus, filling up my suitcase, and Julia's, to bursting point.

On 21 December, I dressed to impress in a three-piece brown suit over a white shirt and tie with cream Elton John block-heel shoes. Towing two obese suitcases and two heavy holdalls between us, Julia and I left Lancaster to spend the night at Heathrow. We faced no fuss at the check-in counter early the next morning despite our luggage being well in excess of 30 kgs each and got ourselves into the spacious upper-deck cabin to a heady air of cigars, cigarettes and alcohol. Those were the days before headphones, private entertainment systems or GPS flight tracking feed; just a large common screen playing a movie with a free flow of beverages and lunch with a choice of red or white wine served in classic crockery and wine glasses – in economy class!

As I was anticipating the adventures to come, I couldn't help remembering Mummy's last letter to me. *How tall are you now?* she'd asked, not having seen me in almost six years. How tall Prasad, Viji and Tom must be, my sister, Shanta, too. And surely Mummy must've felt a lump in her throat like I did when I sent out the unexpected telegram: *Mohan arriving 23 December 2 pm Trivandrum Airport.*

Julia and I disembarked at Santa Cruz Airport at 10 pm Indian time on the 22nd. Dim yellow lighting and a foul, musty smell filled the air. I have to admit I felt a burning shame. Bombay's airport, workers, facilities and trappings looked primitive, to say the least. By the time we'd located the Indian Airlines counter to confirm our following morning's connecting flight to Trivandrum, it was one o'clock. Counters closed, another airport night. On grubby benches feeling restless and uncomfortable, having to keep watch over our suitcases between catnaps.

Early next morning, we freshened up as best we could in overused, undercleaned, sloshy, smelly toilets and reached the Indian Airlines queue to be told that with our pending status we could only get onto a connecting flight the following day. 'Please understand, sir, many, many Kerala peoples coming for Christmas holiday from Gulf,' sputtered the man at the counter with a smug Indian airport staff finality before shouting, 'NEXT!'

Seeing no point in arguing, I did an orientation of the building and found the office of the Indian Tourism Board. The manager in charge parroted his Indian Airlines counterpart. 'Sir, this is normal problem this time of year. Suggest you take bus from main station to Mangalore. From Mangalore take train to Trivandrum. Suggest you take taxi to bus station now.'

I looked at my pocket global atlas/traveller's map (carry one to this day), and his suggestion seemed plausible to cover the thousand-mile journey from Bombay (Mumbai) to Trivandrum. The man pocketed my tip, summoned an Ambassador car taxi and gave the young driver in need of a haircut and shave instructions in Hindi. Before leaving, I sent a *Trivandrum flight cancelled* telegram to Mummy so she would not make the arduous 120-mile journey on poor roads from our village in Thekkemala.

From the moment our taxi began navigating Bombay's treacherous roads, it was an unremitting onslaught of dreariness. I could feel Julia's anxiety. She was not ready to break ground into unpredictable territory. I too was sickened by Bombay's dirty, tired, overpopulated, clamorous state – waves of harassed faces, beggars, touts, angry horns, angrier vehicles in perpetual hot pursuit, packed buses with people dangling from doors… The only thing bearable was the mildly sunny weather after England's winter chills, which was not impressing Julia, so I assured her with nostalgic fervour that the south was not like the filth Bombay was flinging at us. Sunil, our driver, slowed down and cut into a narrow dirt road passing through a shanty town, eventually stopping at a shady lay-by next to a large, dusty tree plastered in posters depicting two angry young men brandishing pistols to the word *SHOLAY*.

'Bus stop, go Mangalore,' announced Sunil. No way the crudely built shack overlooking a parched playing field and cluttered low-slung cottages was Bombay's central bus terminus! There was no mistaking we were in trouble. I was transported to Prime Minister Indira Gandhi's authoritarian proclamation a few months earlier when announcing India's state of emergency, which had just come into force: 'There is nothing to panic about.' Like Mrs Gandhi's political opponents and the country's dissident media, I knew I had every reason to panic.

Seeing Sunil get out of the car, I transferred my Swiss army-type knife from my holdall to my suit pocket, instructed Julia to remain in the car and went out to confront our driver, now opening the boot. 'Close boot! Drive back airport,' I ordered. Sunil's response was something mutinous in Hindi to make it clear he had other intentions.

At that moment, two light motorcycles with four ruffian types sped in our direction and the riders jumped off their vehicles. Two of them stood guard as the burlier two came straight for our suitcases, shouting at Sunil in Hindi. I held my ground, pushed the two and a scuffle broke out. Sunil remained by the boot, Julia sprang out of the car screaming in the direction of some youngsters playing street cricket as I kicked one assailant on the shin and punched and felled the other. Seeing the other two rushing to aid their accomplices, I took out my knife and waved it about, but they stopped in their tracks at the sight of yelling youngsters charging in our direction.

As luck would have it, and true to the Indian cinema rule of the day, a police jeep swooped and screeched onto the scene when the main action was over and as the gangsters were speeding off with the boys giving chase. The two policemen had some harsh words with Sunil before taking our statements. Apologising profusely, they explained that Sunil would drive us back to the airport with them following right behind, after which the crook would be arrested and the tourism office manager questioned to see if he too was involved in the syndicate.

Back in the safety of the crowded airport, we thanked the officers, who advised us to catch a plane to the south. We took their badge numbers and later wrote to their superiors in Bombay commending their efficiency and compassion. The Indian Airlines information officer was sympathetic to our plight, and since all connecting flights remained overbooked, we were put on a semi-diplomatic official flight to Belgaum (now Belagavi), where we were told we could take the bus or train the rest of the way to Trivandrum. The small, one-propeller plane with five seats on each side landed in Belgaum, where the setting sun had turned the sky a splash of orange.

We caught the airport bus to the main bus station about two miles away and booked a 9.30 pm night coach to Bangalore (Bengaluru), a twelve-hour journey with breaks. We hung around the bus station and had some street food with bottled Coke until the interstate coach rolled up. The bus quickly filled up with travel-hardened Indians and we set forth in darkness.

The views that unfolded outside my window were heartbreaking: men, women, barely clothed children sleeping on pavements, under bridges, by open sewers, in the company of dogs, cows, pigs, no street lights, hawkers selling food with candles or Petromax lights… After centuries of British imperialism in India? Surely these weren't the scenes that attracted the East India Company's commercial pirates and the despotic British Raj? How could this decay have been called the Jewel in Britain's Crown? Unless, this was the outcome of centuries of pillage and corruption… the cow milked to death then banished to the slaughterhouse.

In the thirty-six hours since departing Lancaster, Julia and I had only had a handful of hours of sleep. Out of sheer exhaustion, we nodded off. Not for long. We'd made the mistake of choosing the back-end seats of the bus, now speeding mercilessly on bumpy, windy roads. Julia kept squeezing my hand and it was that way all along. The coach made about three toilet-cum-street coffee stops, where each time people openly stared at Julia. At 11 am the following morning, on the eve of Christmas, we arrived in one piece at Bangalore's main bus station, with another 342 miles to go. We caught a taxi to the domestic airport about ten miles away only to find out all flights to either Cochin or Trivandrum in Kerala were fully booked until 4th January 1976! In utter despair, we headed to Bangalore railway station instead, getting there at around 4 pm to again be told no tickets were available for the 10 pm train to Cochin. Recalling my father's wile from my last India trip, I settled on a shrewd-looking porter who understood English and explained my intentions: if I offered a bribe to the officials in the ticket office through him, could he possibly get us two berths? His grin said it all. 'Yes, sir. Sure, sir.'

Yet another telegram went out to Mummy: *Arriving Cochin 25 December 11 am.* For my generosity, our grinning porter managed to get us a self-contained berth with a wash area and toilet – desperately needed after two days of dust, dirt and a brawl. We changed into lighter clothes for the following eleven-hour journey to Cochin. We arrived on time to blue skies and the beautiful diversity of Kerala's emerald landscapes, but no Mummy or brothers. Not wanting to waste time, Julia and I caught another train from Cochin to Thiruvalla and arrived at 4 pm. Having come to the last lap of our journey after three days of harsh travelling, I was overcome by an expectant adrenaline rush. I changed back into my suit, the collar of my white shirt bearing a ring of grime, ready to impress my folk when I got to my village of Thekkemala in Kozencherry, still about an hour away. Outside at the taxi stand, we caused a small stir when locals gathered around us casting curious looks, sniggers and whispers at Julia, who began blushing like a hapless *memsahib*!

It was hills, fields and palm trees all the way to Thekkemala. Once we'd reached the single-street village oozing tranquillity, the driver asked me for my father's full name, essential for direction-enquiry and as good as Google Maps back in the day. It is an old Indian convention to attach the family, village and sometimes caste identity to one's name. At the first mention of Kalayil Puthuparampil George, we were straightaway guided to the house.

At 5.30 pm on Christmas evening, I was eagerly flinging open the iron gate of my family home for our taxi to enter the green driveway hiding a portion of a pitched red roof. A lone young woman with cascading black curls, in a flowing white skirt and with a long necklace over her blouse made her way to the spacious verandah. How strikingly beautiful my sister looked. I saw in her Papa's square face, chiselled jaw, thick arched eyebrows, keen slanted eyes and light complexion. As Shanta and I embraced, my second brother, Viji, hollered a hello from up a slender guava tree, clad in shorts and a familiar beige patterned shirt I'd worn in Malaysia.

The taxi door purred shut, Julia stepped out, my siblings' eyes dilated. I'd skipped the detail of my friend travelling with me! At that moment, a little boy bounding our way stopped to ape the other two. 'Servant boy,' explained Shanta, recovering her composure. The boy's eyes stayed fixed on Julia.

I was dismayed to find out we'd missed poor Mummy, Prasad, Tom and our uncle who had gone to Cochin in a taxi to receive me. With nothing to do but wait, Julia and I were given a property tour in between Shanta and me catching up on our lost years. All my siblings were home for the Christmas holidays, the boys from the Quilon boarding school and Shanta from the All Saints College in Trivandrum. Rightfully or wrongfully, I perceived their situation as a cruel denigration of what life might have been in progressive Malaysia if they hadn't been flung into stone-age India! They'd be in choir practice or piano classes in KL, evolving with international movies, music, fashion trends…

It was a typically spacious Kerala house, elegant in its simplicity. There were plenty of wooden doors, windows and pillars, six large airy rooms, two separate lounges, three bathrooms and a big kitchen with water supplied by a pump connected to a garden well, two outhouses for crops and implements and fertile acreage. Shanta plucked some limes to make us cool lime juice using homegrown palm sugar and ice cubes from our old fridge Papa had carted from Malaysia. The F&N glasses used to serve Julia and me were familiar too. Refreshments gulped down, Shanta showed us to my room, which had a sturdy wooden double bed as its centrepiece. My sister discreetly left us to sort out our suitcases, not quite able to hide a sheepish smile.

We were chatting in the main lounge – Shanta and Viji spoke in heavily Indian-accented English, while they said mine was like "English people's" – when the others arrived. Under the low lights, everyone dispersed into the background. Mummy came straight for me and I melted into her. Decades later, when the composer AR Rahman in his Oscar-winning speech (best original score, *Slumdog Millionaire*) mentioned a famous Hindi film line *Mere Paas Ma Hai* (I have Mother), I could feel him. Tears coursing down her cheeks, Mummy cupped my equally teary face in her rough palms, wanting to know how I was, why the delay, if I'd had anything to eat... I just couldn't answer her. My mother tongue was tangled in my throat and it was unthinkable to respond to her in English, the language bursting at the tip of my tongue. To cover my predicament, I held her in a tight embrace until my Malayalam vocabulary made a slow return. Julia was quietly observing everything, unaware the playwright of *her* dramatic scene was already packing his luggage in Malaysia.

South Indian men's oedipal obsession with their mothers isn't unlike the momma's boys of Italy, whose mommas feed and clean up after their grown boys while often sidelining the girls. Likewise, misogyny's prevalence in my family was laid bare to me on that trip. My well-educated, relatively exposed sister would not think of putting on a badminton skirt for a game with me as Julia did, nor would she join us boys on our expeditions and neither was she expected to. I don't know if I'd have been as bothered by her restricted freedom, her *I know my place* conduct, had I not been exposed to Western customs. I was certainly making comparisons to my English girlfriends and was wondering how much my sister could have benefitted from equal treatment. I was also seeing the impact of Papa's crippling mollycoddling of his only daughter. My sister, for her part, had always been under his spell, devoted and docile to his puppet mastering – at a time when India's first female prime minister was throwing men with the effrontery to oppose her into prison!

Mummy looked neat and petite as ever, her beautiful olive skin creaseless, her features small and delicate but for her cheekbones that rose prominently whenever she had a big smile, like she had the whole time that night. My brothers' facial features had changed, especially little Tom, who was only seven the last time we were together and was now a teenager. My mother's casual greeting of Julia in her broken English was a welcome relief after all the awkward stares my friend had been getting since arriving in India. The house burst into life with Mummy's insouciant grace, bringing to full bloom the spirit of Christmas, a time when I always remember her invocation of the words of the Saint of Assisi: 'It is in giving that we receive.'

Like always in my family, it was a simple Christmas focused on reflection rather than revelry. We said a prayer and with warm hearts enjoyed my mother's mutton fry and creamy chicken *kurma*, following which I brought out all my gifts for the family, including whole new wardrobes for my brothers to share between them.

After staving off jet lag for three days, Julia and I only woke up for a very late lunch the following day, by which time Prasad, the eldest of my younger brothers, had returned from the post office after sending a *Mohan home* telegram to Papa.

There followed a few halcyon days crammed with long catch-ups, exchanges of photos, strolls around the village and Mum beaming at villagers stopping to gawp at her lively brood, without fail noting, '*This* is your son from England, Kunjamma?' We also played badminton on the court of a nearby uncle's house, attracting curious crowds ogling Julia's whiteness in her Fred Perry skirt over frilly knickers.

Then the telegram from Papa: *Arriving Trivandrum Airport tomorrow afternoon.*

Our hypnotically restful spell felt broken, and I noticed that Mummy's face hardened too. It caused in me a sudden pang of anticipatory excitement and anxiety, like in school when I'd be pleased with a borderline pass and at the same time dread the showdown awaiting me at home. As the hours passed, I grew more restless and could only snatch a few hours of sleep. Early the next morning, Prasad, Tom and I took an express coach for the five-hour journey to Trivandrum Airport.

Papa was his usual sharp self with smiles and pats for his boys along with an unmissable scrutiny-filled look flung in my direction. During the journey back in a taxi, the conversation hovered around how my brothers were doing at boarding school, with indifferent interludes about my progress in England. There was a lot behind Papa's impassive face from the way he was not making proper eye contact with me. I gathered he must have somehow got wind of my English *friend* in his house. KP George was in *Spycatcher* mode, the popular BBC television series about a WW2 intelligence officer and specialist interrogator that he made me watch with him on our RCA during our Prang Besar years.

When we arrived home, it wasn't just the sun's rays dissolving on the horizon; my spirit too was doing the same. With my father, there was nothing of the emotional drama of a few days ago, just a nod of acknowledgement at the wife he hadn't seen in a few years and a pat on Shanta's head. A heavy hush settled over the living room when Mummy made a stiff introduction: 'Julia. Mohan's friend. From England.'

There might have been a very brief appraisal of Julia before Papa launched his interrogation. Shell-shocked Julia tried to keep up with KP George's succession of blunt personal questions: age, what she was doing, what subjects she taught, what her father did… I grew increasingly helpless as each of Julia's brittle responses was received with scorn. Papa was not bothered about hiding his contempt – took me right back to his clashes with Mackintosh and the lot. It got worse when he began throwing around his stentorian views on his distrust of the English, the brutality of empire, "unreliability" of white women, at which point I intervened and got a burning earful in Malayalam, which was just as well for Julia.

The confrontation only passed when Julia walked away in tears. The aspersions cast on my girlfriend were totally unnecessary considering marriage was not at all in my mind, and I was embarrassed and furious with Papa. I also knew very well I couldn't make a middle-class English schoolteacher like Julia understand that my father's outburst was owing to more than the Amritsar massacre, the Bengal famines or Winston Churchill's policy failures. There was also his sly ambition of "saving" me for marriage to a Malayali girl of our type, willing to offer a mouth-watering price for my husband services.

So I did the best I could with Julia. After some gentle pacifying, I told her she should now understand how I felt about her mother's attitude towards me and coloured people in general, calling me a bounder to my face. It followed a muted reconciliation over dinner, with no apologies from either party, just everyone behaving as if nothing had happened.

We rang in the New Year at Thekkemala's prominent Syrian Orthodox church where, among the big hair and winged eyeliners of sari-clad women, and safari suits, tight polyester shirts and flared trousers of its men, I stuck out as the "foreign return" and Julia was the star attraction. Thankfully, attention quickly drifted to national matters. One name and one word dominated conversation in the church and at the homes of the multitude of relatives we visited during that period: Indira Gandhi and Emergency. Not to be outdone, I spoke about England's own revolutionary female leader, the new head of the Conservative party, who, like Mrs Gandhi, was already showing a penchant for the iron fist. The excruciatingly male-dominated discussions were sustained on the rising stars of the two international stateswomen, an irony clearly lost there. In an uncanny coincidence, when both women were prime ministers, Margaret Thatcher would escape an IRA bomb assassination attempt on her, while Indira Gandhi would perish in a gunfire assassination, just fifteen days apart.

After taking in the glorious sights of Kerala, from the Malabar coast's stunning beaches to the arresting hillside tea plantations of Munnar, established by the British to produce *English* tea, Julia left for England in early January 1976 saying the trip had opened her eyes. I waved a guilty goodbye to see her leave alone, wondering if eye-opening meant she had imbibed whatever it was that the Beatles had wanted to during their widely covered first trip to India. When John, George, Paul and Ringo sported facial hair, wore marigold garlands over Indian clothes, appeared to have lost sense of time and posed in suspiciously pot-manifested tranquil positions. Makes me wonder if India might just have contributed to John's crossing over from one ruinous empire to take up citizenship across the pond at the new empire builder stocking up military bases and "territories" in place of colonies.

Papa was to return to Malaysia a week after Julia, during which time there were many more family gatherings… and several heart-to-heart talks between him and me. Leaving nursing was good. Banking job was good, although "just a clerk". British PR status was good – measure for measure for "the rivers of blood they'd spilt on our soil". Impressing Adidas and Yonex representatives to land both the prestigious sponsorships of all my sports gear was a mere umm. Doing well in my A-levels was good but "send me a copy of your results" – to think not even Mr Shorrock had scrutinised my certificates when employing me! My travels and explorations were "a waste of money". However, my man-about-town jollies were all right. But marriage was a different business altogether. Best left to the experts.

My father was very touched and most impressed by my Wesley friends, particularly Geoffrey and Dave. A return-of-favour exercise saw us making a trip to Kozencherry's high street to select yards of the highest-grade cheesecloth, a very popular summer shirt fabric and cultural identity of the Indian subcontinent. We gave detailed instructions to the tailor for twenty-five custom-stitched shirts. On the return trip from the tailor's, Papa became silent and morose. 'What can they do for the sins of their fathers…' came a sudden cryptic grumble. He proceeded to give the taxi driver and me a brief history of India's (particularly Bengal's) legendary fine muslin textile industry, the livelihoods of thousands, which was ruthlessly manipulated and destroyed by the British.

Soon after Papa's departure, Shanta returned to college, but the boys obtained extensions for some memorable bonding expeditions. We took the village by storm, whizzing about in our stylish clothes, no oiled good-boy hairstyles or typical South Indian moustaches! That did not prevent Mummy from reintroducing me to the dreaded health technique from antiquity in South India: the oil soak and decoction consumption. 'When you are old and have strong teeth and healthy hair, you will thank me,' she said. Thank you, Mummy!

My India trip ended with the most rugged badminton tournament of my life, courtesy of the Muthoot brothers, boys from a prominent business family who actively promoted the event in the upmarket areas of Kozencherry and Thekkemala, using me as their star billing. Over seven nights, we played at the Chengannur Municipality on a dusty sand court with poor lighting, compensated for by big raucous crowds coming from afar. On that high note, I decided I could no longer delay my return to England. On 28 February 1976, after two postponements that extended my stay in Kerala by six weeks, I was finally to take the plane back to England. Mummy, Shanta, my brothers and my uncle were in attendance to bid a highly charged teary farewell. I did an East India Company by carting away to England varieties of roasted spices and nuts, handlooms and fabric, and wood-carved elephants for my English friends.

I wept as I'd never wept before. We all cried, but such scenes weren't unusual at an Indian airport to cause any concern, and so with a heart as heavy as the three-tier Tupperware of Mum-made rice, fish curry, fried fish and vegetables, I left Kerala for Bombay, where I had nine hours to kill before my flight to London. No one took offence at the strong curry and spices wafting out of my tiffin carrier as I polished off every morsel of my dinner, something I knew I would never do in England, knowing how the English looked down on the smell of curry. I washed the Tupperware clean and gifted it to a thrilled airport-cleaning staff.

It was a gloomy, contemplative journey that set the tone for my many future trips to the East, when my introspective nature would kick in to take me through every important experience and try to integrate them.

It appears fitting now that I had made that trip to India with an English companion. To capture the trip's central thesis: the cultures of the east and west are different by design; the twain can only meet when delusions of superiority and indispensability are removed. When real histories are acknowledged and atoned for before they can be left in the past.

## THIRTEEN

# BUILT ON DREAMS

Pink Floyd's *Wish You Were Here* became my anthem in the weeks after my Kerala trip, my mood only improving after beginning my second innings at the Nat West bank's main branch in Lancaster, as a clerk.

It was a new team and new responsibilities under an assistant manager not able to appreciate my easy assimilation with office mates or my closeness to Mr Shorrock. Within a month, Mr Shorrock put me in charge of five satellite branches. Accompanied by an ex-SAS protection officer every morning, I travelled to Caton, Hornby, Hest Bank, Lancaster University and Lancaster Abattoir, opened the branches, served local folk giving me the jaw-drop treatment, closed up and returned to Lancaster to cash up.

There was so much going on in England in 1976. A new prime minister replacing one retiring from exhaustion; inflation and interest rates soaring; an unprecedented heatwave making the Minister for Drought suggest people "take a bath with a friend" (being the '70s, he escaped an uproar, although his title would change to Minister for Floods later the same year!); and one pioneering woman opened her first Body Shop outlet, vowing to save the planet. It was also the year of the Montreal Olympics, my second Olympics since arriving in England. Romania's wonder-gymnast Nadia Comăneci made history with perfect-ten scores, and in one of my favourite events, America's Bruce Jenner broke the decathlon world record, but sporting outcomes were marred by the withdrawal of nearly thirty African countries, in solidarity against the Olympic Committee's decision to admit New Zealand despite its rugby team's tour of South Africa where there was a widely observed sporting embargo of the country owing to its apartheid policy. The boycott took all the shine off the track events.

I marvelled at the willingness of a whole continent to make a sacrifice like that, renewing my interest in South Africa's social and political upheavals. It was only months earlier that the mini-series *Roots* had shocked millions of television audiences with its stark depiction of slavery in America. What a powerful moment in television history that was – certainly churned a variety of emotions in me, considering I was living in a city very much a part of the transatlantic slave trade.

In mid-1976, my brother Prasad joined me in England under my sponsorship as promised to Mummy. I enrolled him in college for A-levels, got him part-time work and introduced him to all my friends. Proud and protective, I was the big brother hungry to launch his wide-eyed sibling into English life. My brother fulfilled the role of the eager, compliant newcomer, loving every bit of his new adventure – excited that the jacket was an article of must-have clothing, loving the music and social scenes and intrigued to find out top-name softcore magazines were just as well known for uncovering government scandals and cover-ups as they were for displaying female flesh! We did morning runs together, played badminton, and soon he was also playing for the Wesley Club. All my friends extended the same welcome to Prasad as they did me, and he got on well with everyone.

It struck me then how badminton was charting my journey in England. By then, I was a familiar face on the circuit, with many friends all over the country. As was the convention, for each tournament an English family would host me – in on Friday, out Sunday – taken in cars to their beautiful homes, given supper and always a full English breakfast before matches, same as their sons. I'd play singles, doubles and mixed doubles, about fifteen rounds week in, week out, and would invariably be in all three finals, finishing well past midnight. Parents would sit in the halls watching us play, tartan blankets on knees as there was no heating, waiting for me to finish the championship, although their sons would've lost early on, sometimes carrying on till about 2 am. Such was their kindness. They were also well informed, had a good impression of Malaysian players and were doubly delighted to host me as

I was the only Asian player on the scene for the fifteen years of my badminton career in England. The exposure was nerve-racking for one coming from a culture of straight talking and used to rushing in, but what better way to learn than from first-hand observation of English ways – to appreciate the importance of context to understanding what an expression actually meant ("interesting" could mean "you're talking rubbish", so reading between the lines was a social skill!) and more importantly the value of patience, holding back and emulating.

I ended another tireless year in England appreciating how fortunate I was to be holding employment at a time when the country was in deep recession and the government at the mercy of the International Monetary Fund. The trend continued into the new year, but with the security of my job and my badminton success, my star was soaring. It also felt wonderful to once again be representing the bank at monthly badminton championships on the Continent, every visit a rich, immersive experience draped in amazing European culture and thinking.

The middle of 1977 was an exciting time for the bank as we were working on a special commemorative coin for the Queen's silver jubilee celebrations. On the other hand, upstart punk rockers the Sex Pistols had a rather unsavoury idea of immortalising the occasion. Having already courted national-level controversy by being the first to swear on live television (Thames Television should've known; their guests' first single was titled *Anarchy in the U.K.*), the group rained on the Queen's parade by releasing their incendiary single *God Save the Queen*. The song was banned by the BBC and many radio stations, which created a mad buzz to send sales rocketing.

It was a very different England those days. The economy and politics might have been in paralysis, but its music scene was outrageously progressive and the football and its commentators were absolute vintage! A new sound, talent or radical band broke out every so often, and the beautiful game was played on muddy, soggy fields where brutal tackles and marauding tactics were fair play that roused crowds in stadiums and down every pub on a Saturday – an unashamed whetting of the male ego. Not for the sanitised world of today's cucumber sandwich supporters as I call them.

On the Saturdays I was going to watch live football by myself, I'd be on tenterhooks right from the moment of thumbing off well in advance, to any stadium. I was hellbent on experiencing as many stadiums as I could. Once there, I'd take time to find my bearings, to know where the entrances and rickety turnstiles were, where the ticket louts lurked, and be mindful of gangsters and police watching each other at work. No tickets at booths, then you were in the lap of the gods. It could come from another spectator unable to go in for whatever reason, or you negotiated on the black market with the lout. I was never a precious one, and it has worked for me in Wembley, the Boca Juniors' stadium, World Cups, the Olympics and F1. Inside the stadium terraces, it was all about endurance. The unpleasantness of the whole experience, where you could suffocate, get injured, stabbed or even die, meant most of my friends preferred watching from the comfort of their homes, but they enjoyed listening to my stories of jostling and chanting with charged-up men reeking of a foul concoction of alcohol, tobacco, piss or worse; with whom celebrating a goal from the home end meant bringing down the stadium. Such was the fan-player interaction, an experience that is simply not available anymore.

What a contrast that was to the time two years earlier when I'd hitched to London on a Thursday afternoon and got into Wimbledon on Friday evening to camp in the open field to a great atmosphere of buskers, and burger and fish and chip stalls; the following day standing in a mile-long queue for a ticket to watch Arthur Ashe demolish Jimmy Connors and become the first black man to win the Wimbledon Tennis Open in a match swirling in controversy between two contrasting personalities, but in an atmosphere without an iota of the feral spirit of a football stadium. What an insight it provided for me into English identity and class: football for the working classes, tennis and cricket for the more elite and rugby union for the posh!

In June 1977, Prasad and I entered a nervous phase with his A-levels approaching. I was helping him prepare and our emotions were congruent. A lot was riding on the outcome because Papa's original plan had been to use his considerable influence in Kerala to place Prasad in the Indian Navy. My father by now had retired, cashed his sumptuous provident fund, resettled in Kerala and fulfilled his fatherly duty to his only daughter. Using the lump sum from the sale of our Trivandrum house as collateral, my sister Shanta was married off to a hotelier, a "Malayali green-card holder from America" as I was informed in a rare letter.

When Prasad's college days came to an end, I had one less responsibility and began to seriously think about pursuing a university degree. The choice of Law was influenced by Geoffrey's invigorating discussions of his practice and stories of his nephew Nigel Knowles, son of his brother Kenneth Knowles, also a partner in Whiteside and Knowles. Nigel was doing Law at Preston Polytechnic (University of Central Lancashire).

'Merchant banking? Why would you want to be a banker, Phil?' I recall Geoffrey's protests. His confidence in my intellectual ability was a welcome tonic to my deep-rooted self-doubt when it came to matters of the grey cells. Once again, I was at the familiar crossroads of giving up an assured future for the unknown.

I applied to Preston Polytechnic to do the LLB and, on the strength of my A-levels, decided to also try for Manchester University. Both institutions offered me a place but I opted for Preston because Manchester being forty miles south, I would have had to stay in the halls of residence, which I couldn't afford without my healthy bank salary. Being in Morecambe, I could commute daily and also carry on doing casual work at weekends to supplement my meagre student's grant from the Lancashire County Education Board (having paid income tax throughout my stay in England). With a heavy heart, I gave the bank four weeks' notice.

In other crushing news, the A-Level results came out

and Prasad had done very poorly. In disbelief and shock, I wrote to the examinations board for a review. I needn't have. I felt just as much a failure as my crestfallen brother. Perhaps I was operating with unrealistic idealism, in part because I'd been assigned the moral responsibility of ensuring my brother was led down the right path. The situation was made worse when Papa ordered me to send him back to Kerala. Prasad, however, was adamant about not leaving England, and between us, it was decided he would re-sit the following year.

In September 1977, at the age of twenty-five, I began my Law degree.

'*Oh, Yangtze River full of fish,*' Nigel Knowles greeted me in his typically eccentric English manner as his car rolled up with two other occupants, Baker and Anderton. It was my travel arrangement for the thirty miles from Morecambe to Preston Polytechnic. I took my seat behind Nigel in his red mini Gambia 1275GT. Lovely car, though not as attractive as my dream machine, the Volkswagen Golf series. I'd go on to purchase sixteen of the VW GTI over forty years. We drove off with Fleetwood Mac's *Rumours* blasting on the cassette stereo system, and fun was had by all on that journey and for the whole of my first year travelling with the boys.

The head of school in his induction speech stressed the importance of the library for learning law as there were only twelve hours of lectures a week, the rest of the time to be spent in the library preparing for tutorials. It immediately struck me as I'd been conditioned to believe the library was where you picked up peripheral knowledge, "finding out useless things" in Papa's words. As a matter of fact, my earliest visits to the university's library were to get my fill of current affairs, and September 1977 is etched in my mind as the month of death. Steve Biko, the founder of the Black Consciousness Movement, died in South Africa from police brutality, a medical student aged just thirty, and T. Rex's Marc Bolan died in a car crash in London at the peak of his musical career two weeks before his thirtieth birthday. It felt surreal to be reading about the deaths of young people in the throes of success or fulfilling their ambitions, especially Bolan, whom I'd seen up close in performance at the Great Hall.

Fraternising with a different set of people in the university's vibrant environment did not faze me as I'd learnt to roll with the punches in the social arena. The big lectures too were manageable. What I found unnerving was sitting in a small circle with tutorial lecturers expecting us to engage with them on topics of law and general discussion. These lecturers made it very clear from the start that polished articulation was a trait I needed to develop to serve me well in my future line of work. It was completely different to the English banter I was accustomed to, leaving me often tongue-tied and self-conscious. And there was nowhere to hide.

I liked tort law right away, taught by Mr Hart, who had no time for loafers and whose air and utterances took time to be understood for their rebukes. During his lectures, Mr Hart threw us the type of glances that suggested he thought half the occupants did not belong there! He was proven correct when of the 260 students that started, only around sixty would complete and graduate. His tutorials always felt like inquisitions in the way he would drill and probe until he was satisfied we had acquired sufficient understanding of a case's facts and legal principles.

My first year stretched me to my limits, leaving me demotivated many times, thinking of the lucrative, secure life I'd squandered with the bank, and I would feel its impact throughout my law studies.

Steve Krebs, a young Jew who, like me, did not live on campus and Tina Howe who was also in the mature student band like me became my friends in need. We stuck together, understanding each other's tutorial struggles, exchanging support and empathy as we made the library a second home, along with hanging out regularly at the Lamb and Packet pub, which served good music and equally good minced curry rice. We were in the same tutorial group from year one to year three and formed a study group for discussions that went a long way to alleviate the tension before tutorials and helped me slowly become more comfortable with opening my mouth.

Not all lecturers were of the same mould as Mr Hart or the endearing Mr Graham Stephenson, our Contract and International Law lecturer, who in one moment of exasperation memorably rebuked, 'You lot might as well be doing needlework!' Many of the lecturers were quite young, often failed lawyers opting for academia to make a living. Some of the male lecturers attended our parties and it was not unusual for them to take off with female students, which did not augur well considering our internal exam papers were marked by them. Those incidents made for first-hand inside knowledge for later in my court actions representing clients against academic institutions!

By not living on campus, I missed out on the total student social life experience, but I could tell the atmosphere was no comparison to what I'd experienced through badminton and concerts at Lancaster University. Nevertheless, there were many university socials that my gang and I were a part of and we ended 1977 witnessing disco and American culture filtering in. By the time we'd begun the second year, the class had dwindled to half its size.

Prasad and I were drifting apart and the imminent fallout happened after a short visit to Kerala in mid-1978. I went alone to face Papa, whose wrath was barely assuaged by the Rodenstock German spectacle frames I'd bought for him upon special request. I might have been a second-year Law student but stood no chance of defending myself against the accusations flung at me.

'*You* let him fail...'

'I did my best, Papa. Even helped him with lessons.'

'*You* helped him with lessons? I sent Prasad to a *boarding* school in Quilon, remember that...'

'Education is different in England, it's not just about learning and memorising... was tough for me too, you know. And I had nobody to help me.' Encouraged by what I'd assumed to be a softening mood, I went on. 'British education is of a higher standard, Papa. Very different to what it's like here...'

I should not have said that. Especially not after finding out my father had newly joined the Indian Congress

Party and the Wisemen's Club (akin to the Rotary). And especially not after having already received a couple of castigations for my "increasingly Western outlook". My room emanating *Songbird, Baker Street, Hotel California, Sultans of Swing* and my big Kevin Keegan perm (the rage in England at the time) had been too much for him.

Kalayil Puthuparampil George's silence was stoic, but his eyebrows performing impressive waves told the real story. His hard eyes cut through me. I stared, wondering if Rodenstock frames might soften future glares.

'Shame on you, Mohan! You have become the Englishman's propaganda.' The pronouncement was delivered in method-acting iciness but I was spared further beratement. Even if he'd continued, I would not have argued, purely to avoid conflict.

To make my father understand how I was benefitting from British education, I would've had to confront him with his conceptions of certain Eastern values: the public and private humiliations children, especially boys, have to endure through savage scolding, threats, smacks, belts and damaging imputations (fit only for climbing coconut trees) because the future rested only on titles and papers awarded by select and reputable institutes of higher learning, in systems that rob children of smiles and a spring in their step.

The confrontation, by all means, was not over. What Papa said after the uncomfortable silence to substantiate my so-called English propagandist role made me think what a wonderful lawyer he would've made. There was a method to his madness. 'They plundered this country to enrich themselves and left us in a total mess. Millions of our men, women, children died in famines, and now they're making babies out of test tubes! Nice culture, Mohan. Full of divorces, abortions, artificial babies.'

I was completely dumbfounded by how he linked my moral degradation to the first baby successfully born via in vitro fertilization in the world – a historic event that had happened in Lancashire of all places!

Another nightmare I had to endure on that trip came in the form of stacks of albums and studio photos playing out my sister's impeccably loud, garish, most *grand* wedding, which included a massive parade of cars and more layers of gold on my sister than Technicolor could do justice to. A wholly different world compared to the framed black and white tastefully simple image of my parents as newlyweds in KL, surrounded by artfully organised family and friends!

'Did Shanta require extra luggage to take all that ransom to America?' I was close to asking Mummy but refrained upon seeing her state of triumphant bliss.

There were no tears that time on my return journey to England, neither at the airport nor on my flight. Just an uneasy tug in my heart where Prasad was concerned and when recollecting the stingers from Papa. The split with Prasad happened when he no longer showed interest in re-sitting the A-levels and felt he could manage his future in England. He moved out. Two years later, the grapevine would deliver the message of his marriage to an English girl. News that devastated my parents, who could not understand my inability to rein in a brother who'd chosen to leave the nest, let alone that he even had that freedom of choice.

Upon Prasad leaving, I moved to another flat in Morecambe overlooking the sea, at a cheaper rent with no central heating or double glazing so I could buy my first car, a second-hand brown Hillman Avenger. My rudderless lifestyle was back on song. There followed a great time of partying and socialising, but Coach Chan did not forsake me. I managed not to go overboard like many other students around me, who went on an alcohol, drugs and sex bender – a lifestyle that would come to a screeching halt with AIDS.

I continued to play for Wesley and found a great doubles partner in Peter Brogden, a PhD in Chemistry student at Keele University who'd share my badminton journey for eight years, winning a shedload of tournaments. I had an offer to play for Lancashire, instead, opted to be a freelance Malaysian player, a fine move I'd realise in later years as it paved the way for me to play with visiting Malaysian players, most memorably the Sidek brothers, Misbun, Razif and Jalani.

During the semester holidays, I held down three jobs. At a Ladbrokes betting agency, as a stevedore at Heysham Port and at the Oasis gaming centre. What I would not do was return to the pier's Miami Bowl where I'd worked as a bartender during my A-levels. I was that put off by its post-concert drunken brawls and rowdy behaviour – the antithesis of the Great Hall's decent vibrancy. I had no desire to return to the name-calling, foul-mouthed put-downs or violent skirmishes of Miami Bowl's inebriated male patrons "catching" me serving their cheeky women drinks or escorting unsteady ones to their cars. The Miami Bowl scenes inevitably pop up each time I watch major football matches involving England, feeling as anguished as the women and children in English homes wishing their men weren't coming home, especially if England lost. As a concertgoer, however, I have many fond memories of the Miami Bowl. One that resonates to this day is meeting The Drifters when the American group were on tour. Life came full circle that evening. Mr Simms of Prang Besar Estate would've shared my excitement knowing of my little misadventure of signing off my oil palm census report as *The Drifters* instead of Philip George!

Having little money and battling the uncertainty of whether I had the mettle to get into law practice forced upon me the need for frugality, a quality that remains with me and ranks as high as good personal hygiene and immaculate orderliness. I would not pass an opportunity to make some extra money, so when I found out Dave Ashcroft needed a foundation dug to build a granny flat adjoining his house, I offered to take on the job and spent one month single-handedly digging with a shovel while missing my *changkul* (hoe) of Malaya! The shovelling and carting away soil and stones using a wheelbarrow to then transfer them to a tipper truck was gruelling, but I enjoyed driving the truck to the local tip and Dave paid me handsomely.

My semester breaks weren't all about grim labour. I still played badminton and hitchhiked on a whim for a concert, movie spree or theatre in London… attending the sell-out Andrew Lloyd Webber/Tim Rice musical *Evita* while being disappointed it wasn't my favourite Julie Covington performing *Don't Cry For Me Argentina* on the night, springs to mind. There were also my jollies with Geoffrey at the Old Trafford Cricket Club, or gardening or clay pigeon shooting in Shefferlands. Early shooting lessons with Geoffrey will never leave me, especially my first experience.

'Relax. Synchronise your eyes and fingers…' he said, placing the shotgun on my left shoulder over my thick donkey jacket. 'Bend your neck, look straight ahead like you do with a shuttlecock. Listen for the sound of the pigeon's release, follow the target until it's at its summit then click the trigger. Take into account the bullet's lag factor…'

It would not have been as terrifying if I wasn't being watched by twenty or so other expert regular shooters, one of whom was Bill Braithwaite, a vet from Garstang and a 1970 Olympics gold medalist!

'No pressure,' Geoffrey assured me as he adjusted my neck and shoulder and held my right elbow in a resting position. 'You'll be fine, son. Just go for it.'

Hearing those words instantly motivated me and I did exactly as instructed. I blanked out the audience, held the heavy gun, heard the words "ready, pull", and the next thing I knew, the clay pigeon target was disintegrating to pieces.

'BULLY!' the crowd cried. I had no clue what the expression meant, but the proud smile on Geoffrey's face was a *res ipsa loquitur* moment.

FOURTEEN

# THE OPEN ROAD

The lure of libraries for me would never match that period of my tertiary education. Apart from the university's library, I also frequented Morecambe Library, a treasure trove of national and international magazines and newspapers. My gateway to the world!

A unique structure consisting of three linked octagons and a modern interior, Morecambe Library played a big part in my life. In May 1978, while engrossed in my private sphere, the intimacy of my hushed space was ruffled. It was an attractive young girl stacking up books on the nearby rack. A face I'd seen before at the birthday party of my mixed doubles partner but had to make quite sure.

'Hi, are you not Janet from Carol's birthday party?'

'Yes.'

'I'm Phil George.'

'I know who you are,' she said, her blue eyes locked onto mine. 'I've heard about you. You think you're the bee's knees, don't you?'

I did not know what the expression meant, but beyond the slight scorn, she displayed a flirtatious overture and I decided to ask her out.

'I'll think about it.' Janet returned to shelving, I to my law books. Neither could have foretold that library move of mine would one day make us Mr and Mrs George.

During the summer break after completing my first year, I decided to embark on a road journey to South America for the 1978 Buenos Aires FIFA World Cup. Flying into the Argentine capital was the popular option, but my long-term *Butch Cassidy and the Sundance Kid* hangover kicked in and I chose instead to take the road less travelled. A visit to Morecambe Library beckoned. I explained my intention to Magda Gillow, the chief librarian, who had become a good friend. The matriarch of Morecambe Library was always in Jean Brodie-like prime. With eyes in the back of her head, she knew every inch of her territory and possessed admirable command intuition. Magda knew exactly what I required. And more.

'You do know the country is under military control, don't you, Phil?' A conversation ensued on how the junta had "disappeared" thousands of Argentinians into torture centres to never be heard of again. She wouldn't hear of my plan to hitchhike. 'You want to think about that,

Phil. Dangerous, you know.' Magda followed it up with advice on travel logistics: some basic Spanish will help, take enough sterling, local currencies can be got on the go, youth hostels and backpacker outfits aplenty in the cities hosting matches, you'll need some luck to get tickets, grease some palms perhaps, no guarantee buses and trains will be reliable, best to give ample allowances…

Armed with a large sheet of four A4-sized papers I'd taped together, a large atlas on South America and some old travel books, I found a big enough table to splay my ware and chart my route with grid points from Houston Airport in Texas to Buenos Aires. With Mummy's oft-repeated mantra ringing in my ears, "When a job is once begun, do it well", I worked on identifying the path I'd be taking, covering Mexico, Guatemala, Honduras, Nicaragua, Costa Rica, Panama, Colombia, Ecuador, Peru, Bolivia and my final destination, Argentina.

Establishing the distances from one point to another, modes of transport, estimated travel time and cost… suddenly the trip did not seem difficult, or far-fetched. Within a day of research and planning, I had a credible route map to which I kept adding data as the days moved forward.

In all those years, I never forgot that feeling of exhilaration that washed over me when the Limau Manis *sakai* burst out of nowhere to give me a sight to behold; and a lifetime's lesson on what can be gained from being exploratory and interested. Such precious encounters do not happen to ships that languish in harbours, only to those ready for a spin in the choppy seas. I've kept my connection with that part of me that knows how to be in the flow of fun, of taking my chances, being in unknown places or striking up conversations with strangers.

You can imagine how I looked forward to my South America adventure. I thought about it on my morning runs, on the bus, during my part-time jobs, at the badminton courts, in my sea-facing flat…

With £600 to last the three-week trip covering twelve countries, I left London Gatwick at the start of summer on Laker Airways to New York and then on Pan Am to Houston. With my UK permanent resident status, I was able to obtain a British Certificate/Passport which allowed me to travel to the US and South American countries without the need for a visa. That did not mean one did not face some hassle from immigration officers.

'Sir, could you please tell me why you have a stamp of Iran in your passport?' asked the immigration officer at Houston.

'It sounded like a nice place to visit. I just applied, in case, you know, I get the opportunity…' My cheeky reply was dismissed with a derisive grunt but the officer let me get on with it.

After a dinner of shockingly large steak, french fries and a mixed salad with dollops of sauce and relish, downed with a bottle of Coca-Cola, I spent my first night in the land of the golden arches at Houston's big Greyhound bus station.

I caught the first train to San Antonio and from there a train to enter Mexico. There was no missing the slogan "LARGE AND IN CHARGE" scrolled in bold lights across a billboard close to the Mexico border. Fitting indeed considering how big everything was in America, from its meal portions and its buildings to its people.

On the journey to Monterrey, the contrast was immediate and glaring. Endless sunshine, open blue skies, brown roads, weather-beaten faces, ramshackle homes... a distant world so far away from huddled, punctilious Europe.

The Central America stretch flew by in buses and trains. In the small hours between a bus or a train to catch, I strolled along narrow streets, dusty roads or crowded markets in cramped cities, communicating in simple English and a range of hand and head gestures. I put up in cheap hostels and motels close to stations, ate steaks and *prosciutto* sandwiches, drank coffee from street carts and water off public pipes. People in regular modern clothes or wrapped in colourful indigenous attire went out of their way with their kindness when they found out I was headed to the World Cup, pride gleaming in their eyes. Not one hid their shock to find out I was from Malaysia, living in England or was of Indian descent. I wasn't shocked either when they probed me with personal questions. No missus? Girlfriend?

There was not a moment or opportunity for me to feel any fear, not even as I headed further south to violence-ridden Colombia. Bogota, where I spent a night in a youth hostel, felt like it carried an air of defiance, likely owing to its drug cartel notoriety, but that was as close as I got to Colombia's dangerous reputation. My mind grew dim only when I witnessed the poverty and dread in the dense slums that launched the revolutionary thinking of the bearded one as his Norton 500cc went on its purposeful dreams.

All along Peru and Bolivia, the call of the Amazon was ever so strong. That I was skipping Brazil pricked my heart and increased my determination to make amends another time. I would too, more than two decades later, by which time ancient Amazon was shrinking at the speed of a chainsaw humming through a rain tree.

I reached La Paz after hitching a ride in a Jeep. Central La Paz, the world's highest capital city, offered great cityscapes, and its cobbled streets and rickety houses with straw roofs intrigued me. As did its high-spirited, slovenly children watching over sacks of carrots, chillies, sweet potatoes piled on pavements; and stout women in colourful ponchos and bowler hats squatting atop boxes and sacks, laughing and calling out to me in a language I wished I could speak. I was happy to oblige when one pointed at her cheek in return for a tangerine she offered me. Another woman said, 'Good…' making a circular motion around her middle as she handed me a small steel cup of *yerba mate*, a bitter herbal caffeine concoction. As with toddy in Kerala, I did not acquire a taste for it.

I checked into a modest guest house managed by a friendly lady. 'You know him?' she asked, catching me staring at the sidewall containing a framed picture of the all-too-familiar angry gaze of the beret-clad icon who'd followed me all through Latin America. I stared because the photograph of Che Guevara was placed right next to the Virgin Mary. The Argentine Cuban was familiar as one of the many things that Morecambe Library had taught me, but on that evening I experienced him as an apostle of revolution.

From La Paz, it was another long bus journey into the northwest of Argentina via the spectacularly multicoloured gorge of Quebrada de Humahuaca in San Salvador de Jujuy, whereupon I transferred to a Jeep with four others. The Jeep rose and fell while the landscape shifted from mountains and dramatic rock formations to multi-hued valleys, towering cacti and snowy salt flats. There was a stopover at a mountain pass so we could catch the sunset. I sat by myself, taking in the view of the sun gleaming and dropping into the immense mountains. Against the backdrop of such pulsating beauty, I longed for the company of one who had mocked me for being the bee's knees. Just as quickly, a calmness came over me – I would not have traded the reward of travelling alone for anything, the power of making my own choices, knowing I would stand or fall by them.

After a night's halt at Salta, I shot off by train to cover the 900 miles to reach the first of my World Cup cities: Cordoba. I arrived at night in a city full of football life and vitality, locals and foreigners of many extractions spilling out of bars and pubs. I asked my way around to an available youth hostel where I booked in for three days and finished the day with my favourite *empanadas*, a cross between the Malaysian curry puff and Cornish pasty, but with more spice and kick. I finished off the meal with a Colombian coffee.

My first live World Cup match was Scotland vs Iran, ending in a 1-1 draw. I was hoping for a Scottish victory since England did not qualify. A couple of matches later and having learnt how to work the black market for tickets, I travelled south to Rosario for an electric match between Argentina and Peru, in a stadium dominated by the white and blue of the host country.

I spent the last leg and week of my South America travels in Buenos Aries, the big, busy World Cup city reeling in conflict from the vacuum left behind by its beloved president, Juan Peron. Excitement and curiosity building, I made my way through the docks populated by Italian immigrants living in their fabled colourful houses, to a hostel in scruffy La Boca, home of the world-famous Boca Juniors and Maradona, where passion for football was as intense as its immigrant spirit. At long last I was in the heart of the Argentinian Superclásico! The one sporting event to attend before you die for football enthusiasts, when Boca Juniors and River Plate come together for a gladiatorial clash.

I made it into the Estadio Monumental for the final between Argentina and Holland to witness Mario Kempes drowning in confetti when he broke the duck in extra time and Daniel Passarella lifting his country's first World Cup trophy. A World Cup mired in controversies, conspiracies and volatile politics could not derail Argentina's jubilation. Under the huge Argentine flag waving over our heads, the atmosphere was absolute mania – passionate singing, cheering, chanting, sobbing; reminiscent of scenes in England. Except, the noise, energy and passion were amplified. I'd thought the electrifying Kop section of Anfield was the business, but football's grip on Argentine culture was another level altogether.

Jostling out of the stadium after the final, with the locals continuing their frenzied celebrations, I did not feel conspicuous. Floating with the crowds, I landed at a local *parilla* for grilled steak and sausages to loud music and couples breaking into the tango. It was easy to embrace the atmosphere and fall in love with the unique intensity of Argentina and its football. For most of the trip, I was sweaty and dirty and lacked sleep and rest, yet a prescient intuition told me I would return, and return again. To my Argentina!

I left Buenos Aires on Iberia Airways via Madrid, proud of the good service rendered by my "map" drafted in Morecambe Library. It was an eleven-hour flight to London, occupied by the colourful reels playing in my mind of the most out-of-this-world journey.

I returned to England to my new lady-love Janet for a period of intense romance before she would break my heart and go off to Newcastle to pursue a degree in Librarianship and Russian. By then, I'd been made to understand what bee's knees meant. What I couldn't understand was opposition leader Margaret Thatcher's statement at the close of 1978 that "People (Britons) are rather afraid that this country might be rather swamped by people with a different culture". It did not feel right to be accused of "swamping" Britain when all I was doing was working extremely hard and contributing to its economy. It felt even less right when Thatcher's Conservative Party took the lead over Labour the following month.

At the time I began my final year of law in September 1979, the IRA was gaining the upper hand. The nation was shaken by the bombing at the House of Commons, killing the MP Airey Neave, and another bomb, killing Prince Philip's uncle, Lord Mountbatten. The biggest news, however, was Margaret Thatcher becoming Britain's first female prime minister.

Hot on the heels of her appointment, the "trial of the century" came to an end, another hot topic for discussion at university and with my Wesley lot. Jeremy Thorpe, the charismatic hope of the Liberal Democratic Party, was acquitted of charges of conspiring to murder an alleged former homosexual partner (he was purportedly in an affair before homosexual acts were decriminalised in England in 1967). The decision favoured Thorpe, but the scandal effectively killed the voracious human rights advocate's chances of reviving his party or his political future, just as it seemed like we were looking at a credible third force in the two-way battles of Labour and Conservative. It's worth thinking about how Jeremy Thorpe might have handled Margaret Thatcher's vow "to bring back respectability and societal values" into the system, meaning a return to Victorian values tossed out in the previous decades. As Thorpe's star fell, Thatcher's rose. What a way to end the unrestrained 1970s!

Steve, Tina and I operated like a deer clan in the way we looked out for each other. I was also friends with their families and would occasionally stay with Steve's family in Prestwich, a wealthy Jewish suburb in Manchester. Steve's uncle was the main doctor for the Manchester

City Football Club, and his father Max would sometimes take Steve and me to watch home matches, with special seats next to the directors of the club. Steve's parents were also members of *The Village*, an exclusive squash club frequented by top Jewish professionals and businessmen, whose Rolls-Royces and Aston Martins decorated the club's car park. Squash came on my radar.

My visits to Steve's family opened me to quite a bit about Jewish culture, and also about the long-standing political conflict between Israel and Palestine. Israel's "progress" in the West Bank and Gaza Strip was a topic of particular interest, and Morecambe Library's ever-reliable resource centre furnished me with the required information to ensure I was able to participate in their conversations. On one such visit, the library gave me the brainwave to make a trip to Israel for the summer break of 1979. *Go to the Kibbutz*, suggested a magazine, of the little settlements in rural Israel that allow volunteers from any part of the world, usually young people, to spend short periods in the running of the communes in return for food, lodging and friendships. It was all the invitation needed for one with the impulse to catch the moment!

I flew into Tel Aviv from London Heathrow on a shabby El AL (Israel's national carrier), served by a crew unfamiliar with customer service, and food about as palatable as their service. Six hours later, I was glad for my British Certificate/ Passport as my Malaysian passport prohibited me from entering the conflicted state. A courtesy bus took me to the Kibbutz Program Centre in downtown Tel Aviv, where I filled out forms to obtain a volunteer visa for my six-week stay. From there, more volunteers joined and everyone was dropped off at their respective kibbutz north of Tel Aviv. My kibbutz, Kfar Hanassi, was more than a hundred miles north of Ben Gurion, a two-hour drive, and I arrived around midday with fellow volunteer Russell Scott from Sydney. We were shown a room with four bunk beds right around the corner past a swimming pool.

Meals were served buffet style and Russell and I got to meet half a dozen others – prosperous Ivy League types from England and the US who rejoiced in post-meal conversations on the Gaza Strip, West Bank, Golan Heights… Every once in a while, my Morecambe Library spirit would rise, invariably causing heated arguments when I brought into conversation the creation of Israel from the soil of Palestine with the aid of British and American settler colonialists and in doing so robbing natives of their ancestral land and source of livelihood.

I was glad of Russell's company as we went about enjoying our little chores, and he'd happily hop on every time I took the kibbutz's small motorcycle to venture outside. As inviting as the kibbutz's swimming pool was in Israel's sweltering weather, I was more drawn to be a part of the ordinariness happening outside the shelter of the commune. The weeks passed slowly and I kept getting transported to South America more and more, feeling stifled by the orderliness of the kibbutz and the sidelong glances of company hostile to dissent. It wasn't with any sadness that I boarded my return flight.

Steve, Tina and I graduated together with all their

families attending our convocation. It was quite the occasion, yet, I did not feel like I'd achieved a milestone since I was aware of the difficulties that lay ahead. During that time, law graduates were allowed only one sitting at the Law Society Finals, and more than sixty per cent failed it, including Nigel Knowles, dashing any hopes he might have had of joining Whiteside and Knowles.

Geoffrey expressed his desire of wanting me on board Whiteside and Knowles, which was added pressure for me as much as it was an honour. That, and his nephew Nigel's inability to pass the qualifying exam, triggered fear in me. I decided to take a gap year and postponed my place at law school in Chester and Lincoln's Inn London, to give me time to work out whether I wanted to stay permanently in England or perhaps return to Malaysia. Geoffrey was pleased with my decision.

It was a time when my savings had depleted as I'd taken leave from work during preparations for the finals, and the gap year meant going back to juggling part-time jobs. I particularly looked forward to my stevedore job at the James Fisher & Son dockyard in Heysham Port, which was ad hoc but well paid. Thirty-five pounds a day for back-breaking, risky work of heavy lifting, stacking and storing. Big money those days. Hordes of men would turn up very early every morning hoping for supervisor Jack Lyons to pick them.

It took about two weeks of being turned back every day – walking miles in bitter weather to and from Morecambe and Heysham to save money – before I was finally selected for regular work. I spent the entire winter of my gap year working there whenever picked. By five in the morning, I'd be ready in my jeans, long tee-shirt over a fleece, work boots, and a donkey jacket and gloves to keep out the cold wind blitzing from the Irish Sea, for the five-mile walk to start work at six o'clock. In wintry weather, work conditions were more challenging; injuries and even deaths weren't uncommon. For certain in this day and age, any of the dangerous dockyards would be sued for breach of health and safety regulations, but none of that mattered to my new mates used to the hard side of life. What a difference to my Middle-England friends! This lot were absolute workhorses. Their ways were rough, they drank hard, half the time their language was unsavoury and they functioned on a shorter fuse, but, they were no shirkers. Reliability was an essential quality to be on the regular roll call; otherwise, one was booted out.

Without a doubt, that was a period of character development for this pipsqueak, as Geoffrey used to call me. Walking home after the sweat-drenching labour each day, I could feel exhaustion trickling through me and went to bed with tired arms and body. All the same, the experience was not loathsome as I loved the satisfaction of knowing I'd given it my all. Additionally, the work environment was not fun starved because a tight comradeship and spirit of bonhomie subsisted among the workers, which enabled me to endure the gruelling conditions.

My fitness and exuberance were not missed on Jack, who took a shine to my work ethic and held me in some esteem as a law graduate. He would later become a client of mine, so too a number of my co-workers, mainly for injury claims. I did not know then that my genuine interest in connecting with people was to significantly impact my future career. As was the case with Magda. That bond forged in Morecambe Library led to Magda cooking meals for me and me for her and her American boat-builder partner Nathan, and, upon my suggestion, the couple visiting Kerala and staying with my family. She would later appoint me her lawyer and joint executor of her will. The story of my life.

It is noteworthy that during my gap year, between 1980 and 1981, the three countries I was associated with were undergoing major political shifts. In Britain, the grocer's daughter turned prime minister Margaret Thatcher was bent on building her legacy around eradicating "socialist thinking"; Malaysia had its first prime minister not from the pedigree of the ruling elite in Dr Mahathir Mohamad; on the other hand, political pedigree and family lineage made a comeback in India, with old prime minister Indira Gandhi returning as its new prime minister. The triumvirate of dynamic, notoriously divisive personalities would forever divide opinions. The 1980s promised a torrid ride.

FIFTEEN

# TRUTH IS A TRICKY BUSINESS

Little money, plenty of freedom, three jobs, heavy badminton and squash, fun aplenty; my gap year was going great. Snap! John Lennon shot and killed outside his apartment in New York. The 8th of December 1980 became the most intimate memory attached to my gap year. A period filled with watershed moments.

For the boy who had arrived in England ten years earlier to catch a glimpse of his idol, I never fulfilled that wish. The Beatles split up that year and John left for America to battle for his green card and never set foot in England again. He was all over anyway, records, papers, TV.

In the mid-'70s, I watched the BBC's "Whispering" Bob Harris in dialogue with John Lennon in Manhattan, and it felt like John was talking to me directly when he teased, 'Hello, England, keep your chin up. We'll meet again.' Above all, I loved his style, cheeky genius and his total ease with confessions like 'I've always been a little, you know, loose...' John also talked about Elvis Presley never having stepped into England. Made no difference, he said to Bob; England still fell for Elvis's music and adored him. They didn't have to see Elvis; they *felt* him. John Lennon too was that and more for me at the time.

I was entering my flat after a morning practice when I was taken aback by female wails coming from the flat below mine tenanted by some university students. Squash rackets still thrust on my back, I made my way down when first one girl then another made their way to me to break the news. The three of us huddled in a group hug, the girls unbothered by my sweat-sodden tee-shirt or that we barely knew each other. We spent the next few hours in my flat, keeping our private vigil until midnight over copious amounts of tea and cheap white wine from Povey's, the stereo tirelessly playing John Lennon.

The week after, I joined thousands for the commemorative vigil in Liverpool, a jam-packed evening of Beatles mania and a powerful ten-minute pin-drop silence. I harked back to the way my father and friends mourned the assassination of President John Kennedy when I was a schoolboy, but the way John Lennon brought people together was something else altogether. The spirit of the rebel Beatle has travelled with me through his words, particularly his openness in acknowledging that the Beatles got their music from the blacks, as he frequently called on the influences of Chuck Berry, Bo Didley, Little Richards or BB King. It was something I would recall to Bob Harris after a concert at the Great Hall over a pint of Tartan, leading to a discussion on the huge freedom the 1970s afforded to produce extraordinary music and journalism missing in the post-Thatcher era.

Margaret Thatcher was the other major newsmaker, steaming ahead with her mission to divert the course of the country from socialism – and persistent winters of discontent. 'This lady is not for turning,' she warned. 'No more spending money like water... that dream is over.' Her national interests explained in robust spirit, about a free-market economy and the independence it brought to people, such as the tricky Right to Buy council houses scheme, appealed to the working classes. In a similar mood, she went about privatising national assets and taking on the unions, the Labour opposition and the European Union during a tenure coinciding with her political soulmate and new American president Ronald Reagan, and the personable Soviet Union president Mikhail Gorbachev. The warpath suited the Iron Lady.

My badminton reputation paved the way for my membership of Morecambe's Concorde Squash Club, a restless den of iniquities and egos. I was already familiar with the sociology of sports and sports clubs in England: some plebeian, certain others closed to the plebs. The Vale of Lune Harriers, Vale of Lune Rugby Union, the Bowerham Tennis Club, the Wesley Badminton Club, the Lancaster Boys Club, the Governors of the Lancaster Boys' Grammar School... a diplomatic roll call of the East India Trading Company after its loot! I was aware of why Princess Anne represented Britain in equestrian at the 1976 Olympics instead of, for instance, a track event. But I did not give sporting snobbery much importance, being spared this distinction wherever I played. In fact, the Concorde Squash Club was quite eager for its first coloured member to market their club, just as I was happy to flaunt my head-to-toe Adidas- and Yonex-sponsored gear.

The club had a tradition called the ladder challenge. There were 275 players listed on the ladder and members were allowed three challenges upwards from anywhere, usually from the lower rungs. If everything went your way, one could reach the top in about two years. Additionally, a newcomer to the club was entitled to one flying challenge – the chance to challenge anyone on the ladder. A win meant an overtake; a loss landed you at the bottom of the pile. Placing my faith in my supreme fitness and badminton training, I opted for the flying challenge, going for the club's number one, a local star and a bank manager. My challenge was accepted and I booked three forty-minute sessions – a feat, considering the great demand for courts – so I could pace myself and play a tactical game. The news caused the kind of stir the club's powers had been hoping for when they waived my annual fee!

On match day, there was a packed audience for the "audacious duel". Many were simply curious to see the arrogant twat taking on their number one. How could they have known I was winged by badminton, and great muscular endurance and aerobic capacity thanks to Morecambe Promenade, the Trough of Bowland and, increasingly, the Lakes? It took me the full five sets and a little under two hours to prove to the stunned spectators I was not out to lunch. I became the toast of the club and was always on the radar of the ladder challenge – and young married women stuck in stale marriages looking for excitement and dissolution of their marriages. It was all so transactional and disposable; having small children was no matter.

Realising how deeply I'd been sucked into England's social environment, it was easy to edge out a return to Malaysia. I realised my decade away from Malaysia had forged a deep chasm between me and my Malaysian family and friends. I didn't think I could span that chasm. My decision called for a visit to Shefferlands.

I always made a special effort when headed to dinner with the Knowleses. It was never short of formal, with Joan being a Cordon Bleu-type cook and Geoffrey with his good taste. Over a mouth-watering pineapple roast gammon, I informed my delighted hosts of my decision to stay on in England. My announcement dominated conversation after that, over liberal downing of Geoffrey's favourite Martini Asti Spumante, Italy's refreshingly fruity dry sparkling wine never in short supply at Shefferlands' cellar.

By the end of the night, I'd almost landed myself the position of a peon/articled clerk at Whiteside and Knowles and will never forget the gleam in Geoffrey's eyes or the affection in his voice when he said, 'I'll see you at Skipton on Monday. Goodnight, son.' I felt the gift of grace at that moment. It allowed me to trust I'd be taken care of even in the toughest of times.

Monday morning in Skipton Street in Morecambe's heart was for Geoffrey to get the green light from his partner, Anthony Collinson, to take me on board. Whiteside and Knowles was established in 1888, and upon the recent death of his brother Kenneth, Geoffrey was the only Knowles left in the firm.

I made my first visit to Whiteside and Knowles, a charming end-of-terrace property with offices spread over four floors; the fortunate ones had views of Morecambe Promenade and the sea. From the crowded waiting room, I was whisked upstairs to the inner sanctum of senior partners Geoffrey and Anthony Collinson, waiting to put me to the sword before offering me the job.

Every inch the astute, discerning lawyer, Tony was well aware of me through Geoffrey, although that was our first meeting. The whole office by then knew of my racket adventures. If the man I was going to work closely with for the remaining months of my gap year had any reservations about my suitability to undertake articled clerkship being an unknown quantity when it came to the law, Tony did not show it.

I started the following day at Whiteside and Knowles with a room and a telephone all to myself, bubbling with enthusiasm and high spirits, fired up to make a good impression on the glittering elite, as I saw my seniors. A big deal for one still wandering through life haphazardly and feeling vulnerable as a late entrant to law, being at the mature end of my twenties by then.

There were three other solicitors besides Geoffrey and Tony, all males, and fifteen female administrative staff. Tony Collinson, only three years older than me, was buff from his horse riding and did power dressing in a quintessentially English way. In Jermyn Street suits, complementing coloured braces, smart ties and shoes, coupled with his appealing etiquette and capacity for presenting his arguments with erudition, Tony aligned perfectly with the culture and ethos of Whiteside and Knowles. When the early impression of the suits, his exquisite desk set comprising Montblanc fountain pen, ink blotter and silver hallmark paper opener withered, I was able to connect with Tony's earnest desire to fortify the firm. Tony was a perfect segue to Geoffrey's ebullience and no less a pleasure to work with. I found it endearing that he was a man of integrity and goodwill, if a little stately – he still signs off our WhatsApp exchanges with *Best Wishes*.

One of my earliest tasks as an articled clerk was to hold a watching brief as Tony's legal assistant (glorified note taker) in the town hall courtrooms at Lancaster Magistrates' Court. Caroline Swift was the barrister defending our client Peter Patrick against criminal charges of unsafe asbestos removal at his business premises. Barristers were prohibited to work in chambers with solicitors until multi-disciplinary practices were allowed from 2010 onwards.

Over coffee, I observed Tony, Caroline and Peter discussing the merits of the allegations and analysing the defence and tactics. There were common interests to keep the mood upbeat, all three being members of the Vale of Lune Harriers and the Pony Club. Just listening to their chin-wagging made me feel privileged. Caroline's tête-à-tête with the boys ended with 'Hell will break loose if Bobby Sands dies' when the court usher called us to enter the cauldron of the solemn law lords. I had no idea who Bobby Sands was.

On a day of good legal arguments and production of doubt, our client was acquitted to the joy of all concerned, not to mention Whiteside and Knowles' office account. 'Cakes for the office,' declared Geoffrey, as the articled clerk (me!) brought in the good news. The articled clerk also took some mental notes: build a pyramid of legal players and experts and play the game like the cross-court jump smash. Smash at the right moment. Importantly, bank on disclosure.

Bobby Sands did die. In Her Majesty's Prison Maze, Northern Ireland. His funeral procession attracted tens of thousands of mourners for whom he'd become a martyr. Militant, insisted Margaret Thatcher. Belfast burned, the Troubles escalated, and it was all the discussion in my office and on the streets. The media went to town on the Irish Republican Army's Mahatma Gandhi-like hunger strikes; the "dirty protest" of the political prisoners' refusal to wear prison clothes, demanding instead clothes from their homes; Mrs Thatcher's deceitful approval (passing them new clothes instead of the ones from their families); Bobby Sands winning an unexpected snap by-election from his prison death bed; him dying a month later as Bobby Sands, Member of Parliament…

Why would masses march behind a militant's coffin? Why would an Irish Catholic man disobey the Pope (John Paul II had sent an envoy to urge Bobby Sands to give up the hunger strike)? Was Margaret Thatcher a murderer as they claimed? What impacted a community to push a man behind bars to political status despite the British prime minister reminding them he was a convicted criminal?

Upon Sands' death, Mrs Thatcher would say, 'He chose to take his own life. It was a choice that his organisation did not allow to many of their victims.' Popular media did not probe into the historical context of England's political meddling in Ireland, a discord stretching back centuries. There seemed little desire for understanding the minds of men imprisoned within walls, faeces and urine, reading Mao, Che Guevara or Ho Chi Minh. Whomever I spoke to about the matter summed it up rather vaguely: 'History of religious kerfuffle, you know... the Catholics, Protestants...'

A bee settled in my bonnet. I imagined the IRA's unification desire and its guerrilla offensives as being no different to what Ho Chi Minh's National Liberation Front wanted for Vietnam. The insatiable bee then flew to the radical thinking of the social, cultural and political tyranny South Africa's Steve Biko gave his life for and what Nelson Mandela was fighting for from behind bars. It wasn't hard to see that prison hallmarked many a revolutionary's legacies. Mandela, Gandhi, Bobby Sands. Men of different colours, of different continents, yet sharing a common nemesis. In my opinion, no amount of revisionist history can change the fact that Margaret Thatcher committed atrocities against Irish Catholics in Northern Ireland for legitimately resisting England's brutal occupation.

Weeks after Bobby Sand's death, more IRA prisoners died of hunger strikes, causing unrest in major cities around the country. England, however, unchained itself from such troubles to jubilate in its crown prince's marriage. Riots and street disorders were temporarily replaced by an exultant pride in watching Prince Charles marry Lady Diana. The new princess heralded a new era. Not long after, her brother-in-law Prince Andrew heralded another one as a helicopter pilot and navy officer travelling thousands of miles south of the Atlantic Ocean with a fleet of warships to fight a distant war on occupied islands. I was intrigued because of the Falkland Islands' proximity to Argentina.

When it was time to start law school, I gave up my place to do the Bar Vocational Course, opting instead for the one-year Legal Practice Course (LPC) at Manchester University, seeing that solution-seeking and liaising with a range of people came naturally to me. The strangling demands of the LPC and having only one opportunity at it meant it was not possible to sustain my job at Whiteside and Knowles. I had to manage with my savings and the welcome contributions from two new friends I gave a lift to university, together with the discretionary grant I received from Lancashire County Council for the LPC fee, without which I would have joined the long list of law graduates failing to become solicitors because of finance.

The LPC was a completely different pressure from the law degree, mainly because the lecturers were tough industry practitioners. Tutorials for the seven subjects required a much higher level of commitment and I missed the company of Steve, who was doing the Bar, and Tina, who'd settled to being a housewife. Badly needing a lifeline, I turned to music, undoubtedly a great mood-lifter and energy-booster all my life, but I least expected the whimsical purchase of a classical opera album to do the trick during my LPC struggles. It didn't matter that I couldn't make out the words; just looping Luciano Pavarotti belting *Madam Butterfly* in the background as I studied was so strangely comforting!

Taking the place of Steve and Tina was my new friend Pru Beevar, with whom, one year later, I drove to the *Daily Telegraph* Manchester's printworks for its first publication containing the LPC results. We weren't the only ashen-faced ones at the side entrance of the post-press area unable to enjoy the sensory pleasure of fresh paper coming hot off the press. It was midnight and the course of our futures was inked on a particular page of that newspaper we'd been impatient for the lorries and vans to deliver to vendors and paperboys in the morning.

Keeping Mummy's prayers in my heart, I received a warm copy of the *Daily Telegraph*, barely breathing until I saw my name on the list, with Pru's. We kept our joy muted… in our midst were several other bent heads shedding tears for the end of their legal paths.

My privileged position dawned on me on that return journey home. I was holding a job in a reputable law firm without clearing the LPC; in fact, I was back at Whiteside and Knowles right after completing my papers, even before the results were out. Securing a training contract with a legal firm to undertake the compulsory two years of vocational training to qualify as a solicitor was highly competitive. It could take years of waiting, and some just never went into practice. In my case, my principals in Whiteside and Knowles, Geoffrey, Tony and new associate Charles Wilson, furthered my cause by backtracking my training to the time I began work, which meant earlier completion for me. I couldn't help reflecting on how badminton had dealt me a good hand with my chance meeting with Geoffrey immediately after landing in England, but I also knew it was not just an accident of circumstance that got me there. I'd earned my stripes.

I moved house yet again. To Sunset View, a bedsit flat owned by a wealthy solicitor better known for his properties and yacht moored at the Morecambe Bay Yacht Club than for upholding high standards of legal practice. Geoffrey and Tony were right with their cautionary advice of dealing with him when, within a few months into our contract, my landlord wanted vacant possession of his property. He was evicting me and a middle-aged couple occupying a flat in another part of the building. I took on my own defence and represented the couple as well. There was not a chance of him getting a court possession order as we had the security of tenure under the Law of Equity and the Housing Act.

The dispute was resolved without the need to go to court and under the circumstances the solicitor was forced to offer us substantial compensation in return for voluntary possession. Geoffrey was tickled pink with the way I'd turned the tables on and made money off an established solicitor used to worming his way out of tricky cases.

Margaret Thatcher scored an even more miraculous victory. Things had been going so badly for her that her popularity stood at an all-time low. *She's not going to make it to term two* was the widespread belief. As luck would have it, the Falkland Islands fell on the beleaguered prime minister's lap. Most Britons had no clue where the Falklands were or how Britain had acquired a territory more than 8,000 miles away, but "Argentina Invades!" sounded grave enough to raise hackles. The legality, and morality, of Britain's claim over the Falkland Islands that lie off the coast of Argentina mattered not to a woefully ignorant public being sold on the British-territory-invaded narrative.

Margaret Thatcher saw her opportunity. Raising the heat of xenophobia, she dispatched the military task force from Portsmouth on 2nd May 1982, with the nation waving the Union Jack. It took her popularity to nearly eighty per cent. It was a season of high emotions – the press on a mission to promote the retake of the islands, and jingoism ruled newsrooms with headlines like *GOTCHA. Our lads sink gunboat…* It was a moment I felt I'd lost the England I knew. I suddenly felt like a nigger in the woodpile, a slur once directed at me without malice by a close associate.

The rhetoric was no different in American media bent on creating revulsion for Argentina's domestic human rights woes under the junta. It's no secret that Thatcher was assisted by the United States with intelligence and military equipment. Or that as a payback for the weapons Britain was supplying them, Thatcher also received intelligence from another South American dictatorship sitting in power after a coup d'état by its ruthless junta over a democratically elected government following the assassination (later determined as suicide) of Chile's President Salvador Allende. The US had decided the Chilean people were wrong in voting for a left-leaning socialist government. Neither Thatcher nor Reagan conveyed revulsion for the dictatorship of General Pinochet, although in Chile too, people were being "disappeared" just like in Argentina.

When the Falklands War ended, hundreds of Argentines, British servicemen and Falklands natives had lost their lives, almost half of them from the controversial sinking of the cruiser *General Belgrano*. On a business trip to Buenos Aires in 2001, I would experience the aftermath of that tragedy through the recollections of a young man whose college lecturer father lost most of his class of boys conscripted to the *Belgrano* – all no more than twenty years of age. I'd see first-hand the sheer futility of wars stemming from invasions, of countries never learning from their failures and continuing to fill up history chapters with pyrrhic victories.

The *Belgrano* was sailing away from the British task force and outside the war waters, but Thatcher claimed otherwise to Parliament and gave orders for its sinking, as was revealed by her senior government officer in the Ministry of Defence, Clive Ponting, in papers that came to be known as the Crown Jewels. The papers, sent to the attention of firebrand Labour parliamentarian Tam

Dalyell, ended Ponting's career, and he might have gone to jail in 1985 if not for a bold jury that saw merit in his "interest of the state" defence. Revelations at the trial and the equally controversial Official Secrets Act used to charge Ponting attracted huge interest, and the country was exploding in debate. It was happening at the time I'd completed my training and was admitted as Solicitor of the Supreme Court of England & Wales. The case evokes special memories of my admiration for Tam Dalyell's uncompromising courage and tenacity. And Ponting's gallantry when he said after his acquittal, 'I did what I did because it was the right thing to do.'

A year later, an Argentinian maestro would show Thatcher's England how it felt to use trickery and get away with it. With a goal handed by God. Maradona would go on to admit two things after that 1986 World Cup. Football and politics go hand in hand and, yeah, his controversial goal felt like "picking the pocket of an Englishman".

The Argentinian icon must be grinning from heaven's gates, watching Leo Messi bring home the World Cup trophy for the third time and seeing the EU deliver a diplomatic blow to Britain by referring to the disputed territory by its Argentine name, Islas Malvinas.

## SIXTEEN

# THE BALLAD OF EAST AND WEST

I began my career as an associate solicitor at Whiteside and Knowles prepared to face resistance from clients known for appreciating the discerningly cosy English-room feel of our lounge while flicking through *Horse & Hound* magazine sipping Fortnum & Mason tea in fine bone china served by familiar faces devoted to the firm.

Whiteside and Knowles' client associations were chiefly provincial, lacking London's cosmopolitan flair and interconnectedness, yet we attracted the Lord Shuttleworth or the Duke of Westminster types who preferred us to London lawyers. I had much to live up to!

Law being the domain of white, wealthy, Anglo-Saxon society meant I needed to work much harder than my English counterparts to prove my worth. On top of the obvious "impediment" of my colour, I stood no chance of matching certain posh accents or impeccable turns of phrase and had to devise ways to not let all that affect clients' judgement of my abilities. To my benefit, I'd picked up much about client mindsets and vulnerabilities from Geoffrey, who instilled in me that the reverential respect clients had for our firm came foremost from earning their trust.

From the outset, it was clear I was on trial. Passing the two stages of reading law and knowing how to apply the law felt like nothing when faced with my ultimate test of convincing contemptuously quiet, attentive clients that I was their man. Mind you, they were far from hostile or unfriendly, just bewildered at the prospect of having to "divulge the size of their underpants", as Geoffrey put it, to a brown solicitor.

Just as I wasn't wonderstruck for too long by my seniors at the firm, I applied the same attitude to my clients. Clients who always came neatly dressed and never late. The phone might ring at 9.55 am to tell me that a Mrs Bragg was in the waiting room on the ground floor for her 10.00 am appointment.

'I'll be down in five minutes. Please make her some tea, Chris,' I'd say to the receptionist, knowing how important it was to ensure Mrs Bragg was not too unprepared for her introductory session with the new solicitor blemished by a permanent tan. No tea or coffee was ever enough to conceal the awkward silence, nervous eye or God knows what running through their minds when I entered the boardroom! Suppressing the tension building up inside me, also pretending not to have noticed Mrs Bragg's sharp intake of breath, I would proceed to gain her confidence, at which point the warm-up statements and questions from Mrs Bragg would come up.

'Mind, I wasn't expecting someone new...' 'Why am I not seeing Geoffrey/Tony/Charles...?' 'They said Philip George, so I assumed, you know... that's an English name...'

*'I do not have an English name. It's a biblical name, not the chattel or ownership of the English. By the way, the apostle St Thomas arrived in the ancient world of my ancestors in Kerala, to spread the word and baptise my forefathers. And since AD 52, we've been having names from the book. Also, long before St Thomas arrived, that strip of southwestern India overlooking the Arabian Sea was already a flourishing maritime trade centre. You'll be surprised to know, Philip, George and many a Thomas were long in the local mix, to the shock of Portuguese explorer Vasco da Gama when he arrived with his missionaries in 1498. A whole century before Britain's East India Company joined the exploitation.'*

I'd have loved to impart that lesson to my client, but, as a rookie solicitor on a mission to impress, what I did was carry on with the sabre rattling until the client dropped all traces of disapproval and discomfiture. Without fail, they would thaw. Crossed arms would loosen, tone of voice would soften, smiles would relax... My work took over from there and I'd be free of the further need to convince them that I was indeed a qualified lawyer; that I had obtained my degree from an English institution; and, no, I wasn't Muslim or Hindu.

Such encounters and the subsequent solid relationships I built with my broad client base of townsfolk, farming families and landed gentry from all corners of Lancaster and Morecambe, covering Sunderland Point to Skipton and Carlisle to Manchester even, took away the drudgery of a profession needing long hours of hard work and meticulous analysis. The reward wasn't just a healthy bank balance, more than that, it came in the form of appreciation and adoration from my clients, such as the delightful Mrs Hunneybell insisting I spend New Year's Eve night with her family at her lovely Overton country home, to partake in madcap celebrations and conversations meandering to Henry the Eighth, Anne Boleyn and Elizabeth I.

Holding the law with reverence and being committed to the needs and best interests of the client, I took nothing for granted. Neither did I shy of taking any litigious cases that came my way, no matter how mundane or complex; and usually because Tony and Charles preferred not to take them on. I did not attach any standard or requirement for the type of case or client I would act for but had a soft spot for the disadvantaged and migrant communities who gravitated towards me. One such interesting friend turned client was Bruno Brucciani, a second-generation Italian whose family owned Morecambe's landmark Brucciani ice-cream parlour-cum-café looking out to the bay. We bonded over our love for driving and quality cars and when done with talking about what makes our machines cause our hearts to go aflutter, our discussions would meander towards the social and political developments of Italy, Malaysia or India, the common struggles of immigrants arriving in Britain or America often with nothing but dreams and the willingness to work hard to materialise those dreams while faced with prejudices. As was often the case, I also got on famously with Brucciani's extended family, which would have some bearing in the distant future when choosing a country to call my home.

In those early days, Geoffrey's obvious soft spot for me was most useful, and it wasn't just pertaining to work. Once, when I needed to run an errand, I asked if I could take his brand-new Chrysler. Knowing how much I admired it, he gave me the keys just like that, although I wasn't used to its power steering, having only driven it once before. While parking at St Nicholas, I lost control of the steering wheel and scraped it against an iron barrier, causing a nasty dent. My heart sank thinking Geoffrey was surely going to disown me!

'He's in a meeting now. You're going to get into big bother with him, Phil,' warned Mandy, Geoffrey's secretary. Two hours later, Mandy called me to his room.

Geoffrey's only contribution from the moment he saw my wretched, crestfallen face was two words. 'What happened?' I explained. His face transformed into a dangerous crimson, yet he refrained from giving me a mouthful as I'd seen him do numerous times with others. The awkward silence that followed was clearly instructive – I left the room as feebly as I had walked into it. In a small seaside town like Morecambe, where everybody knew everybody, and everybody certainly knew me, *Phil crashed Geoffrey's car* spread like wildfire, especially on the badminton circuit. Like me, everybody was surprised I escaped my mentor's wrath scot-free.

There was no blotch when it came to my work because I did litigation with precision control, the same way I planned my travels, played chess or prepared for a badminton tournament – everything I learnt from Geoffrey and Malaya. There is always a lot of Malaya that drives me still, the same way it helped me organise my forty-year legal career in England. My psychiatric nursing experience too gave me the edge in assessing and evaluating a client's mental and emotional state. I took great care towards ensuring my clients felt completely safe in disclosing even the minutest of detail to advance their case in court. Such emotional investment led to many clients remaining with me for their lifetimes, often making me executor of their wills. Some left me legacies; many would recommend me to their friends and family, contributing to my meteoric rise in Whiteside and Knowles.

On the personal front, Janet and I resumed our relationship when she returned to Lancaster to work as a legal cashier at a well-established law firm across the castle. Within a short period, we had invested in a flat in Castle Court by Lancaster train station, where due to tradition-minded restraint she wouldn't spend the nights with me. She'd drive to our flat every morning from where we'd leave for our respective offices to be reunited in the evening for dinner before she drove back to her parents. Mrs Stubbs took to me straight away, not so Janet's father.

Mr Stubbs had made clear his dislike of me from the time I was a mere articled clerk at Whiteside and Knowles. He was disturbed by my ladies' man reputation, rightfully so, and alarmed by my "differentness", understandably, considering his parochial affiliations and general stodginess. He was being a protective father, struggling to cast away entrenched prejudices, convinced it was for his daughter's own good he was barring me from their house for Christmas. Defiant daughter would still bring me home-cooked Christmas meals and gifts. A pair of silver cufflinks, in particular, remains a cherished keepsake.

By the time Janet arrived at our house, I'd have finished my morning run and be kitted out in my Jermyn Street clothes, always in a double cuff shirt following Papa's style, with Janet's silver cufflinks, tie in a Windsor knot, Crockett & Jones black brogue shoes and Burlington pink socks. I'd pop my Bridge satchel bag containing work files and my big Adidas holdall with five squash rackets into my red Golf GTI to arrive at my personal parking spot by eight o'clock to let myself in. My second-floor office was at the front end of the building with a view of Morecambe Promenade and the Irish Sea.

Geoffrey, Tony, Charles and I would start the morning over coffee and tea, current affairs and sports. Some days we'd gather in Tony's office for a meeting over lunch or I'd meet up with Geoffrey and Tony at Morecambe Golf Club instead. Such lunches with Geoffrey and Tony led to unshackled conversations over a range of matters legal and otherwise; got rather irrational at times, not that any of us cared as we marched in synchronicity.

Despite the pressure to perform, Whiteside and Knowles provided a congenial, cooperative work environment where I quickly earned the nickname Peter Pan for my abundant energy and not looking my age. Geoffrey and Tony were well liked for the interest they took in employee welfare, and for their generosity: annual pay rises, long bank holidays and Geoffrey's much looked-forward-to Friday lunch treat, not to mention annual Christmas gatherings. It was no wonder legal assistants and administrative staff who started as teenagers right after leaving school stayed until retirement.

My average day's work would read something like: 10 am Mrs Bragg (dog attack), 10.30 am William Spencer (car garage dispute), 11 am Hilda Hunneybell (inheritance dispute), 12 noon Olwyn Davies (house sale), 12.30 to 1.30 pm lunch (grab my standard issue Marks and Spencer Wensleydale and carrot chutney sandwich on the way to a 40-minute squash ladder challenge), 2 pm court hearing, 3.30 pm Mrs H Rooney (family dispute), 4.30 pm Barry Stimpson (clinical negligence claim), 5 pm Fiona Hatton (matrimonial dispute), 6 pm Kathleen Hogton home visit (personal affairs).

I particularly enjoyed home visits for the opportunity to build relationships, and made them part of my service protocol. Geoffrey had placed the ladder for me to climb by taking me along to visit Whiteside and Knowles' clients sprawled across the Yorkshire Dales, the Lakes and the Trough of Bowland – everywhere from market towns to desolate valleys and moorland hills. We could do Bentham, Skipton, Garstang or Kendal with our eyes closed! I also got a sense of achievement from knowing I was already a familiar face to many of our clients owing to the *Lancaster Guardian* or the *Morecambe Visitor* carrying my pictures following badminton victories.

Of the many memorable visits, one remains so fresh in my memory, although it wasn't strictly a home visit. It was to Lancaster Moor Hospital to attend to two elderly clients who had lost their mental capacity. As receiver via the court of protection, it was my duty to continue supervision of their health condition and financial affairs. I drove into the institution to the same echoes of woe and familiar faces, this time to question and direct the charge nurses and doctors on the standard of patient care being provided to my clients and how they were progressing. What a role-reversal moment that was! Humbling too, as everyone was truly delighted with the way I had "made good" of my life.

From very early on, Geoffrey made sure I was mindful about not allowing clients, especially ones with influence and power, and there were many, to ever have control over me. 'Francis Drake had to finish his game of bowls before he went to defend his fleet against the Spanish Armada,' I remember him saying once, composed and serious, unusual for the thorough fun-lover with a hankering for the naughty. He repeated the statement another time after we'd all attended the funeral of an established local solicitor from another firm. An emotional Geoffrey continued on a no-holds-barred rampage that would have burnt the ears of the demanding wealthy client, who, in his opinion, had sent the solicitor to his untimely death.

My thoughts at the funeral were squarely on the combustible state of mind the poor solicitor must have been in. The misery, pain, anguish he was unable to overcome. There was total merit in Geoffrey's allegation since I too put extraordinary effort into my work, combing through facts and arguments, spelling out specific laws, *ratio decidendi* and *obiter dicta*, amounting to bundles of legal papers sorted and arranged neatly in my spic and span office.

What I would not do was take my cases to bed and spoil the few hours of my precious sleep. Once again, it was the indoctrination of badminton into my construct that came to my rescue. I balanced my work without abandoning my usual rigour of badminton matches at county, town, club levels and continuous ladder challenges from others at the Concorde Squash Club. With age catching up, it was getting harder to maintain my winning standards, but I felt no inclination to stop, slow down or settle within comfortable parameters. The physical and mental pain from the constant adrenaline rush was bearable because I relished testing my limits and, importantly, retaining my slim frame. The minute my head hit the pillow, it was always for restful sleep. It is why badminton remains top of my gratitude list.

In all of this, I also made time for Janet. We hit the road as often as we could on the weekends going around Britain. It was not unusual for us to drive miles for a concert at Birmingham's NEC, cheering and singing along to the Police or Jules Holland. We also had an unforgettable fortnight in France. My ever-reliable GTI carried us, our ridge tent and two-plate gas cooker with a medium-sized gas cylinder through towns and villages. The sunroof open, stereo speakers blasting Sade, Roxy Music or Grace Jones, and Janet map reading from a foldable Michelin road map guided by my skeleton route map, we took the no-toll scenic roads all over the French countryside, through the champagne route from Châlons-en-Champagne to Joan of Arc's Reims. We pulled up at fields and woods, stopped for local fare at quaint cafés, set up tent at campsites, shopped, cooked and ate by grassy banks after a swim in a clear spring and slept in pumped-up air beds.

We roamed freely, occasionally treating ourselves to a Bed and Breakfast, and drove up to Toulouse to catch the Police in concert. Never had *Every Breath You Take* meant so much. From endless revelatory conversations, Janet and I discovered so much about each other. I got to know all about the Greenham Common protests she was very passionate about – a series of campaigns and pickets by hundreds of thousands of women protesting against nuclear weapons being stored at the former American base on British soil. Fines, court cases and imprisonment could not deter the powerful fleet of women from all over Britain who would stand their ground for almost two decades.

We covered the luminous South of France, finishing off in Nice and Monte Carlo before heading back to Calais for Dover, amassing about 5,000 miles. My life was transported to a new, exciting, sophisticated trajectory with an assertive, companionable girl whose simple elegance and self-worth I found most alluring. We were easy lovers, not in each other's pockets even though by this stage we were joined at the hip. We'd come far. From purchasing a flat together to Janet accompanying me to the Law Society in London for my admission ceremony, clapping proudly as I received my scroll in the company of Lord Denning and fellow esteemed law lords. Yet, even a joint mortgage in our names, implying permanency, did not drive either of us to push for the inevitable.

My career in Whiteside and Knowles off to a flying start, my love life going great, I received a letter from my father. It was carefully composed and constructed (dictionary at the ready!), asking to see my original Solicitor of the Supreme Court of England and Wales admission scroll. *I do not want any photocopies* was stressed. And duly noted. It didn't require cross-examining skills to see through my father's motive.

After a seven-year interval, in June 1985, I returned to Kerala for a two-week visit, with bloated luggage as was expected, without a game plan to counter the impending encroachment into my personal life. I figured I'd just say I was not ready to renege on my unspoken vow to remain a bachelor. If only Papa knew about my carryings-on with my Aston Martin gang at the Red Well pub, playing DJ at parties in Shefferlands or "scoring" after a 2 am finish at the Great Hall, which I must say nullified the long, vengefully cold walk back to my nurses' residence during my Moor Hospital days…

Papa only waited until I'd finished my first satisfactory fish curry meal before getting down to business. My damp hand still smelling of Mummy's freshly ground masala, I dug out original copies of my certificates, which he perused through like they were school reports. My brothers Viji and Tom had disappeared. I had to face the disciplinary hearing on my own.

'Mohan, this lifestyle cannot go on. You must settle down, you are over thirty years old. Do you or do you not realise it? There are some very good alliances, and the marriage broker is only waiting for these.' The reproval ended with Papa flapping my hard-earned papers.

I wasted time muttering about needing time to build my career and not being in a hurry to settle down, not in the least with anyone his broker was going to pitch at me. That part about Papa's broker did not leave my mouth.

The next day, a corpulent, moustachioed, keen-eyed man clasping a paper folder under one armpit descended on our house to ensure my limbs were intact, my senses functioned to satisfaction and my papers were genuine. Papa endorsed the visitor as an *international* broker. Broker beamed at the proclamation. I missed Janet desperately and wished I'd brought her with me.

It took the *international* broker only two days to return with a "perfect proposal" that deserved a declaration. 'Mr KP George, it will be a mistake if your son turns down this alliance.' The "mistake" I was about to make was a Malayali doctor from Manhattan, New York, whose parents were ready with a £100k dowry. It was hard to tell which of the two men was drooling more at the hundred thousand pounds sterling. I glanced from man to man, then Mummy, feeling so disconnected. I returned the small album containing photographs of the Manhattan doctor to my tormentor, repeating my reservations about marriage. To ease the tension, I said I'd consider it on my next visit.

Broker took in the irritation on my face, finished his cup of chai, huffed around as if making completely sure his chance at a sizeable commission had indeed totally evaporated and strode out, accompanied by a red-faced Papa.

Despite the strain in my heart, I avoided any mention of Janet, although I was used to being open with my parents about my female friends galore. I didn't see any point. I was also not completely sure about the course of my future. There was no one I could confide in, having grown far apart from my brothers, especially Viji, whom I noticed looked lacklustre and was spending a lot of time huddled in his room.

Papa went silent, keeping his indignation beneath his cold, unyielding eyes, his way of coming round to the fact his pawn had let slip a golden opportunity. I maintained prudent silence.

On the same day, news hit Indian newspapers about the Heysel Stadium disaster during the European Cup final between Liverpool and Juventus, killing thirty-eight spectators. A horrific tragedy that brought out the disturbing face of English football hooliganism and resulted in all English clubs being banned from Europe for five years. Being so far away and in a country not in the least interested in football made it difficult for me to come to terms with what had happened. I needed to know what exactly might have transpired or where culpability lay and badly missed England's media, particularly its sports coverage. How was I going to manage the remaining eleven days without football updates? And Janet.

Every morning, I waited for the khaki uniform on his rickety bicycle to bring Janet's letter. I devoured each *par avion* like a dog with a bone; she wrote such beautiful letters! Papa and Mummy got suspicious at the amount of mail I was getting, but neither confronted me and I was happy to keep my own counsel. How I wished circumstances were different with Papa and I could have been honest and open with him, the way my lover expressed herself so freely to me. If the emotional gulf between us hadn't been so wide, I might at least have written a letter to my father about what I certainly could not share with him in person.

*Dear Papa,*

*I wish I could make you, just for once, sit down and listen to my thoughts and feelings. Make you understand things from my heart and mind. I do not care for your clan or producing progeny to carry our lineage. If I must marry, it will be for love, not your hundred thousand pounds, Manhattan apartment or well-brought-up Malayali girl. What even is the guarantee I can repay your Manhattan girl with whatever expectations she has with that much investment into the game? I wish her well, Papa. I wish you'd wish Janet well too, Papa.*

*She's this girl I've been seeing for a few years now, very well brought up too if that's really your main concern. Kind, considerate and sensitive, she doesn't flinch to tell me off when I get even a little too big for my boots. She says adorable things like 'Put that in your pipe and smoke it' when she feels I need to be more assertive and stand my ground – not unlike what you used to do with me, Papa.*

*Janet's been by my side through thick and thin, in the times I've had to fend for myself. None of you knew about my nose operation, yes, I had one at the Beaumont Hospital in Morecambe. I'm sure you'll like Morecambe when you visit in the near future, hopefully to watch Alan Bennett on the television. If you are able to understand Alan Bennett's dry northern wit and humour, it makes you become part of England, it is so Lancashire working class. You'll appreciate it. I only managed to crack it with Janet next to me.*

*It was Janet that visited me at the hospital with a present that made me feel like a million pounds. A shirt, bed trousers and a dressing gown she had made herself with cloth she'd purchased from the local market. It was terribly touching and loving. Can you understand that, Papa?*

*I cannot understand how on the day of the operation following a pre-med injection, I went to the bathroom, fell forward, hit my left cheek on an iron radiator and almost blacked out in the arms of a nurse. My doctor was immediately summoned to ascertain if the surgery could go ahead. It was a moment I realised the power of being a lawyer and a local high-profile person – badminton's taken me places you know. Between tactful interjections, I assured my consultant surgeon, Mr Bullman, that the hospital was not looking at a clinical negligence action. The last thing I knew as the anaesthesia took over was Mr Bullman saying Singapore is a beautiful place! It's a thing, you know, to overlook our good old Malaya for that little dot in the south.*

*I woke up two hours later looking marvellously monstrous in a mask-like bandage over my nose and face with cocaine stuffing up both nostrils. By my bedside, holding my hand, was Janet. She broke down in tears when I opened my eyes. You see, she had never seen me in a state of rest. Ever. You know how I'm always buzzing around doing one thing or another, the number of times you and Mummy have scolded me for not being still. I don't know if you'd have cried for me, Papa, Mummy certainly. Anyway, Janet told me later that she went into shock seeing me lying in bed in that state as she had never known me to be anything but healthy. A testament to my badminton, won't you say?*

*So you understand why I'm lost in your house, longing not for your affection but for that par avion to arrive from England every day? For those beautiful words in her letters startlingly different to yours! What were you thinking writing to your thirty-three-year-old son about bringing his original certificates to solidify his prospects for a suitable match?! How can you even conclude I want to go the well-trodden path of marriage and procreation? Tell that to your parochial clan refusing to assimilate and embrace all as one. Plenty of them around London, preaching "our people, our church, our ways". No, Papa, I will not be turned into them.*

*Philip George*

I returned to England on 17 June 1985 to Janet at Manchester Airport. As I came out, I instantly caught her eye and I knew. We fell into each other's arms for a long embrace and that was when I asked her if she'd marry me.

'Of course.'

## SEVENTEEN

# AM I NOT A MAN AND A BROTHER?

Janet and I were caught up in the excitement of our marriage. With only one stumbling block: I needed to ask for her father's blessing so we could properly announce our engagement.

To my advantage, I knew Mr Stubbs was resigned to the fact he did not have the option to decline. It also helped that on the day I was going to ask for his permission he was engrossed in the French F1 race on television. Team Renault did me a favour by doing well to lift his spirits, giving me the perfect opportunity to bring up the matter of "what you probably know I'm going to ask for…" After some assurances on my part to quell Mr Stubbs' remaining misgivings about me, he said yes and we shook hands.

Janet wrote a lovely letter to my parents addressing them as Papa and Mummy and received an unequivocal reply: *We will not be able to attend. Have a good day and life ahead.*

Being a talented seamstress with a good eye for clothes, my bride-to-be decided to make her own wedding dress after a Laura Ashley design. I opted for a classic double-breasted dark grey suit with a white double cuff shirt, to be worn with Janet's cufflinks, and a spotted red tie – caught up with the outrageous yuppie demographic of the 1980s.

On the eve of the wedding, after heavy bar-hopping, and piss-taking by friends – the wager had been on lifelong bachelorhood for me – I spent the night at my best man David Ashcroft's house. Under soft grey clouds, I returned home the next day to get changed and arrived at the Hest Bank United Reform Church on the morning of the 21st of September 1985 for a Protestant marriage.

The heavens opened, the church was in full celebratory mood, with friends, family and clients, and the union was solemnised. Cousin PC and wife were the only family from my side. How could badminton not have been part of such a beautiful memory? For the afternoon reception following the ceremony at the Old Rectory near Hornby, I was taken by surprise to see my friends holding rackets to form an archway for us to walk under as Janet and I made our entry to a rousing welcome.

It felt awkward referring to Janet as my wife in my speech that drew laughter when I openly complimented her on her bee's knees comment I found attractive, but not as awkward as hearing Janet's father in his speech say, 'I thought he might be a philanderer like the Monocled Mutineer.' When he added how pleased he was that I was making an honest woman of Janet, it was clear the man was speaking purely from a position of love.

My best man gave a suitably funny speech, bringing up the Cliff Richard *Bachelor Boy* analogy, thirty-three being a late age for marriage at the time, and how he had kept me imprisoned the night before to ensure I turned up in good shape for the big event. It was still pouring when we left straight for our honeymoon in the Cotswolds. Upon our return, I finally carried my wife upstairs to our Castle Court apartment, which stood right next to Lancaster railway station where I'd first landed in 1970.

I felt loved and safe with Janet, enjoying the natural comfort that came with the compatibility we shared. Nothing was unsettling; no big compromises were made; we were both highly organised. She, in addition, was passionate about cooking and delighted in surprising me with her experiments. She was a girl you picked flowers for and I did. The one thing left was to introduce her to my childhood playgrounds and my family.

In the meantime, I continued to juggle sports and work commitments with my Filofax being full of life, regularly travelling for litigation matters or conferences. It was continuous pressure, which I could cope with because I loved my work, kept strict boundaries on time and worked with a team whose judgement and integrity I trusted implicitly. My forte lay in the way I built up my pyramid of experts and barristers and trained my legal assistants and clerks. Before long, my office staff operated like me and I was able to delegate, not abrogate my responsibilities. This allowed me to be out of the office as much as I wanted, knowing the office was in capable hands.

My career trajectory shot up because I had a good set of barristers, the likes of Tim Horlock, Paul Gilroy, Nicholas Hinchcliffe and John Dowse, all Queen's Counsels in top chambers earmarked to go up the ranks, and they would too. We formed a lasting friendship network, going all the way to them attending my retirement party. We worked with a reliable team of experts from all fields of dispute: a range of medical experts, surveyors, consulting engineers, welfare officers, private investigators, the police and, unavoidably, underworld figures.

In 1986, given my legal aid work and actions against medical professionals and hospitals, I was invited to join the AVMA (Action against Medical Accidents, a UK charity for patient safety and justice) and APIL (Association of Personal Injuries Lawyers). They were opportunities to team up with eminent solicitors and barristers and engage with medical experts for the exchange of knowledge and experience. I was often the only non-white involved in discussions and seminars at these associations providing great fodder for the mind, also the development and expression of strong views on any subject of discussion. In addition, I joined the International Bar Association (IBA) and the CCLA (Commonwealth Lawyers Association).

My confidence and stature grew from such exposure. No longer hugging the coast, I was sailing with the wind. I began taking on class actions, mainly seeking damages for clinical negligence (breast implants, drug claims, tobacco addiction, etc.). My client base expanded and I needed to regularly commute between London, Manchester, Birmingham, Leeds and Newcastle, something I thoroughly enjoyed, be it taking the train or whisking in my Golf GTI, epitomised by its burst of speed and power.

The trouble with me is I never see the hopelessness of a legal case until the disclosure stage. I do not allow my feelings to prejudge clients, as was the case once when an unwashed, scruffy young man came to consult me because he was hearing metal noises while asleep because of something "installed in his head by the MI5" and that they were controlling him like a robot. He wanted to take the government to court under legal aid. 'Show him the door' was the advice from colleagues, but I gave him an hour of my time, signed him to a legal application form, dictated a proof of evidence, to the amusement of my secretary, and sent it off. The rejection from the Legal Aid Board came saying there was no merit, to the relief of Tony and Charles and the laughter of the office girls! I didn't know it then but on account of such cases, I learnt to experience hope, joy, despair and disappointment, while cultivating practical wisdom.

Another area to give me fulfilment was mentoring young people, something not many established firms did, or did with enthusiasm. Schools, colleges and universities wrote in requesting us to take pupils, and I averaged about twenty mentees a year, selecting them mostly from underdog institutions. None of my colleagues wanted that extra bother with their busy schedules. It was additional work, certainly not for the sake of appearances. Upon selection, I interviewed each candidate with their parents, kept a file for each one and wrote a pro forma evaluation report for their teachers.

Shy, gauche teenagers unsure about their futures came, not knowing what to expect. I instituted a "watching brief" experience – let them watch me guide my secretary or sit in on client meetings, took them into the boardroom for staff meetings, on site visits and to the courts to learn from observation, instead of having to labour by the photocopy machine. We got into discussions about films, music, sports or current affairs. I'd talk to them about the thrill of an early-morning run in the snow or winning a squash ladder challenge, at the same time keeping up with their developments. Most of all, it was such a pleasure to share their excitement when Geoffrey, Tony or Charles acknowledged them or a judge in court stopped to ask them, 'Did you enjoy the proceedings today?'

The impact of it would only dawn on me when weeks, months, years later, the mentees or parents wrote beautiful letters, emails and now WhatsApp messages about how invaluable the internships had been. By retirement in 2013, I had mentored around 600 boys and girls, who went on to become postmen or doctors, many lawyers, some taxi drivers, one or two long-distance lorry drivers and a few high court judges. My one regret is that I never had a single non-white applicant for mentorship.

Pleased with my work and the substantial income I brought in for Whiteside and Knowles, I was ready for a long holiday combining Malaysia, Singapore and India. What thrilled Janet and me more than the thought of spending Christmas and New Year with my family in Kerala was my first return to Malaysia after sixteen years. I longed to take Janet to all my old haunts, to make her try all the food I grew up eating and possibly meet my Kajang friends. Hitherto, my only connection to Malaysia came from visits to Bryanston Square's Malaysia Hall, to keep abreast with home matters via Malaysian newspapers and, of course, savour authentic *nasi lemak, laksa* or chicken rice.

Early December 1986, Janet and I joined a long queue at the Air India counter of London Heathrow's Terminal 3, worried about our good-looking but whopping luggage. By happy chance, a member of the Air India ground staff selected us to be upgraded to first class, which took care of the excess luggage nightmare. It emboldened me to purchase even more duty-free gifts at Dubai Airport, which at the time was no more than a camel shed. Dubai was our transit en route to Bombay, from where we were to fly into Kuala Lumpur's Subang International Airport. Cousin Rajan and I were going to reunite at the airport after not seeing each other for almost twenty years. After his studies in India, Rajan had returned to resettle in Malaysia and I'd managed to track him down.

Re-stepping onto the soil where I was born felt like watching a movie in colour for the first time; everything brightened up and sprang to life. I was moved to tears. I would've willingly withstood a thousand "waste of space" or "fit only for climbing coconut trees" taunts for that moment of pure nostalgia. I could immediately smell Kajang's smoky satay, hear the Jalan Sulaiman boys, feel the energy of Prang Besar, see the Limau Manis *sakai*... Janet squeezed my clammy hand.

My eyes dancing and darting, we went through immigration and passport control, handing over our disembarkation cards containing the warning in bold letters *The Penalty for Drug Trafficking is Death*. The faces of Kevin Barlow and Brian Chambers flashed before me. Malaysia had only recently made international headlines for hanging the two Australians for trafficking heroin into the country.

Conspicuously missing at the airport was English, from signboards to conversations. It was mostly Malay, as were most of the ground staff. Some of the women were in headscarves to match their flowing attire – a complete contrast to the scene of 1970. We collected our luggage, now fatter from Dubai's liquor bottles, and headed outside. I immediately spotted Rajan, looking good in a cool blue batik shirt and neatly trimmed facial hair. Between hugs and tears, we were instantly transported to our Kajang High shenanigans. Janet blended in with ease with our incessant chatter as we piled our bags into Rajan's Mitsubishi, the Japanese company where my cousin worked.

I said my first hello to Kuala Lumpur in classic Malaysian style by chowing down a bowl of creamy Chinese curry *laksa* at a hawker stall outside the airport area, breathing Malaya's air! The stage was set for what was to come the following six days.

My Kajang boy avatar remained for the entire ride on the federal highway fringed by billboards displaying colourful faces endorsing familiar products.

'Look at that! That wasn't there before!' I kept going to a bemused Janet, who'd endured years of my Malaya ramblings. I hadn't anticipated such rapid growth for KL; it seemed like there were few spaces in the city without ongoing construction.

By the time we arrived at Rajan's two-storey house in Federal Hill, we'd done so much catching up on our lost years. Janet too might have shared our childhood in the way she participated in the repartee. There was the old fire in Rajan, and he was beginning to see Malaysia vicariously through our eyes, such was the immediate bond between the three of us.

The early-morning atmosphere in the East was so pleasant, and the thrill of being back provided me with extra energy for my morning run from Federal Hill to the Royal Selangor Club, past the National Mosque, Lake Gardens, the old railway station and back via the National Museum and the Majestic Hotel. The cold shower that followed was both invigorating and sentimental. Back to Chandrika bar soap!

We hit the road the next morning with Rajan driving, starting at St Mary Syrian Christian Orthodox Church in Brickfields, where I was baptised, then walking the length and breadth of Jalan Tuanku Abdul Rahman's busy corridors of cobblers, key makers, *kacang putih* sellers and blind men playing the harmonium *and* old-timers at the iconic Coliseum Café and little watch shop asking after my father. The tailor at Globe Silk Store who made my suit for England was there too!

The biggest highlight was the trip to Kajang, made all the more nostalgic as Rajan too had not visited our old haunts since returning to Malaysia from India. Prang Besar Estate's reputation for being a well-managed plantation producing the best and highest-yielding rubber trees had undergone a complete reconstruction. Glades of dense palm trees, their unruly fronds atop woody trunks obstructing sunlight, replaced elegant rubber trees. Clear rivers and streams were now cloudy waterways. The spirit of the estate was in a geriatric state, just about staying in business. Its staff terraces and grounds bore few traces of the estate's past glory. My old house was still standing, occupied by a Tamil estate conductor who kindly allowed us access, and in that short tour, I showed Janet where I hid my *Playboys* in the built-in *almari* of my old bedroom.

I was distressed to see old dirt roads overgrown and stacked with piles of decaying palm fronds and stems, providing mulch and habitat for rodents, monitor lizards and cobras, making it impossible for us to locate the way to Limau Manis.

We continued Papa's "transfer trail" by visiting Galloway Estate from where my whole family had left for Kerala, leaving me behind. Galloway remained a sleepy hollow and I showed Janet the cement badminton court I built with the estate and *kampung* boys. It all looked rather small and untidy to my days. We then took the Dengkil road, past my bicycle stand at the Chinese medicine shop and the old graveyard, to Sg Buaya, Papa's final estate and from where I left for England. Worn-out Sg Buaya's noticeable change was the presence of Indonesian labourers. 'They get in easily on boats and ferries. Once they're here, they're free to stay as long as they please the police. Some get red, even blue ICs, it seems. It's our Indian workers born here that cannot get their ICs. Don't know what's going to happen to them when they are forced out of these estates.' Rajan shrugged as he spoke.

On that dismal note, we took a long coastal drive along Dengkil, Banting and Morib, making *rambutan, nasi lemak* and *chendol* pit stops before heading to Kajang town for satay, as mosques in the vicinity began their midday call to prayer. After lunch, we wandered around Jalan Sulaiman, searching in vain for Chong See Lin, Evelyn Chan and the others, before making an emotional visit to Coach Chan's badminton hall.

Tours to our former schools gave the clearest picture yet of the transformation Malaysia was undergoing – a foreboding experienced by both Rajan and me. At Kajang High School, we got permission to take photographs and also managed to speak to some teachers and boys milling about terraces and classrooms who looked happy, in a subdued, timid way. Tall, slender, waif-like Janet with her blue eyes and short brown hair elicited *Lady Diana* whispers as we made our way to my favourite Low Ti Kok library, past the hall where I'd organised retiring headmaster Mr Yeoh's farewell to the music of the Beatles. The library was mere space, absent of *Pathé News, Life magazine, London Weekly Illustrated, World Atlas*...

'Next time you visit Malaysia, I don't think this library will even carry the same name,' Rajan murmured. I feared he might be right. A mono-race hegemony hung at my alma mater, gnawing at its character and constitution, but according to one male Malay teacher, the school remained highly desirable in the area. When I asked for whom it was desirable – seeing that there were few Indian faces among teachers and students and even fewer Chinese – his conviction snapped. Rajan did not engage in the conversation. As he would say later, 'You have the sanctuary of a British passport.'

I left Kajang High School feeling the real cause of future troubles for Malaysia lay there in the ruinous, polarised system being called education, breaking away from beautiful, free Malaya. Mahathir's Malaysia was as stifling and fettered as Thatcher's England.

Janet and I next flew into Lee Kuan Yew's carefully constructed Singapore for a three-day whirlwind tour covering Raffles, Changi Beach and Sentosa Island, with drop-ins at relatives, the kind of my clan who had no qualms casting the judging eye and passing uncouth statements such as "I don't see this marriage lasting" to our faces. Janet cringed. All I could do was give her the *let them be* eye signal.

We returned to Kuala Lumpur for another two days of food trails and exploring the magical world of Sungei Wang Plaza, the Ali Baba cave of KL, amply endowed to conjure up any merchandise on a tourist's list, where you could find the rare artisan to repair your Rolex or yuppy Chinese salesman to guide you through "what is fake, what is not" while pedalling "the latest arrival computer". We left Sungei Wang Plaza's labyrinthine network of shops and kiosks with twelve more Yonex badminton rackets to the four I'd brought with me from England and more pairs of sneakers and shoes since things were true to Sungei Wang's permeable slogan: Cheap.

When we left memorable Malaya – Tunku's Malaya being how I'd rather remember my country – it was Janet that was in tears.

Lugging a typically Indian traveller load, to Janet's chagrin, we left Subang International Airport for Cochin, again escaping excess baggage charges after another upgrade, this time to business class. We couldn't escape the greedy eye of Indian customs, though, but KP George's firstborn was at the ready to part with some Sungei Wang shirts and shoes. We soon exited in Cochin looking like professional athletes, carrying massive Adidas bags full of rackets and a top-range Gunn & Moore cricket bat for my youngest brother, Tom.

'We might be Richard Burton and Elizabeth Taylor,' remarked Janet, referring to the stares and attentive treatment we were getting by virtue of our outward appearances and Janet's whiteness. I will admit I was glad at how distanced I'd become from my cultural roots.

Papa and Viji were already waiting. Curiously, both embraced Janet affectionately while I was dismissed with greetings in Malayalam. We took the back seat, wedged between our bags. Viji, in the front, also had his arms full. On the three-hour journey to Thekkemala, Papa attempted a tour-guide narrative for the obvious benefit of Janet while

I played spoilsport upbraiding his boast whenever I could – the first time I had dared wrangle with my father!

'What palatial building? That one is so run down I'm shocked people live there. You should see KL's buildings now,' I'd say, or 'You call this a road? You should see KL's roads now.'

At each point, Janet's hand would find its way to mine through the heavy partition for a reproachful squeeze. When I looked at her, she mouthed *let him be*.

The sun was retiring by the time we pulled up at our house to see Mummy, Tom, servant boy Shibu and Papa's pet mongrel, Jimmy, congregated on the porch, along with neighbours eager for a look at Philip George's wife, so they could be the first disseminators of the news. Seeing the two women I loved the most falling into a warm, affectionate embrace, I had to blink away tears. The audience grinned and gawped and it wasn't long before Lady Diana cropped up again. Thekkemala's villagers hardly ever saw white people in the flesh as Westerners mainly flocked to Bombay, Goa or the Himalayas. It was long before Kerala's natural beauty and backwaters became international tourist attractions. Yet, everyone knew Diana.

Janet got on famously with my parents and brothers, earning Mummy's "she's not proud" appraisal. Why wouldn't my mother be impressed when Janet pulled up her sleeves to help with chores, including hand-washing clothes by the well, serving lime juice to visitors or shooing out Mummy and her helper from the kitchen so she could prepare a meal for the family all by herself, being an expert in Malaysian and Indian cooking by then?

Mummy's facade of docility was noticeably relaxed, as was Papa's spitfire personality. There was a strange new order in the house, with my mother giving Papa the occasional instruction, scolding even, and not getting any reaction from my father, who enjoyed pottering about the grounds with Jimmy, dressed down in a cotton tunic shirt and *lungi*.

Janet was game for a gritty itinerary starting from the Malabar coast to the western ghats – what I call experiential learning! She never flinched at being squished on the occasional bus ride on bad roads, or worse, at India's notorious public toilets. Not even during the one time she suffered from Delhi belly while touring. My brother Viji was particularly comforted by Janet, who saw through his troubles and did what she could to help him gain confidence. Viji came with us on all our trips and was a much happier boy than the sullen recluse he was at the start. Tom couldn't get enough of his Gunn & Moore bat, and Janet and I went to the cricket ground to watch him impressing the local boys.

Then came the moment my wife would talk about for weeks after our trip, which I'm sure will never leave her memory. A big lorry had toppled near an embankment not far from our house and lay there for three days. On the morning of the fourth day, there was a commotion as the village thronged the embankment.

'Owner has brought an elephant to lift the lorry,' Mummy explained, not in the least expecting Janet to say she wanted to be part of the scene.

'No! No! Don't go,' my mother warned, perhaps

concerned about the excitement her English daughter-in-law was going to cause, or how she might manage the hordes.

Janet left on her own. I watched from afar, my camcorder capturing her in the full glare of day, sticking out in a red cropped-sleeve blouse, patterned maxi skirt, tinted sunglasses and gold bracelet family heirloom from Mummy, mingling with crowds more excited at *Lady Diana* than watching the atavistic phenomenon unfolding before them. The lord of the jungle was performing a spectacular JCB task of hauling the heavy mud-caked vehicle.

That evening, when I brought up the matter of the Maharani treatment she received from my people, as opposed to the disdain my lot got in England, Janet could see my point. Unlike the "you've got a chip on your shoulder" or "you're reading too much into it" charges thrown at me by long-standing English friends unable to understand what they do not wish to. Perhaps if they too disposed of their straw hats for a first-hand experience of the elephant god Indians identify as the remover of obstacles, their veil of ignorance might just wilt and make them ride past mere "awareness of discrimination prevailing in the system" and push for honest reviewing, restructuring and reforming of hypocritical policies.

Our return trip luggage was considerably lighter, containing lots of nuts and coconut *chamanthi,* a condiment Mummy had taken days to make. Viji was going back into his shell, but not before pleading with Janet to take him with us to England. I would not entertain the thought, largely owing to the Prasad episode. Mummy tried appealing to me but I gently let her down.

The one incident that left me permanently scarred happened in the summer of 1987. The Wimbledon Ladies' Final between Martina Navratilova and Steffi Graf was to begin on television at 2 pm on a Saturday. After my regular run that morning, I proceeded to wash my latest pride and joy, a Monza Blue Golf GTI 16v, a process that would take around three hours. I was grubby, hadn't shaved and was still in my sweaty running gear when Janet suggested going to Sainsbury's for our weekly grocery shopping before I went in and settled down for the tennis final. I quickly put on a sweatshirt over my top to cover my appearance.

Within a few minutes of being at the delicatessen counter in Sainsbury's, two uniformed policemen passed us, giving me a good look-over before heading upstairs to the offices. I might have recognised one of them. Janet and I carried on loading our trolley and made our way to the long queues despite many tills operating. The same policemen strode towards me and one began his imperious questioning about what I was doing there when I'd been banned from the store for shoplifting two weeks earlier! Customers stared, eyes passing involuntary judgement, and I could see the colour rising in Janet's pale face.

I could have torn a strip off the men. Instead, I explained as calmly as I could that it was a case of mistaken identity, offering my opponent a path to amicability. At that point, the other officer recognised me from badminton and began explaining to his colleague, who by then was in full enforcer-of-justice form to accept his junior's reasoning.

That is, until I told him he was dealing with a Whiteside and Knowles solicitor. Looking like a ripe Italian *pomodoro*, he turned on his heels without even an apology, unimpeded by the grievance he'd caused me. I stopped him in his tracks and took his name and badge number. We headed straight to the local police station to discover my badminton friend Keith Lowe was the sergeant on duty. Highly embarrassed and profusely apologetic about the "mistake", Keith took down the details of my complaint.

Strawberries and cream and all things Wimbledon set aside, Janet and I drove to Shefferlands, where Geoffrey listened sympathetically. Then he said something that did nothing to mitigate the anger boiling within me. 'Get over it, my lad. These types of mistakes can happen. Just treat it as a joke. It's good for your character building.'

Geoffrey said it nonchalantly, without the intention to hurt. Yet, it pricked my heart quite forcibly. A joke? No, I was not getting it. What I was getting was the clear message that only the one experiencing it can truly understand the pain of racism. Not willing to let the matter rest as a "mistake" or "joke", I sought my remedy in law. Apologies were issued and grovelling attempts were made by the chief constable, who visited me in my office. I turned deaf to hollow reason.

The fiasco ended with Lancashire Constabulary's indemnity insurance compensating me within a year with substantial damages with costs after issue of proceedings, and a letter of apology from the station. In small-town Lancaster and Morecambe, where news travelled fast, Philip George became the target of Chinese whispers. For months, friends and acquaintances kept bringing up the incident, the innuendo being that there was no smoke without fire. I was able to handle the insinuations but it left an indelible mark on Janet.

The same year, I relented to Janet's pestering about having Viji over. We organised my brother's place and accommodation at St Aldgate College, Oxford, to do A-levels. As Viji's visa came through, we planned to coincide his arrival at London Heathrow with a holiday in America to reconnect with my sister, Shanta, and meet her family in Atlanta. In the land of Martin Luther King, CNN, Coca-Cola and *Gone With the Wind*, I made several discoveries. My dowry-guzzling brother-in-law was no chief executive of any big hotel. He was no longer even in the hotel industry where he had worked as an assistant manager. He was now a self-employed car salesman dealing in repossessed cars. George Mathew was friendly enough in a matter-of-fact way but was noticeably distant, even cold, with my sister and their two perpetually anxious children, my nephew and niece, who, once they'd warmed up, clung to Janet and me. My sister was a shell of her bright, bubbly self. Behind Shanta's smiles and cautious words, her discomfiture was obvious, making for a distressing few days.

George played tour guide around Atlanta while my sister preferred to be holed up in the house, except on the Sunday we went to their local Syrian Christian church to meet my creed – zealous upholders devoted in equal measure to the pursuits of theology and prosperity, measured by where and what you studied, what you did to bring home the bacon (and how much), what you drove and your marital status (married within the clan, progeny).

The scene was agonisingly similar to the lot in London that I was keeping at arm's length. For one who loathed ostentatious displays and was the brake to my tendency to splash out on designer clothes and cars, Janet was not impressed.

## EIGHTEEN

# SOMEHOW, I REACHED THE SHORE

I functioned on adrenaline and bravado not just in sports and work but also in life, taking Janet on a whirlwind ride of wining, dining and plentiful travelling. I might have been headed towards the path of the ideal life of growing old with the girl I loved, in a beautiful house, children in tow, several notches up the social ladder. It was an achievable dream and I bulldozed towards it, doing things the only way I knew. My way. At some point, it was going to backfire.

Upon our return from America, Viji stayed with us for two weeks before we sent him to his college in Oxford.

My brother lacked confidence and needed cajoling before he would settle into college life. Our weekends were taken up visiting him or him coming over to our flat, which after some time both Janet and I found exasperating. He gave us a tough time every time he had to return to his accommodation, becoming miserable and needy, especially with Janet. "Clings to my petticoat", was how she described him and how right she was.

We ushered 1988 in by purchasing a big house on Roosevelt Avenue in Lancaster on a higher mortgage, a decision that did not please Janet's sound sense of economics, a quality I admired but frequently challenged. It wasn't that she disliked our well-appointed new home; it was probably all happening too fast and she was finding it hard to cope with the changes.

My lifestyle and habits were not much different to how I lived as a long-time bachelor – minus the dalliances with lady friends. The focus was on the demands of my work, including taking up several courses a year to keep up to date with the law and legal procedures, while maintaining my badminton and squash routine, regularly returning home after midnight, in a bad mood if I lost a match. Sundays were often with Geoffrey at the Old Trafford cricket ground or at events such as the Burma Star (Death Railway) Veterans' Annual gathering at Bolton, a sombre, serious gathering where I stuck out as the only not-old-not-white person. Didn't matter, as there was mutual respect and a great rapport.

What more could a man need? The answer, from the benefit of age and life's many slaps, is emotional intelligence. My vitality and competitive nature that Janet found attractive were losing their appeal as our lives centred around my career and upgrading. 'We're not an ordinary couple,' I'd say straight off my designer labels, not without conceit, failing to see it for the vulgar display of ego it was. More damaging was the erosion of the easy spontaneity and serendipity we used to enjoy. The simplicity and comfort of cosying up to Pet Shop Boys' *Always on My Mind* in our old two-bedroom walk-up flat was reduced to me telling Janet to keep quiet when she voiced her displeasure at my occasional garish behaviour at parties where I indulged in farcical keeping up with fellow "successful" Joneses, or when she chided me for purchasing something expensive and characteristically preposterous on a whim.

Such emotional disagreements became more frequent, and the key building blocks of our young marriage, especially our close connection, began unravelling. I did not act on it. What was her problem?, my ego demanded. I provided a respectable detached home (with a high-end SieMatic kitchen!), contributed the bulk to our joint savings, took her to parties, got her expensive gifts and was faithful to her. Couldn't a woman contend with that! Geoffrey had taught me to never ask a question to which I didn't know the answer in any cross-examination.

Like water swirling in a basin, the cracks in our marriage got bigger very quickly and in no time, from her endearing 'Think you're the bee's knees, don't you?', Janet, with her understated sensibility, made another startling assertion: 'Where's the nice Phil I used to know?'

How hopeless my careless flippancy must've been for her! When we finally had a heart-to-heart talk, my insensitivity to Janet's feelings originating from a lack of perception of married life became clear. All I could offer Janet was remorse for neglectful behaviour. It was too late to impress my wife with compassion and empathy. The big talk ought to have happened in small doses over a period, perhaps then the young woman before me, for Janet was nine years my junior – but far more mature emotionally – might have had the motivation to ride the east-west divide laid bare before her from our travels and her exposure to my family's vices and virtues.

As I went about focused on providing and social climbing, which felt very important to me at the time, her family and friends came into the narrative more and more. Janet decided to return to her parents. No amount of my bravado could mask the immense pain I was under – to think it came on the back of Liverpool's stunning loss to Wimbledon, who made FA Cup history with that shocking victory in 1987. Liverpool's worst-ever defeat loomed like a bad omen for me.

The spilt was to take effect in a week, during which time it was back to our pre-marriage arrangement. Janet came every weekday morning to dress for work, returned in the evening, changed into leisure clothes then went to her parents'. Her clothes remaining in our wardrobe provided me with a small sense of security that she might change her mind. In typical Janet style, she made various to-do lists in chronological order, prepared weeks' worth of food labelled with names and dates and arranged them in the freezer. In anticipation of how broken I was going to be, the cashier in her too kicked in; she attended to and tied up all our finances in an orderly manner.

In the middle of that week, to take my mind off my troubles, I drove Viji to Preston College to look at degrees he could pursue on the assumption he'd obtain the required A- Levels. From my Golf GTI parked by the side of the road, I noticed a Preston Corporation double-decker bus slowly making its way up the hill from behind. I was about to open the door when the bus knocked my car on the driver's side, throwing me to the dashboard and back, causing a loud bang I instantly knew was bad for my beautiful machine. Apart from shock, I did not sustain external injuries. Viji remained fastened to his seat.

'Stupid Paki!' the young driver shouted as he too alighted from his vehicle for a brief, colourful exchange of words. Looking at the mangled rear of my car, I was in no state to lengthen the confrontation. I called the police and my road recovery company, who took my car on a loader and sent us back to Roosevelt House to find Janet packing her clothes. She kindly dropped Viji at the train station to make his way to college. Viji remained in shock, more from the news of our separation, and left looking like he was struggling to reconcile himself to the idea of no more Janet. Janet then drove me to the Royal Lancaster Infirmary where, after an X-ray, I was fitted with a neck brace and discharged with painkillers. By the end of the day, it wasn't just my marriage that was wrecked. Whitehouse Motors called to say my car was a write-off and offered a Ford Escort courtesy car until I obtained a substitute. Two years later, I would win my case against Preston Corporation for compensation. But on that night, I went to bed with a throbbing headache, the start of a cycle of immense physical and emotional stress.

Saturday was split day. On that dreaded morning, I left after giving Janet a peck on her cheek. To avoid the heartache of watching her officially leave, I booked myself into a Bed and Breakfast in the Lakes for a weekend of runs and scrambles up Helvellyn Mountain, a vital lifeline during my years in the north of England. On Sunday night, I drove back hoping and praying. It was not to be. A dismal, desperate house watched me wiping away tears.

What would ordinarily send me over the moon – Hadwins Volkswagen from Grange-over-Sands delivering a spanking new red Golf GTI to my Skipton St parking spot – wasn't moving me an inch towards restoring my emotions. A stiff neck and headaches from little or no sleep also put paid to badminton and squash. I was drifting into a wicked spell and it began affecting my performance at work, and Charles and Tony took me to task.

On Janet's suggestion, as she was seeing him too, I began visiting our GP, Dr David Elliot, for counselling, to discover it was easier to open up to a stranger than to close friends. Dr Elliot prescribed anti-depressants and sleeping tablets, both of which I kept at a tempting distance as I knew they'd affect my performance at sports and also due to my natural aversion to drugs. I also made visits to Vicar Collinson, who had married us. Like Dr Elliot, the vicar too allowed me to spell out my guilt, although in his case, it didn't feel like he had my interests at heart. I was baffled when the vicar suggested that 'In the circumstances, divorce might be the best option.' It was still the early stages of our marital discord, a time when Indian parents, uncles, aunties, friends, even marriage brokers would descend on the warring couple with full moral authority *to put sense in heads*, a lifeline not open to me in the West.

My friends did not know Janet well enough to be non-partisan, and I was not comfortable unloading my burden on anyone, pride being a serious impediment. My close circle was aware of my troubled marriage and despite their time-tames-all-grief advice over meals and drinks, I walked a lonely road, reflecting on the cost of my brash "hey, look at my amazing life" brags, for Janet and I were the couple that seemingly had it all.

Where the vicar failed, the Old Testament handled my suffering better. Humbling myself to its tales of creation gave me immense comfort, as Mummy had always assured me. And some hours of sleep.

Things remained cordial between Janet and me and she agreed on a date for our third wedding anniversary that September, which fell on the day of the Law Society's Autumn Reception at the historic Levens Hall in Kent Valley near Kendal. Janet knew its importance to me. We got dressed at our house and left in my new car, prepared to play happy families, an act preserving the thin thread holding us together at that stage. Weakened by misery, I was at Janet's tender mercies but was not about to throw in the towel without a final attempt at redemption.

The Levens Hall reception was courtly; the company distinguished; the food par excellence. Yet, I could only partake with indifference, being in constant constraint wondering how my plan for later was going to pan out. When we left late in the night, I drove towards the Lake District instead of Lancaster, requesting Janet to give me a chance. She reluctantly agreed, saying she hoped it wasn't anything extravagant or expensive, adding quietly, 'This is already painful enough, Phil.' Choosing not to respond, I turned up the volume of my state-of-the-art stereo to play our favourite songs, including Soft Cell's *Say Hello, Wave Goodbye*. At Janet's favourite Swan Hotel we spent our final night together in its honeymoon suite, the single red rose and Moët & Chandon Champagne untouched, inducing not reconciliation but tears for both. It was curtains.

Word of our official separation caused shocked friends to rally around me even as I was advancing towards an emotional breakdown. There was still the embarrassing prospect of dealing with my parents, who in turn would have to bear the shame of producing the family's first divorcee.

At this time, client turned good friend Vicky came around saying she knew just the way to get me out of my gloom. Rather, just the destination. Not wanting to be too far away from Janet, *just in case*, I tried the I'm-not-ready-I-need-time routine but eventually agreed to Vicky's coaxing. As I warned earlier, my life was about relentless pace and action, with no room for pausing and reflection as my next calling was never too far off. That next calling, according to Vicky at least, was Ibiza. 'Two weeks in Ibiza should sort you out, Phil. I don't like seeing you like this.'

On that assurance, Vicky, her boyfriend, Peter, and I flew onto the Spanish island. We hired a car at the airport and made our journey through breathtaking stretches of the Mediterranean Sea, straight for Santa Eulalia, a home away from home for the English as I found out. The promenade fringing the beach was sprinkled with English pubs, cafés and restaurants, taking me right back to straitlaced Morecambe! Ibiza's reputation hit me right away: a tapestry where boundaries did not exist, where David Bowie or Freddie Mercury could mingle undisturbed, and where Phil George was thrown into madcap indulgences. Drinking, dancing, frolicking into the night, mainly with English holidaymakers, was the operating rule of my friends and they got me involved too. There was a heavy scent of sex, drugs and booze at parties and clubs where Vicky ensured everyone knew Phil George needed pampering.

The very next day, I booked the earliest available return flight. The shortened length of my trip by no means diminished the decadence of the remaining days. The island had me in a miserable state and I was losing my identity on a trip not disposed to resolving any of my problems. Half the time, I was making desperate attempts to stave off Ibiza's lust. Thankfully, I found Mark Elliott, whose father was the acclaimed British actor Denholm Elliott and whose mother owned a lovely bar in Santa Eulalia. It was a welcome respite to have Mark and another friend taking me around in an open army Jeep to experience the soft, spiritual vibes of Ibiza's verdant hills, villages and magical coves and bays as opposed to our night-time adventures at

KU, Europe's premier nightclub of the era. If I was flushed with the collapse of my marriage, Mark harboured his own demons, but those calming drives redeemed Ibiza somewhat.

Denholm Elliott hosted us to dinner, Vicky as usual doing the honour of informing the uninformed of my floundering marriage. The announcement made the *Raiders of the Lost Ark* and *A Room With a View* star focus his attention on me. He proved to be as great a conversationalist as he was a scene-stealing actor. On those stimulating conversations and certain awkward encounters, I aborted my stay in Ibiza, to never return. It was only when I arrived back in Lancaster that I felt normal and grounded again.

Next to tread into my troubled radar was a member of my Malayali clan from London. Not deterred by my "arrogance" in not wanting any part in the clan's goings-on, my relative Jacob had been pursuing my case for some years. Having heard of my marital troubles, Jacob and his wife visited me unannounced. He appeared optimistic about getting Janet and me back together, and such was the fragility of my mind that I allowed them to visit Janet's family. A decision that stands out as one of my biggest errors of judgement! When I was journeying life solo, making my own decisions and reaping its benefits and consequences, I never felt lost. On the contrary, I often discovered how capable I was. Letting go of that hard-earned self-belief led me to my freefall.

Falling for Jacob's persuasion, I also attended a bible centre in North London for the experience of a Malayali

Christian Fellowship gathering. Sunday evening from eight o'clock to midnight was "testimony time", where about forty individuals were scheduled to go up on the stage and spill their guts to the 200 hawk-eyed congregation, to be followed by a cleansing session of prayer and recitations. Not being on the list, I observed from the back row of the auditorium the courage of those publicly washing their dirty linen. When the last confession was over, Jacob and another got on the stage for an announcement that gave me instant chills.

'There is one special person in this audience who is suffering, and Jesus awaits with open arms to shower him with love and make him safe. Let's all listen to his testimony and pray for him.'

All necks turned towards me. The back doors were locked. To a standing ovation and passionate *praise the Lord* chants, I floated towards the stage's classic single steel microphone. Baying ceased, bottoms dropped on seats, it was showtime! I vented my spleen without effort, by the end of which everyone wanted their turn at embracing me like I was some prized new convert. On the drive back to Lancaster, I felt violated and deeply embarrassed by what I had done. The magnitude of my fall from grace made me wonder what next…

A double whammy. Janet had removed all her belongings and left a note on my bedside table, weighted down by the gold bangle Mummy had given her: *This belongs to your family and I reluctantly return it. You will always be in my thoughts. Please take care and look after yourself.*

As the first move towards formalising our separation, Janet and I sold Roosevelt House and I moved to a townhouse in Tower Court for a lonely Christmas, to end 1988 mourning the girl who ruled my airspace for the good part of ten years. The new year began with divorce proceedings issued by Janet, with the decree nisi (provisional decree of divorce) arriving in March. The pressure was unbearable. I went on a shopping spree trying to buy my way out of my misery: a house in Tower Court from David Ashcroft's building company, an apartment in St George's Quay, and a top-floor split-level penthouse in Swan Yard overlooking Lancaster Canal and St Peter's Cathedral.

The next body blow was to my future in racket sports. Trudging up the hills in the Lake District with some friends, I felt a sudden twinge in my right knee, which with my sergeant major attitude I ignored to my peril. Through the pain, I played in the Lancaster University Annual Badminton Tournament. It turned out to be a cruciate ligament tear, needing surgery – the first of my five surgeries over the years on the same right knee. That surgery was performed by a consultant orthopaedic surgeon at a private hospital in the Lake District.

In a familiar scenario, I was wired up to drainage, blood and saline solutions with Janet holding my ring hand. We had a tender moment, rekindling hope in me. Perhaps the decree nisi could be rescinded? That hope was dashed when a nurse opened the door for my next visitor – a striking blonde model. Poof went our moment and Janet immediately excused herself. It was back to the

Old Testament and replays of Black's *Wonderful Life*. The operation proved to be a case of clinical negligence and my only recourse was to bring an action against the hospital. I would recover substantial damages and costs but at the expense of my knee.

The decree absolute was pronounced in May 1989, dissolving my marriage. Two months later, I moved into my scenic Swan Yard penthouse for a pleasant discovery – my next-door neighbour was Arthur, my PE teacher during A-levels. He and his wife, Eva, had represented Wales in football and hockey respectively and, despite being retired, retained their athleticism and remained great ambassadors for sports, which I consider prized traits. On top of being sporty, the pair were enthusiastic and always ready for spur-of-the-moment escapades, signalling straightaway a friendship for posterity.

As was my foible, I bought a new black Volkswagen Corrado to match the feel of my new house and to help me sustain my rediscovered groove. It worked. Until 25 October 1989.

I was towelling down after a shower, having just returned from a high court trial in Manchester. My landline rang at that unusual hour way past midnight. '*Achachen* (big brother), I have bad news.' It was Shanta calling from Atlanta. 'Papa passed away from a heart attack. About half an hour ago, at the Kozencherry Muthoot Hospital. I am leaving in three hours. Are you coming?'

Talk about nothing going right when you're down and troubled! Ring Janet was my first thought as I put down the phone. My mind was still in conflict when the phone rang again. My friend Elaine, whom I'd visited on my way back from Manchester, was checking if I'd reached home safely and I told her about Papa. Being a ward sister, she understood my pain and was also aware of my Janet hangover. Pouring my heart out to her about Papa certainly helped me get through the night. It was approaching 4.30 am. I put on my running shoes and returned at 6.30 am for a cold shower. After informing Arthur and Eva, I went to Whiteside and Knowles to rearrange my appointments.

Getting a ticket to India proved less of a hassle than the trouble the Indian Embassy put me through before issuing a visa. It was a good thing I got a night flight since the hours in between were needed to battle India's infamous red tape debacle. 'Sir, what is the proof your father is dead? Show me the telegram. How do I know you're telling the truth your sister called from America to tell the news? I need to see some evidence,' the officer demanded. Exhaustion aside, I wanted to jump-smash my tormentor, but I had my eldest son duties to perform for Kalayil Puthuparampil George. Out came my handy Filofax to my rescue. After scrutinising my diary to ensure the contemporaneous notes corroborated with my version of events, law-and-order bound civil servant accepted my request. In absolute overkill and pent-up anger, I then produced my Law Society and Solicitor of the Supreme Court of England and Wales identity cards, plus my Whiteside and Knowles business card, to give the man a lecture on customer service and empathy, in full view of others too. It was the least I could do.

Papa's Padmini was waiting outside Trivandrum Airport, the one he drove to receive me and Janet on my last trip. In his place was a driver, and a tearful Tom. We embraced and I took over the wheel, requesting the startled driver to sit in the back. Tom began filling me in. After dinner at around 9 pm, Papa felt some discomfort in his chest. He went to rest, with Jimmy under his bed. When the pain became intense, Tom and Mummy helped him into the car with Tom taking the controls. 'Jimmy began howling and Papa said to him, it's all right, I'll be back soon,' Tom said, welling up. When they arrived at Muthoot Hospital, only two miles away, Papa was settled in a wheelchair while the hospital staff searched for the missing key to the ICU, during which time my father breathed his last, in that wheelchair, in that upright position. The horror of negligence! Everything about India caused me anger and irritation.

Arriving in beautiful sunny weather to crowds lining our driveway, I pulled up at the main entrance dominated by off-white cotton sarees. A chorus of feminine wails erupted when I stepped out into an atmosphere thick and heavy in gloom. My stony mask was well fitted only up to the point when Mummy was in my embrace and I heard her say tearfully, 'First Janet, now your father.' My tear glands opened big time as I rocked in my mother's tight hug, setting off a fresh round of wails, and howls from Jimmy.

An elderly uncle interrupted our grief, breathing in my ear, 'Funeral at ten tomorrow. Much to organise.' As he detailed what needed immediate attention, my head spun at the thought of fulfilling my father's demands to perfection, as nothing less would satisfy KP George. Incidentally, it was something I was used to doing for clients as executor of their wills back in England, but with the aid of an efficient undertaker who took care of the nitty-gritty.

My to-do list from Uncle:
- Formally inform church authorities.
- Ensure availability of bishops and priests. (Papa had left instructions; he wanted them all in attendance!) Arrange cars for the entourage.
- Place notice of death and funeral in the *Malayalam Manorama* for tonight's circulation.
- Notify grave man.
- Place order for coffin for delivery by 7 am.
- Arrange for the ambulance to collect body from the hospital mortuary at 8 am (together with the death certificate).
- Organise glass hearse to move body from house to church.
- Marquees, chairs, tables and food for 1,000 people.

A Heath Robinson funeral awaited! First things first. I drove to town to change the £10,000 I'd brought in anticipation of the funeral expenses – on the black market, of course – for a more favourable rate. Armed with my satchel loaded with juice that can move mountains in India, I prepared to play the biggest role of my life.

All items on the list ticked, I returned home to private moments with my family and some rest on the bed I last shared with Janet, feeling guilty at failing to blot out the longing for her to be by my side. I still had company: Jimmy under my bed and my Sony Walkman playing the just-released *Sacrifice*, which felt like Bernie Taupin had written it especially for me. Elton John's crooning and the occasional doggie whimper harmonising with the tears on my pillow took me even further from sleep. Tired of trying to induce sleep, I got up at five for an early-morning run against the already busy Indian traffic breaking laws, spouting carbon monoxide, blowing horns and throwing me and my shorts curious looks. I couldn't be bothered. My endorphins kicking in, I felt energised.

After a shower by the well in full view of Thekkemala's brightening sky, pulling pail after metal pail of water using the thick rope attached to it, I got changed and set off to collect my father.

Tom and I settled Papa's coffin in the ambulance for a one-hour spellbinding journey back home, dominated by flashbacks of my last Kerala trip when KP George finally opened up during my "cross-examination" of the man unused to talking about his harsh early life or his vulnerabilities since the torch was only allowed to shine on his achievements and his authoritative persona. Mummy and Janet silently watched the three-hour session as Papa revealed everything: the early death of his mother, leaving Kerala without informing his father to travel by road, rail and sea for Malaya, surviving the Japanese invasion, conflicts with European bosses, marriage, children inter alia. Once out of the witness box, his teary eyes held what I like to think was a measure of respect for his firstborn. I'd finally had a proper dialogue with Papa and could see things from his point, without disdain. I also awakened to his famous statement *Our country is India*, especially when I derided him for leaving behind Malaya's comforts. As I write today, it is Giuseppe Mazzini that resonates with me. *Slumber not in the tents of your fathers.*

The ambulance pulled up to the porch of our marquee-clad house hosting hundreds of mourners at the forecourt and other parts. Tom and I did the honour of carrying the coffin to a linen-covered table. Shanta, Mummy and some ladies cleaned and changed Papa into his favourite shirt and the ill-fitting suit of 1970 he had had tailored at the Globe Silk Store in KL at the same time as mine when I left for England. Tom and I had other matters to attend to, in other words, dipping into my satchel to pay the waiting florists, the marquee company, caterers, hearse men, taxis…

The bishops and priests with their entourages arrived in impressive ceremonial black robes, showpiece headgear and flowing wizard beards to give KP George a service of pomp and pageantry. The service began in our front lounge, where two large framed pictures of Jesus and St George slaying the dragon looked down on proceedings. It was made all the more melancholic by Jimmy's feeble whines. I'd insisted he be there, to the displeasure of people I didn't care for.

The importance of having made the journey from England dawned on me from the sanctity of that moment.

Beyond its obligatory rituals and prayers, the cathartic beauty of deep, intense Eastern traditions and spirituality, of people openly weeping their grief compared to the stoicism of the English funerals I was so accustomed to. Janet would have understood. I was right. Geoffrey had telephoned her and just before we left for church a condolence telegram arrived from Janet to lift my spirits.

For the walk to the church, the coffin was fitted into a glass hearse placed on a four-wheel wooden trolley. What a sight it was to watch a muscled man with a thick rope tied around his waist pulling the coffin from the forecourt to the main road followed by an imposing procession led by me, Mummy, Tom and Shanta. Traffic stopped for the half- kilometre to our Syrian Christian Orthodox church on top of a hill at the edge of Thekkemala village. Locals lined the road to pay their final respects to a well-loved neighbour.

At the main well of the church, the coffin was moved to a large white marble slab table for a two-hour service. At its conclusion, I was handed a thick white silk cloth bearing the cross. Drawing strength from Mummy, Shanta and Tom standing by me, also moved by the dexterous swinging of incense pots by the bishops and priests, I lay the silk on my father's face, hands shaking, tears free flowing. It took me to that childhood memory of my Hindu friend, topless, draped in a white *dhoti*, sobbing, setting his father's pyre on fire for closure.

The lid was placed on my father's coffin for the final time, acknowledged by a crescendo of fresh sobs. Tom, two elderly uncles and I carried the coffin the final fifty yards to the Kalayil family tomb Papa had constructed only the year before. We placed the coffin on two ropes by the edge of the pit, where, upon the direction of the bishops, we lowered it into the tomb.

It wasn't like my father to go meekly. Not even death could vanquish the spirit of the man who had been his own commander-in-chief. One of my poor uncles let go of his end too quickly, causing the coffin to hit the concrete wall and undoing the lid! I instinctively jumped into the ten-foot hole to join my father in his grave, placed the lid back and pulled myself up using the ropes, with Tom and others helping me. Looking back, I recall what Papa said at the end of my cross-examination of his life: somehow, I reached the shore.

## NINETEEN

# THE GREAT HEDGE

If my father lived his life with guns blazing, his presence continued to hover in every part of the house and the village in the days following his mammoth funeral. I felt it as much as I felt a transition, watching Mummy, dignified and stoical, going about keeping the house in order, making meals, receiving guests.

No one offered the "I'm so sorry for your loss" I was used to hearing. Instead, everyone had memory after memory of my father to share in gentleness, through tears, chats and moments of silence. Mummy started to appear more at peace with her grief. I was so emotionally in tune with my mother that I could not miss the appeal in her eyes for what was ahead – the distressing prospect of having to fill the shoes of the man who loved, protected and impressed me as much as he traumatised my growing-up years. Not my soulmate or best friend, but my undisputed inspiration. A genuinely maverick self-taught man fuelled by fearlessness and commitment to what he felt was correct and a predilection for keeping up to date with world affairs.

I returned to England to the sensational news of the fall of the Berlin Wall. Images of thousands of East Germans clambering over the once-feared wall to join their delirious family and friends in the West front-paged print media all over the world. It was the sort of historic event my father would've devoured, and it was coming off the back of 1989's other landmark event: the Tiananmen Square massacre. The curious juxtaposition of these two events was unmissable – one screaming freedom, the other a cruel curtailment of hopes for democratic reform.

I found it a purgative exercise to start my day at work looking through a stack of newspapers splashing stories and images of the tumbling of a pile of concrete responsible for decades of suffering and misery. The big question was whether it was going to lead to the reunification of the once-mighty country, something that rankled Margaret Thatcher, who was openly wary of an expanding Germany becoming too powerful. Thatcher might have been better off concentrating on the matter of gross abuse of power and incompetence stirring things at home.

Strained relations between England and the Irish Republic, as a result of English courts imprisoning Irish people accused of terrorist crimes, was back in conversation with the landmark decision of the Court of Appeal to quash the convictions of the Guildford Four – after the three men and a woman had served *fifteen* years in prison owing to the deliberate failure of the police and the prosecution to disclose relevant evidence favouring the four. At the same time, in a similar case in Wales, the Cardiff Five, all black or mixed-race men, were facing trial after being wrongfully arrested for the murder of a white woman despite evidence pointing to a lone white male killer. These cases didn't just interest me because of their impact on the process of law. I was also keenly following the human cost to the innocent victims, taking me to my psychiatric nurse training and the maxim that justice delayed is justice denied. 'We were brutalised,' said Paul Hill, one of the Guildford victims upon his release, of the humiliation, threats and torture meted out to the four. As a legal practitioner, it was his other statement that I found more disturbing and difficult to reconcile. 'The most insulting part was when the judge said, "At least something has been gleaned from this *unhappy incident*."

Viji, in the meantime, had failed his A-levels and was in a fragile emotional state, not something I could manage at that point, so I found him accommodation near me and also ad hoc jobs, an arrangement I preferred to preserve my privacy and peace of mind.

Back to living in a bachelor pad provided me with a much-needed opportunity for reflection. I was approaching my twentieth year in England, had made considerable inroads into English life and developed both admiration and disenchantment for my adopted country.

For the most part, I was blessed to be showered with unconditional generosity and love, imparted with wit and humour so quaintly English that it had to be experienced, not explained, which I made possible for myself by persistently going after and embracing everything English. Further, my career as a solicitor allowed me to engage extensively with clients and I accumulated a vast network of friends from different levels of society.

What troubled me was, it was rare to find anyone who knew their country's history well, especially concerning European history or its colonial past, let alone the extent of England's troubled legacies. I was also puzzled by how narrow their views were and by the way they would refrain from discussion on matters not congenial to their prejudices and limited worldviews. For most, the empire evoked nostalgia and pride, which was fine; a few admitted to some form of guilt over the incontrovertible brutality of colonialism, but all were clueless as to why many outside their island, especially Indians, loathed Churchill, or why the Chinese harboured such hostility towards them, to the point where neither of these two eastern economic powerhouses is going to blindly enter any post-Brexit free trade deals Britain is trying to seduce them with.

Against this backdrop, I functioned helplessly as friends and the English media tore into communist oppression symbolised by the Berlin Wall, and especially Beijing's mishandling of the uprising that culminated with the Tiananmen killings, spawning articles, books and documentaries on "by far the bloodiest suppression of peaceful dissent in communist Beijing". Imagine my frustration when I tried telling friends what happened in Tiananmen was not by far the bloodiest suppression of peaceful dissent in the world because the British too had opened fire (shooting until soldiers ran out of ammunition) at unarmed Indian villagers attending a political gathering trapped within a walled enclosure, killing hundreds and mercilessly leaving the wounded to die, seventy years before Tiananmen. That cold-blooded massacre in Amritsar (*Jallianwala Bagh* to locals), shocked Indian polymath and Nobel Peace prize winner "Sir" Rabindranath Tagore into renouncing his knighthood, saying, 'Such mass murderers aren't worthy of giving any title to anyone.'

The real tragedy is that such historical facts, crucial towards a better understanding of our world, towards forming gainful beliefs and values, do not reach the ears of British schoolchildren, who remain ignorant, or worse, are fed myths that impair proper understanding of history. It is for this reason, I believe, with post-Brexit Britain's worsening relationship with China, there's a greater chance of the Tiananmen tragedy appearing in British history books than many an "unhappy incident" such as Amritsar or Mau Mau or the Qing Dynasty's Old Summer Palace, the handy work of western colonialists!

Centuries of mess caused by European, in particular British, imperialism, from Africa and the Caribbean to the Americas, the Middle East and Asia require just that – centuries of undoing. It appears to be taking shape. As a forest mowed down knows how to regrow if left undisturbed, these ancient civilisations are rooted enough to find ways to erase imperial edifices and promulgation of borders, boundaries and partitions devised to ferment hate and instil authoritarianism. And plug the damages. While the horrific carving-up of India and Pakistan immediately comes to mind, a much less-known illustration of Britain's noxious divide and control ploy was the Great Hedge, India's own Berlin Wall, built by the East India Company. The impenetrable hedge of thorny trees and bushes used as a "customs line" was devised to give Britain a total monopoly of salt and to curb the "smuggling" of salt by oppressed Indians heavily taxed for it as salt was a major revenue for Britain. Mahatma Gandhi called it "the most inhuman poll tax that ingenuity of man can devise".

1989 was also a time of upheavals and transformation for the legal profession in Britain. In her tenth year in power, Margaret Thatcher's deregulation fervour was as sharp as the shoulder pads of the era and as strong as the power base she shared with Rupert Murdoch, for whom she laid the legal groundwork to expand his media empire and whose ruthless hold over Britain's newspapers she singularly benefitted from. In a politically motivated action, the former practising barrister proposed a radical shake-up of the legal profession to make it more consumer-friendly by wiping out the almost one-thousand-year-old demarcation between barristers and solicitors. Additionally, by allowing both to accept cases on a no-win-no-fee basis, an American practice long considered unethical in England, the integrity of the profession was in jeopardy.

The transformation was set in motion in 1990 with the Courts and Legal Services Act. Apart from moving towards a market-focused approach, the liberalisations altered rules to entry and practice, along with legal aid. Ironically, it was done under the guise of efficiency and improving access to affordable legal solutions... by effectively cutting eligibility for government legal aid. The age of middle-income people having access to financial aid to pay their chosen lawyers' fees to fight their cases through the courts vanished before our eyes. Much of the solicitor's freedom to explore a range of cases and specialise in case preparation, likewise the barrister with advocacy, was being diluted in the name of cost-saving and less rigorous regulation, taking the shine away from the vocation known for its bespoke nature to becoming a service provider.

Even as the Act struck a note of alarm about where the legal profession was headed – *down the plug hole,* said Geoffrey – we at Whiteside and Knowles busied ourselves with courses to keep abreast with changes. Compelled to comply with the government's determination to expose legal practitioners to market forces, we attended workshops in marketing, management, corporate accounts and risk assessment, along with workshops on staff management and setting up a Human Resource Department, thus moving away from our previous way of practising law and serving our clients.

Hoping the start of the new decade might bring me out of my wilderness, I began January 1990 with reconstructive surgery to my right knee after the mess of the first operation because I was desperate to resume playing racket sports regularly, and because consultant surgeon Mr Davies had much experience with operating on professional sportspeople. Surgery went well and I continued working through my recovery.

My work remained the overwhelming constant and I was driven to make my mark in Whiteside and Knowles after my recent ring-rusty performance. Diversity in the accumulation of knowledge and operating with febrile intensity being innate to my nature, I focused on a caseload and client base uncustomary to the others, a freedom Whiteside and Knowles afforded me from the start to the end of my career. I cut my teeth undertaking a range of cases: human rights, defamation, copyright/trademark/patents, contractual disputes, equity, clinical negligence, personal injuries… I took on clients such as a gay patient with HIV AIDS, causing perturbation in the office when word got around about my shaking the young man's hand. My client wanted to exercise his equitable remedy to seek redress for the loss of the matrimonial home he'd shared with his ex-partner, whose handwritten intimate letters caused a full-blown Oscar Wilde scene when read out by the judge at the trial! It was a small victory for my client, who was frail in body and mind and ostracised by family and friends gripped by fear of infection despite the lack of concrete medical evidence on the new virus, understandably so following media reports of medical professionals in gloves and gowns burning the bed sheets of patients. The LGBTIQ community were faced with intense hostility and discrimination. It would be another year of hard fighting before the World Health Organisation removed homosexuality from its list of *diseases*!

Aside from work, I participated in the European Court of Justice networks in Brussels and Strasbourg and the International Bar Association. In Britain, I joined various networks supporting underdogs around England and Wales, such as my pro bono work through a community law centre representing the Cardiff Three's (of the Cardiff Five) appeal led by the renowned barrister Michael Mansfield, whose team I assisted on a peripheral basis attending meetings and doing legal research right through to the time the Court of Appeal quashed their convictions.

The victory felt groundbreaking at the time, but the victims were clearly damaged for life. It was only in 2021 that the former chief constable of South Wales Police apologised to the innocent men, saying, 'It's a time for listening but also a time for acting, a time for the whole of the public sector and the whole of wider society to recognise that racism is still very real in our communities.'

I was the Roy Rogers of law with my spontaneity, energy levels and unpredictability, qualities Geoffrey liked as we were very much alike. He must've seen something in me from watching me run in the snow, dealing with difficult clients, operating a full social calendar or running off to camp at Argentina's Iguazu Falls or climbing the Himalayas... perhaps reminding him of how he had survived the ordeals of the death railway.

I began projecting Whiteside and Knowles into new, lucrative and complicated areas of legal work while remaining an associate solicitor, a fact that did not bother me too much, although I couldn't shrug off the feeling a partnership offer was eluding me for not being of the shade and social background of my colleagues. Despite my considerable contribution, I was conscious of my place in the firm; and it had a significant bearing on most of my legal career. I was acutely aware that had it not been for my fortuitous association with Geoffrey, or if I'd been a Waseem Khan or a Krishnamurthy, my journey would not have led to levelling up with the firm's partners.

In 1990, there was telephone service in my house in Kerala and I was summoned by Mummy to assist with the marriage arrangements of my youngest brother, Tom. Thus, from sorting out one brother in England, I was now on call to perform marriage brokering for another. When some relatives in England found out I was headed to Kerala, in true clan fashion, I was hooked up with "a suitable Malayali girl". Suitable because she was in the same boat as me – soiled goods as we were both divorcees! Although Malaysian, Sara was based in Sydney, but no problem; it was arranged for us to meet in KL after Tom's marriage in Kerala. I decided to dive into it as I missed having a steady partner to share my journey; besides, there was the intrigue factor of the Eastern girl. I convinced myself if it didn't work out the way I was hoping it would, I'd live with the satisfaction of knowing I'd tried.

By the time I reached Kerala for Tom's wedding, Mummy had done due diligence in the way only an Indian mother can, and her verdict on my future second wife? 'Sounds like a *proud* girl.' The code word translated to unsuitability, but I decided to approach the alliance with an open mind. In KL, Rajan, a lifelong bachelor, greeted the news with a sanguine smile, his eyes only lighting up when talking about Janet.

Following one or two meet-the-parents sessions and one private date at the Hilton with Sara, a well-spoken, charming dentist, I flew back to England agreeing to take the relationship forward. A year later, in July 1991, I flew back to KL with my friends and neighbours Arthur and Eva accompanying me. Mummy arrived with the certificate from our Syrian Orthodox church in Kerala nullifying my first marriage to permit me to marry again in the church of the same denomination in KL. Marriage sealed, we completed Sara's permanent residency application at the British embassy, where we were questioned in two separate rooms to assess the validity of our relationship, and left for England.

The first thing I did upon reaching my Swan Yard house was to call the office. To my shock, I was told about the passing of Tony's wife, Carol. Within a short time, I was at Whiteside and Knowles' sombre office, where Charles explained he was holding the fort alone with Tony on compassionate leave. It was usual for the two partners to cover for the one on leave since Geoffrey had stepped down as a partner to take on a consultancy position. After telling Charles I'd start work the next day, it was Shefferlands next to share the moment with a distraught Geoffrey and Joan. The power dynamic might have shifted to Tony and Charles, and to a lesser extent me, but Geoffrey remained the figurehead we all looked up to. Both Tony and I were selected by him to become articled clerks, while he took Charles in as an associate solicitor.

It took me years to navigate my way around office politics, my friendship with Geoffrey notwithstanding – to learn when to offer an opinion, when to keep mum and when to control my reactions. The unshakeable personal equation I shared with Geoffrey acted as the catalyst for Tony accepting me into the fold and we got along. I had little in common with Charles and we stayed afloat. Charles was also not at ease with networking and it was usually Geoffrey, Tony and I that travelled together for social events, charity functions or cricket matches. There was no outward conflict or animosity as we all possessed a strong work ethic and worked hard in one direction. That is not to say nothing was churning behind closed doors; we were a law firm after all, and a reputable one at that!

Everyone, legal assistants and secretaries included, could feel the undercurrent of friction between the two partners, poles apart in personality and pedigree. On my part, I'd been privy to private conversations with Geoffrey when he voiced his regret about Charles not being Whiteside and Knowles partnership material despite being a very good lawyer. On those occasions, I restrained myself from commenting, knowing it was best to play the bystander. My father would've found my self-imposed restraint ingratiating. He'd have seen through my insecurities immediately, just as he'd have known how to deal with my colleagues. Nevertheless, Papa could not have scaled up the hierarchy of a leading law firm in

England, having never waded into Uncle Tom territory. Like I was doing.

Tony's return to work weeks later was to a lacklustre office atmosphere which remained so for months as Charles looked to be taking over his mantle. A rather gloomy prospect for all concerned. Although we had a good understanding, I was unable to broach the subject of his wife's loss and offer what help I could to one whose stiff upper lip I found hard to breach. We weren't on that basis anyway, Tony and I, like I was with Geoffrey with whom I could rattle on about anything under the sun.

My home situation was no better. With my heavy workload and Sara not being able to practise in England as her degree from India was not recognised, we were not seeing eye to eye. It must have been frustrating for her when I told her to just get on with it. We had an active social life, I introduced her to all my friends and she accompanied me to the Law Society autumn function where conspicuously missing from our table was Tony. The misery felt worse watching Charles and his wife leading the show as Geoffrey, Joan, my guests Dave and Jean Ashcroft and I did just enough to pass muster as the night dragged.

Before long, Sara's piano arrived from Sydney and I bought her a new Golf GTI, yet there was no music in our lives. How quickly the hours of happy long-distance chatting while planning our big KL wedding had fizzled out, only for us to discover our tastes and interests differed so much. On a trip to France, staying in luxury hotels, eating luxury food and "sightseeing", Janet resurfaced big time... laying a cloth by the riverbank, cooking simple food on a Bunsen stove, going where the map took us, marvelling at old people with baguettes in their bicycle baskets...

Things got really bad when Sara's parents made an unannounced visit to England in the summer, which was when it hit me how I'd walked into the very eye of the storm I'd consciously avoided for years. The clan's hegemony reared its ugly head. No servants? Still not a partner? Why not a Mercedes? My second marriage did not survive a second anniversary. The soulless, suffocating union ended by mid-1993. I couldn't care for the hole it made in my bank account.

A crisis can spark epiphanies, but only if you pay attention to what it's trying to teach you. It was a lesson I deserved for missing a girl who, upon leaving me, took with her the photographs of her excited self watching an elephant lifting a lorry from an embankment in pretty Kerala.

As my wilderness years wound down, the universe took a break from throwing obstacles at me and I refocused my energies. It began with the heartbreaking decision to lay my rackets to rest. After the third operation on my over-extended right knee for anterior cruciate ligament, now with screws implanted, I was told the bottom half of my knee joint was worn with zero cartilage, so every time I moved it was bone hitting bone. No more jumps and smashes.

To athletes I mentor and just about anybody, my advice is pay heed to your body, follow your instincts, keep surgery as a final resort. As I see it, it isn't too different to the way you conduct litigation. Litigation is built on facts, the law and evidence, but what enhances prospects of success is inclination and aptitude for strategic thinking and good decision-making, skills I honed from the early stages of practice. Likewise, if I had listened to my body and trusted my inner conviction or spontaneous intuition before agreeing to the first operation, I would not have ended with my knee looking like the *Crewe railway zigzag track* as a friend once remarked.

My upturn with Tony began from the time he took me into his confidence about moving the firm forward, a privilege unusual for an associate solicitor. Having regained his strength, Tony looked determined to keep Whiteside and Knowles in the Geoffrey Knowles school of protocols that had served the firm well, seeing that Charles had different ideas. It followed with my first invitation to Tony's classic country home in Borwick, standing on acres of land and a lake giving it its name, Lake House. On that estate, looking like it belonged to a Jane Austen novel, with a bootroom, stables and tastefully dressed rooms displaying stories of his family's rich history, Tony now lived with his two children. He brought the same refined ambience to Whiteside and Knowles, an approach I greatly admired.

Over dinner and homemade slow gin, we got drunk and the floodgates opened on all the closed-door frustrations of partner politics Tony had been enduring with Charles... of Charles's threat to leave for a rival firm, complaining that Tony was not pulling his weight (while recovering from Carol's death), and Tony giving him a small percentage of his share without payment to not rock the boat. Far into the night, it was clear Tony would no longer be hedging. I went to sleep in Lake House's exquisitely appointed guest room thinking about what might be in store for Whiteside and Knowles's future.

A reciprocal visit to my Swan Yard apartment followed in quick succession and from there we nurtured a mutually productive relationship in and out of the office environment, culminating in Tony and Charles inviting me to become a partner in Whiteside and Knowles. It was an equity share partnership with the two partners, involving a sizeable amount for me to come up with after the valuation of the firm's business and assets. I easily secured a loan from my bank and a new partnership deed was concluded in October 1993.

I was never one to look at mountains and wonder what might be beyond, or how being at the crest would feel. I climbed. Becoming Whiteside and Knowles's first non-white partner felt like I had summited a very challenging mountain; of having surmounted slights and privations which entail being an outlander.

To celebrate, I went to bask in the magic of the Lake District and climb Helvellyn Mountain via Striding Edge. It was not a regular climb for I did not wander "lonely as a cloud that floats on high over vales and hills" as Wordsworth described the Lakes so beautifully. My father trailed me in spirit as I ran, walked and scrambled up England's third-highest peak. And at Helvellyn's flat top, we breathed the air of contentment and celebrated beating a myth.

## TWENTY

# THE TRIALS OF PHILIP GEORGE

My road to partnership in Whiteside and Knowles took much longer, but I took heart in the fact I'd done it as a self-starter, a very spirited one with no clue I was going to end up as a lawyer. My perseverance in overcoming bumps along the way had paid off and with it, I acquired the motivation, discipline and a deep sense of how to make the best of my new status.

I phoned Mummy about the promotion to make her understand the importance of the occasion, that I had transitioned from employee to part employer with a financial stake in the firm; that it was a formal acknowledgement of my ability to perform at high levels as well as my good reputation in the industry and community; that from being liked and appreciated, I had become indispensable.

I also told her I found out it came on the heels of Geoffrey's urging to 'Better offer Phil partnership before he ups sticks and moves on' and that he'd said to me, 'Welcome aboard, son.'

'My prayers are always with you. Consider this as the end of your wilderness period, Mohan,' said my mother with prophetic assurance, referring to my seven years of turmoil: two marriage breakdowns, an accident, surgeries and my father's death. In the tender silence that followed, we shared a painful awareness, missing the one person who would've absolutely basked in the news. No one would've enjoyed inventing opportunities to boast about my achievement more than my father, although not without giving me a prickly telling-off for my delay in getting there, in his deliberately patronising manner reserved for "slackers".

It was all the more sad thinking about how eager Papa had been to visit me in England, having already obtained his visa when he died. He would've enjoyed travelling around Europe, especially the eastern half of Europe undergoing political freedom following the collapse of the communist bloc. Papa, Geoffrey and Simms (who gave me my first job at Prang Besar Estate) were my most significant mentors – all larger-than-life personalities and difficult figures to live up to – not helpful with my history of struggles with authority figures. Geoffrey, though, differed with his open affection for me, resulting in our unique closeness, which I suspect was also born of his desire to live vicariously through me.

My network of clients, contacts, colleagues and friends greeted my appointment with a great deal of joy and celebration. It relieved me of the remaining shackles of insecurity curtailing my full potential, especially now that I had the backing of Tony, whose upper-crust client friends were becoming mine too. I was long aware of Britain's class system and its social elites, of old money and new money, of birth, wealth and occupation (or lack of it) being determinants of one's social status and dominance, not unlike caste-driven India. The injustices of both systems have changed little, with the "higher" classes and castes continuing their grip on positions of power, but back in my day as a rank outsider given a free ride with the upper echelons of northern England, I thought nothing of it. If anything, I was taken in by the allure and opportunities available to me from my association with such a company.

More than the increase in income and tax benefits that followed partnership, it was the benefits in kind, the opening of doors, the being seen in a new light not just by clients but also by staff and friends, that made me look in the mirror. The small town Kajang boy glued to his bicycle, its wheels permanently caked with red mud, pedalling on unfrequented paths alone but for his rattan school bag, football boots and badminton rackets (he was going to become world champion!) had recorded his greatest triumph.

Following my latest knee operation, competitive racket sport was no longer a feature in my life, but since I was desperate to accelerate rehabilitation, I switched to intensive running, against the doctor's advice, which was to take up something like white water rafting that wouldn't put too much pressure on my knees. Rafting was not practical for me; nor could I imagine a life bereft of athletic activity. If anything, I was convinced sports would improve my post-surgery limitations.

A big motivation to take up serious running was the London Marathon which in 1994 fell on my forty-second birthday, a prospect I could not resist considering my huge capacity for the adrenaline rush. With six months to prepare, I began a new routine of running about a hundred miles per week by the River Lune on gloomy wintry nights, averaging twelve miles after work on weekdays. On the weekends, it was between eighteen to twenty miles in the company of four friends from the Trust House Forte's health club gym where I was a member, and as my endurance improved, I'd request Arthur to drive me twenty-six miles along the Trough of Bowland and drop me at around Clitheroe so I could run the marathon distance back home.

On Sunday, 17th April 1994, I ran my first London marathon, determined to do the 26.2 miles in under three hours. Around the eighteen-mile mark, I hit the wall, a common problem with runners, which is a depletion of glycogen/energy when the body taps into muscle mass. My legs tightened, I began labouring for each step and sensed fatigue taking over. 'FOCUS!' Coach Chan's order jolted me to tap into my badminton grit and resilience. Hitting the tape in a time of two hours and fifty-five minutes and receiving my first marathon medal produced a surge of wild exhilaration and pride comparable to winning a particularly complicated court case. I wanted more.

An additional birthday gift from the marathon came in the form of the substantial amount I managed to collect through sponsorship from my network of friends and clients, channelled to Lancaster's St John's Hospice, an independent charity providing free palliative care. Whiteside and Knowles were the hospice's honorary solicitors doing work on a pro bono basis, and it was where I referred some of my terminally ill elderly clients.

Being a partner gave me that extra zip and confidence and the awfully important feeling of equality to carry out the goodwill associated with Whiteside and Knowles, the importance of which was firmly drilled into me by Geoffrey.

'Goodwill shows, Phil. A solid customer base means nothing if your clients don't attach a sentimental value to your brand. Nurturing client relationships is at the core of this firm. It's the premium you receive when clients want only you. When they bring their friends and family to you over generations. You cultivate it through the treatment of people; going that extra mile; doing so with sincerity and panache. You have it in you, lad. Just control that ego.'

I shared Geoffrey's vision and took his advice very seriously, although not on the ego front as it was early days still and I continued to indulge my passion for cars and the latest gadgets (the '90s were exploding with the

Internet, mobile phones, PlayStation). For one already known around town as the Golf GTI guy, I would not be able to stop myself from personalising my projection with a custom PG number plate!

Already a member of several exclusive sports clubs and venues, I now had more authority and discretion to network and market the firm, having an open tab to entertain my guests at fine dining establishments, the Royal Exchange Theatre in Manchester or the Glyndebourne Opera House, and in the hospitality boxes of Anfield or Old Trafford (goodbye Kop, Stretford End), Lords for cricket or rugby at Twickenham, all with access to premium season tickets and my own designated car parking space in the grounds a hop and a step from the action.

Now that marketing and publicity were the buzzwords seeping into law practice, Tony and I stepped up our game. One of the best deals we secured was with Corney & Barrow, suppliers of exclusive international wines with an unrivalled portfolio. In an ambience of bucolic sophistication, over a free flow of Corney & Barrow wines literally fit for the Queen, Whiteside and Knowles played host to an evening of wine tasting and purchasing for our more discerning clients and local businesses, including The Inn at Whitewell, belonging to the Duchy of Lancaster estate. On another occasion, Tony and I represented the firm at Lord Reay's stately country house Whittington Hall, south of Kirkby Lonsdale, where the chief guest was the Conservative Party leader and then Foreign Secretary William Hague. Post dinner, select guests were invited to a large drawing room where Mr Hague had agreed to take ten questions. Whiteside and Knowles sponsored a question which I asked as guest number ten. Hague perked up, because, unlike most others, my question was not about land or wind turbine matters impacting country estate owners. You see, I'd met the politician a few years prior at his book signing event and was curious to know his thoughts about William Wilberforce, the man credited for fighting for the abolition of slavery who featured prominently in Hague's memoirs. Sadly, the Yorkshireman's unquestionably impressive oratory did not extend to his answer, which left me none the wiser.

During this period, I also straddled the worlds of advocacy and the arts, my exploration into the arts a long-standing interest sparked by my love of cultures and societies as well as a strong desire to broaden my creativity. I committed what extra hours I had to an appreciation of theatre and studying films and film production, even taking up night classes. A favourite haunt was the Lancaster Dukes Playhouse Theatre. Tuesday evenings was with the Directors Cut group in Preston for a viewing and discussion, over wine and cheese, of classics such as *Citizen Kane, Night of the Iguana* or *Ben-Hur* and critically acclaimed contemporary ones, which all complemented my visits to the Cambridge Footlights, Hay Book Festival, the Edinburgh Fringe Festival and others around the UK. I would also on short notice take off to London or Paris for a film or Berlin for the World Cup Final – on the backing of my well-trained secretary and legal assistant and a mobile satellite phone. The antenna popped out in the 1990s, but Nokia gave me the freedom to work from afar.

My partners indulged my maverick spirit as I got bums on seats as the English say, meaning I brought in a steady stream of business. I conducted personal clinics for clients, which included late-night and weekend appointments to accommodate their work hours and to suit my lifestyle. I frequently visited clients at their homes or in the gym after a workout, the informal venues and atmosphere helping them open up and share their emotions. Such confessional conversations can be a boon and a bane for lawyers because often they stir up powerful emotions of anger, anxiety, deep hurt or frustration, the impact of which can linger long after a case is finished.

Amy's trial, as I call it, is one such memory that surfaces with me. Amy was only four when she first visited me with her parents, who wanted to sue the Royal Lancaster Infirmary for their daughter's condition, believed to have stemmed from the hospital's negligence. I instituted court proceedings for clinical negligence applying the Bolam and Bolitho test, two of the most important rulings with regard to medical negligence, alleging that breach of appropriate standard of reasonable professional care during Amy's birth resulting in oxygen starvation had caused the child's cerebral palsy. Fortunately, Amy's condition was not too severe and she could walk without mobility aids, albeit her gait was jerky and slow. She needed a hearing aid, used purpose-made spectacles and her speech was slow and slurred at times, none of which could hold back her spirited personality.

Every visit was a great bonding time with Amy. We would get into animated conversations, her responding with gestures, stutters, big warm smiles and emotive blue eyes. Over the five years that the case dragged on, I travelled with the family's struggles and the trio became like family to me. I watched Amy grow up to be a smart, sassy young girl with amazing confidence, owing to her parents' unconditional love, care and dedication to their only child. At the trial, the High Court judge chose the defendant's Harley Street expert obstetric over our own and consequently dismissed Amy's claim. The rare loss was a big blow for me and caused me more sadness when Amy's parents divorced soon after.

Needless to say, I derived immense satisfaction from taking on slipshod government authorities operating without care and thought, for which I gained a rottweiler reputation. A good illustration of this sobriquet was when I represented Brendan Davies against the Ministry of Defence (MOD) and the British Government. Brendan had joined the British Army at the tender age of seventeen. During basic combat training over three years, he endured a series of physical and sexual assaults by racist squaddies. Branded a dirty Paki (he was half Asian), he was frequently wrestled to the ground, stripped, beaten, abused and sodomised, causing him to abandon the army scarred and suicidal. Complaints to superiors fell on deaf ears despite the MOD's open campaigns to tackle the problem of bullying since the 1980s.

Gaunt, shifty, unsettled, it was with the company of a social worker that Brendan came to see me. I undertook the case on a wing and a prayer on a pro bono basis because my client had no money to give himself the type of care he badly needed, let alone pay me, and also because Legal Aid funding was denied him.

From start to conclusion, this was the case that benefitted most from my previous training in psychiatric nursing. Accordingly, I gained Brendan's trust and confidence using a highly solicitous approach. The painful revelations came in swirls, which my legal assistant converted to proof of evidence. I pursued the MOD on the basis of breach of employment conditions and negligence under tort law and under common law for trespass to the person, harassment, assault and battery. The MOD with its deep pockets fought tooth and nail for three years. After the issue of proceedings, exchange of witness statements and disclosure of experts on army matters, psychiatric reports on causation and prognosis, the ministry capitulated (a week before trial in the High Court in 1994) and admitted full liability. My client received full damages with costs and my risk had paid off. More importantly, Brendan is now in his fifties, in gainful employment and largely free of his mental anguish after decades of therapy and psychiatric help.

Many a time it was my all-over-the-place visibility, from the squash court and the gym to my social outings – even giving out prizes at local agricultural events – that endeared me to clients to take me on as their solicitor. It was after a casual squash practice that Vic Langley, a Morecambe fisherman, sought me out to ask if I'd represent the local fishermen for loss of livelihood.

The mussel and shrimp fishing business had been their biggest provider for generations, but with Morecambe City Council's multi-million pound sea defence work, their precious sea crop was depleting. Over three years, I carried a heavy burden representing the hard-pressed families at the Lands Tribunal, where despite a marine life professor's expert report backing our claim, the fishermen lost their case for a bigger claim and had to settle for the meagre interim compensation payment.

A generation later, we're watching Morecambe's fishermen face a more serious threat affecting their livelihoods. This national-scale problem brought on by the Brexit fiasco leaves them with products they are unable to export to the European Union Member States, their biggest market. Pre-Brexit promises on quotas and control of domestic waters, one of the biggest drivers for Brexit, are in shambles, while politicians across the English Channel continue to be bogged down in interminable negotiations as the multi-million-pound business struggles with new red tape.

Looking at Britain's post-Brexit woes, I see the continued relevance of Lord Denning's famously graphic description of European Union law in 1974:

> But when we come to matters with a European element, the treaty is like an incoming tide. It flows into the estuaries and up the rivers. It cannot be held back… In future, in transactions that cross the frontiers, we must no longer speak or think of English law as something on its own. We must speak and think of Community

law, of Community rights and obligations, and we must give effect to them.

Similarly, it was during one of my late clinics over a pint of beer at Morecambe's Dog & Partridge pub that I got acquainted with John Buckley, an oil and gas technician who would be the cause of my (and Whiteside and Knowles's) biggest, most high-profile and by far the most yarn-generating case.

John was looking to appoint an executor for his will and knew of me through his late wife, for whom I had drawn up a last will. When he found out I was from Malaysia, the evening's agenda was sealed as we launched into a lively conversation about his experiences laying the pipelines and the infrastructure for the Malaysian Government's Petronas project.

'Red Adair of the oil sector, aren't you?' I remember commenting after listening to his impressive account.

As the night came to a close, John announced, 'You will do!' Little did I know those three words would lead me all the way to Ecuador about a decade later, for the adventure of my life.

My biggest post-partnership highlight was my mother's first trip to the UK in the summer of 1994. Despite being a citizen of the former empire's jewel in the crown, it was an ordeal for her to obtain a UK visa. I'd arranged an appointment for her from my office using my Whiteside and Knowles status. Due diligence done, I could only wait anxiously… picturing Mummy's lone journey. Carrying an overnight shoulder bag armed with a manila file consisting of my letter of sponsorship, reference letters, ownership of real property, recent bank statements for the past six months, passport-sized photographs and completed visa application form; boarding the afternoon Madras Mail train for the interstate travel from Chengannur railway station to the Tamil Nadu capital (now Chennai); arriving the following morning at around ten o'clock.

I only heard from my mother the following night because, being too exhausted for the ten-hour return journey, she'd put up for the night in Madras with relatives.

'You can buy my ticket, Mohan,' Mummy announced, as soon as she heard my hello. 'Young English boy asked me many questions. But he was satisfied after seeing all your papers.' She started explaining how she got a one-year tourist visa. 'He said to me, "Your son is well settled in England. Will you consider staying with him indefinitely?"

"I have my beautiful house in Kerala. Why should I stay in your country?" I replied in my broken English, but he understood and laughed.'

My mother let out a cackle but I was curious. 'Where did you find the courage to say that? I mean, you could have just said no.'

The reply came softly. 'I thought of Papa.'

I spent a lot of my earnings on gaining experience through travel and the acquisition of beautiful objects, especially to mark landmark moments, both to equal satisfaction, so imagine my state at the thought of my mother visiting me in my "home country"! It called for a new toy. Not a Golf GTI, Mummy wouldn't understand my fascination for them, but I knew what she would immediately relate to.

On the day of my mother's arrival, I made the four-hour journey from Lancaster to Heathrow in my brand new metallic black BMW 3 series M Tec sports coupe with a telephone installed and a little exterior aerial on the rear roof. Accompanying me was my friend Vicki Slater, who got an in-depth commentary on the valiant woman making her way across continents to put up with the antics of her twice-divorced firstborn contributing glory and shame in equal measure to the clan!

Orphaned at a very young age, looked down on by her own family, cheated of her inheritance, a married life of selfless devotion and now labouring in the house, garden, paddy fields and coconut groves, Mummy had seen much, but how was she going to handle England with all the plans I had for her? And my plans weren't conventional...

I felt dizzy with excitement when I caught sight of my mother's small dark frame advancing gently. Draped in a new saree, her grizzled hair in a bun, she was wheeling a trolley neatly arranged with large suitcases, toting a brown Emy handbag gifted by Janet all those years ago. She looked anxious but the immediate swing in her mood, the instant toothy smile when she spotted me, sealed the emotion of our reunion. As I held her teary face to my chest, we once again shared Papa's spirit travelling with us.

We set off for Swan Yard, my mother now in the front passenger seat, me giving her an orientation of our journey. Mummy leant back comfortably, her attention more on the car than me, and said something to derail me. 'Nice car, Mohan. Have you said thank you to Jesus?'

As a bemused Vicki looked on, I murmured, 'Of course.'

On the M6 approaching the Lancaster junction, my mother's attention was caught by the Forton Motorway Services set in an unusual hexagonal tower. 'Is that Lancaster Airport?' When I explained what it was, she said it looked like a proper airport, 'Just like KL's Subang Airport,' since she'd not been able to see any of huge Heathrow's towers!

Nearing Swan Yard, I made calls on the car phone to Viji and Prasad (both hadn't seen her in seven years), to invite them to come over that evening. The smile on Mummy's face, whose facial structure was that of my own, carried a slight trepidation. She might have been impressed by my gadgets, my showing off, the way I assumed control or took charge of the agenda, but they were all reminders of the man who "should have been here in my place" as she would lament several times during her visit.

Arthur and Eva, whom she'd already met in KL, and other occupants from our apartments came to greet Mummy, who didn't appear overawed by her new environment, mainly due to her open personality and her previous interactions with the colonial set during her time moving around several estates in Malaya.

Over a chicken curry dinner I made, and in the company of my brothers and niece (Prasad's daughter), my mother's face was a permanent grin. Other such family gatherings during her two-month stay appeared to be leading towards some sort of re-bonding with my brothers, but they would fizzle upon her departure.

Mummy showed no signs of jet lag, a trait I share with her, so once we had the house to ourselves – still exuding the smell of curry – we gabbed into the night about all and nothing. She was impressed by the way I kept my home immaculate and was astonished to know her once-untrained son was cooking, cleaning, washing, shopping and doing just about everything without outside help. When I playfully chided her and Papa for throwing me into the wilderness ill-equipped, and related how shocked I was in my early days to find English boys operating so independently, her face was calm and expressionless. 'You learn best the hard way. I didn't start life knowing everything,' she said, breaking into a small mischievous grin. On that note, I confessed to having sold the gold chain and cross in which I was baptised as a child. I'd been short of money while studying law and was also forced to sell off my almost 400 precious vinyl LPs of top rock groups as well as obscure ones to a backstreet shop for a pittance: £75 (now collectors' items worth thousands)

Mummy knit her brow in grief. I sensed mortification. She reached out to clench my hand and uttered the magic words I wanted to hear: 'It's all right, Mohan. I understand.'

The next morning, my mother got ready in a fresh new saree to match the radiant glow on her face, eager to meet my "England father". She accompanied me to the office where Tony, Charles and the rest of the staff gave her the Queen Mother treatment and she took it all in her stride, telling me when the opportunity arose, 'Your father should have lived to see this.'

No sooner had Geoffrey arrived than he immediately came to greet Mummy with an affectionate embrace. They got on famously and managed to communicate despite the language barrier. For the rest of the trip, whenever I was at work, Geoffrey took charge and showed Mummy around Lancaster and Morecambe and also took her on trips to the Lake District. Mummy enjoyed Geoffrey's wit, charm and generosity. Geoffrey in turn kept her entertained and amused. I can still remember her narrating his experience at the Ashes when Shane Warne delivered "the ball of the century". I was with Geoffrey on that famous occasion at the Old Trafford Cricket Ground. Following a scrumptious lunch of Lancashire hotpot and red cabbage, homemade apple pie and custard, with a pint of Tetley's bitter and gin and tonic, Geoffrey dozed off, drooping with his cigar in mouth, causing his tie to go up in smoke and all-round laughter from members alerting me to wake up my man! I shook his shoulder shouting, 'Geoff! Geoff!' then watched the old boy gently opening his eyes, sizing up the situation with a sheepish grin and patting down his burnt tie, unperturbed by the satire he'd created. That was Geoffrey – absolutely no fuss – even when informed he'd missed a moment in sports history!

Another time, Mummy took me by surprise when she said she'd had a discussion with Geoffrey about Nelson Mandela becoming South Africa's first black president and Bill Clinton (whom she thought was most attractive after

JFK)… before asking me what I thought of the chances of "this young opposition leader Tony Blair" becoming the prime minister of England!

There was a constant flow of invitations from all my friends, including David and Jean Ashcroft and my female friends galore who wanted to meet my mother. Mummy thoroughly enjoyed everyone's company, not in the least perturbed by cultural differences or the generational gap. In just a few days, she got her bearings around St Peter's Road where I lived and on the first Sunday decided to go on her own for service at St Peter's Catholic Cathedral just across the road. By the time I reached the church to walk her back, she had become a mini-celebrity! I could just about make out a tinge of her white saree through the small crowd surrounding her, including the priest, engaged in deep conversation. Being the only foreigner was no burden, she told me afterwards. 'They're just people like us…' she remarked, and I was ever so proud of her. If only I'd had her confidence when I first landed in England in September 1970.

Knowing how much she missed it ever since moving to India, I took my mother to the cinema like Papa used to take us during our KL days, to watch *Four Weddings and a Funeral* and *Philadelphia*. We also watched the 1994 FIFA World Cup Final live on BBC with our favourite team, Brazil, lifting the Jules Rimet trophy. Following that, I took her to see the stadiums at Anfield, Old Trafford and Maine Road, to all the clubs where I played badminton and squash, to my running spots, to the Chancery Lane law society, the Royal Courts of Justice and to the docks in

Heysham, where as a stevedore I was penalised for causing two bags of potatoes to drop.

My mother nevertheless was most looking forward to visiting Whittingham Hospital and the Lancaster Moor Hospital. With just a year to go before its closure, Whittingham was falling into dereliction, compounding its gloomy, ghostly character, and I didn't help matters with my graphic description of its wards, patients, general horror and my own sufferings. Mummy looked around helplessly, then, clutching my arm, began tearing. It was alarming as I'd never known my mother to be anything but resilient, belying her docile appearance, as demonstrated so well by the way she held herself with grace and dignity during Papa's funeral.

In the remaining weeks, we travelled all over England, Wales and Scotland. The biggest highlight was the Edinburgh Fringe Festival, the sort of event you're guaranteed to come away from feeling *I've never seen anything like that*! The music, dances, banter, comedy, plays, sketches, just about anything, ranging from bizarre, funny, raunchy, quirky to the avant-garde, were cleverly crafted, no matter if they were hosted in buses, taxis, on benches or in stadiums over its hundreds of venues. Over three days, Mummy, Viji and I took in nine different types of shows, including at two of the prestigious Big Four venues: the Gilded Ballroom and the Assembly Rooms. For one who used to conveniently find something to do in the kitchen whenever Manolito grabbed a girlfriend for a kiss in the popular 1960s television series *High Chaparral*, my mother had come a long way. She watched unflinching, displaying nothing of her inhibitions from her Prang

Besar Estate days, as a naked lesbian duo performed a live lovemaking act!

On the drive back, Mummy made my day when she appreciated my driving. 'You should've been a racing car driver instead of a lawyer. You drive so much better than Papa.' Taking it as my cue, I told her of my involvement with the Morecambe Car Club, among other clubs, charitable organisations and trusts such as Sandblast, the Lancaster Choral Society, the Lancaster swimming club, Burma Star veterans, British Legion, Morecambe Cricket Club, Morecambe Citizen Advice Bureau, Gordon Working Men's Club…

My moment of glory did not last very long. Somewhere near Glasgow, as I was rattling on, a Mercedes overtook my BMW causing Mummy to remark, 'Does this car not go any faster?' When the woman who is the queen of your heart throws you a challenge, you take it on. I still remember the Cheshire cat smile on my mother's face as I justified her earlier compliment of my skill behind wheels.

My final surprise was elusive tickets to the Last Night of the Proms festival at the Royal Albert Hall in London. It was a glorious night of orchestral classical performances, and Mummy was completely bowled over by the scale, grandeur and mesmerising live music of the evening.

The glint of contentment in her eyes clouded only when the crowd rose to its feet, raising its voice to flood the hall in feverish patriotic fervour. Even without me explaining what was going on, Mummy picked up on *Rule Britannia*. She swung a gaze at me and said something that pierced my conscience: 'Look at these lot.'

TWENTY-ONE

# A LITTLE RESPECT

Mummy returned to Kerala with a very reluctant Viji as his prospects in England were gloomy after failing his examinations and no longer qualifying for a student visa.

There was no break for me from filial duties following my mother's whirlwind visit when soon after I had a cry for help from my sister in Abu Dhabi, where they'd moved to from America. It got the ball rolling for reorganising my diary to accommodate frequent planned and unplanned travels. I arrived in Abu Dhabi without a strategy for resolving my sister's troubled marriage, for that was what she was expecting of me. Having handled many matrimonial matters and being a two-time veteran in the business, I understood the importance of not taking sides and so chose to handle Shanta's troubles the same way... until confessions of physical and emotional abuse surfaced. Big brother emotions kicked in.

My father hadn't spent the majority of his savings on his only daughter's marriage for her to be at the receiving end of a man's temper and violence. Growing up, I'd had enough exposure to know what the toxic combination of alcohol and prejudicial social customs was capable of in Indian societies, and it hurt to see my educated sister unable to assert herself. I only returned to England without harming my sister's abuser because Shanta confessed she felt there was still hope of reconciliation. It would take a few more years of suffering before she would get a divorce, at the core of which, I suspect, was her fear of stigma.

In quick succession, I had to rework my diary once again for a trip to Kerala at Mummy's request and also because I wanted to check on her and Viji. I was taken aback by my brother's transformation in just a matter of months... hair grown out and sporting a fiercely lush moustache. I was even more gobsmacked by Mummy's manoeuvre at ensuring my trip was not wasted. My sullied reputation notwithstanding, she made me part of the selection panel to preside over "interviews" of potential brides for Viji, the only one of my siblings still unmarried. The panel, comprising family elders and Mummy, operated with the steadfast confidence of acting in the best interests of all concerned. Thankfully, Viji exercised his "freedom" to make the final decision. Marriage fixed, I fled to my sanctuary and busy schedule.

Back in Lancaster, I was elated to discover my efforts at pulling strings to book the elusive Golf Rallye GTI were successful. Volkswagen released only fifty in the UK in 1995 and I had to have one! I took Geoffrey on a final spin in my still-new BMW before surrendering it to its next owner and then went off to view Volkswagen's latest model at a showroom in London. It was a moment to relish. A new dream car, no longer hampered by family obligations, and a realisation that solitude was becoming an essential ingredient of my life. I enjoyed being alone; better yet, it contributed to my productivity and general well-being. I was by no means withdrawing from my hectic work schedule or social life; it just felt like I was on the right vector – confidence granted me by my next marathon.

To take it a notch higher from the sea-level London Marathon, I decided to attempt the iconic Snowdonia Marathon in Wales, encircling Britain's highest mountain, its dramatic routes ensuring its reputation as one of the toughest to complete. In 2023, the event organisers announced that the Snowdonia Marathon will henceforth be known by its Welsh name: Marathon Eyri. It's important to note that Wales has faced many discriminatory policies and efforts to suppress Welsh identity under English rule.

I arrived in Snowdon with two friends to spend the night at the Bron Menai, a cracking Bed & Breakfast surrounded by wilderness and big rolling hills tucked on the outskirts of Caernarfon. By the time I hit the sack after a light meal, I'd heard the local legend associated with nearby Beddgelert... of Prince Llewelyn who accidentally killed his beloved dog Gelert thinking it had killed his baby son, when in fact the blood on Gelert's muzzle was from killing the wolf attempting to eat his baby. The stones marking the place where valiant Gelert was buried had become a popular visiting site.

Morning dawned with miserable weather and I was a bundle of nerves thinking about the challenges of the Snowdon massif. When the race got underway, we were already soaking through in heavy rains and high winds blinding views of the surrounding slate mountains. The climb up the steep Llanberis Pass was smooth and I overtook runners with ease, getting into a rhythm right up to the first descent when the trails became slippery. 'Weather like this, best to run as quickly as possible,' cried a fellow runner sporting a 100 Marathon Club tee-shirt, just past Beddgelert village. I picked up speed and made it through the halfway point in 1 hour and 39 minutes, looking good for my target of finishing the course in 4 hours and 30 minutes.

There were other chats and pauses along the way, which was a complete departure from road marathons lined with cheering crowds where your focus is purely on the race. Snowdonia allowed moments for appreciating its spectacular scenery or breathing its crisp mountain air, which many of us did as we ran, walked or hobbled. At mile 22, the incessant bad weather, ascents and descents caught up with me and I was left dragging my knackered legs. Knowing it was the last chunk of the race, I followed a simple strategy: pick a post in the distance, make a run for it then slow down to a power walk before starting all over again. My body adapted. After what seemed like an age,

I made it to mile 24, where the forbidding final descent awaited. Nudging past a couple of runners, I missed my footing in the mud, completely lost control and tumbled down the hill. Taking no notice of my internal pain and ballooning right knee, I picked myself up and crossed the line in 4 hours and 15 minutes. My chip time (net time in marathon language) moved me down to 4 hours 10 minutes and 41 seconds. That solitary Snowdonia Marathon became a life-changing experience, sparking an enduring love for mountains and uphill running, which remains my daily pursuit.

I still run against the wind, no longer as young, no longer as strong, but it would be remiss of me not to mention how punishingly hard it is especially at my age now, far from enjoyable, and sometimes the demons in my head badger me to give up. *Take it easy. Go into retirement. You deserve a break*, they prod. But, I've kept on, never missing my date with nature and always embracing the elements, albeit I do take it easy. I no longer run with a watch. I don't care about pace, strides, cadence or heart rate. Neither do I worry about conditions, although proper attire and shoes that give the best traction are very important. If anything, I find running on inches of snow, in icy conditions, through a blizzard or just feeling the earth under my feet to be quite stimulating.

Following the London and Snowdon marathons, my spirit pointed me in the direction of the Big Apple. Through my contacts in the New York Road Runners club, I secured a gold dust place among its 40,000 runners. Amid Central Manhattan's total carnival atmosphere, I joined runners from all over the world to collect our vest numbers and numbered rucksacks at various designated gates. I struck up a friendship with Eduardo from Tuscany, as we were in the same pan. We did a walkabout around the city and over a pasta dinner exchanged notes on Italy and the Far East.

The next morning, I met Eduardo at the pick-up point where a bus took us from Manhattan to Staten Island via New Jersey. We joined the thousands of other runners in our pen at the start line in affluent Staten Island overlooking the stately Twin Towers, home of stockbrokers and city professionals who gave us a rousing send-off. Just as I crossed the bridge into Brooklyn, my leg began to hurt. I became very disturbed thinking of my throbbing four-time-operated-on right knee. Mr Bollen's warning, 'Stop running, your knee looks like a battlefield,' kept creeping into my thoughts as I felt my knee flaring up.

I completed New York's five boroughs in 4 hours and 44 minutes – way below my target of 3 hours. It was my slowest timing and by far the most painful race. Eduardo was waiting for me to collect our medals together, after which we compared notes with other new friends and I left New York the following day in severe pain from my ripe, swollen knee.

Under the glare of walls adorned with autographed photographs of celebrity footballers, Mr Bollen gave me an earful. The arthroscopy was no good and the sports injury specialist performed the fifth and last operation on my damaged knee. Still in his operating gown, Mr Bollen marched towards me once I came round.

'Fucking hell, Phil, I've never seen anything like this! Why didn't you stop when the pain began? You just made my job really difficult.' I was taken aback to hear the good doctor swear but perked up when he walked away scolding, 'Take up cycling if you must!' That was exactly what I did – gave running a break for a fling with cycling.

Cycling was only a respite as I could not stay away from the lure of marathoning. I loved the whole spirit of sportsmanship and camaraderie that abounds each event. Like any marathon lover would attest, it isn't about how fast you complete a run. Just completing the 26.2 miles is uplifting and I take pride in having completed all twenty-five marathons I took part in until 2006, when I finally stopped. Perhaps I was being reckless, but I put myself through such rigours because of the need to push my limits, a trait I shared with Geoffrey. We thrilled at gate-crashing into out-of-bounds VIP or player areas, even coat-tailing the police motorcade leading the players' coach.

'Cut in!' Geoffrey ordered the time we were trailing the motorcade leading the bus near Edgbaston Cricket Stadium in Birmingham for an England vs Australia match. We parked next to the coach and as we got out, the Australian stars greeted us, mistaking me for English batsman Mark Ramprakash!

'Play along,' Geoffrey chortled into my ear, which I did, feeling like a criminal, especially when Dickie Bird, the international umpire, chipped in with his broad Yorkie drawl a *how do* to "Ram".

My partners at the firm weren't disturbed by my "recklessness" as I never shirked my responsibilities. I have worked from the hospital bed (staff bringing my files in large IKEA bags, taking dictation to the amusement of nurses), or gone to the office on crutches after discharging myself against medical advice, often to conduct recovery with my own style of physiotherapy, which has worked, as would be ascertained by Mr Bollen in his final medical assessment of my knee sixteen years after that fifth operation: '…he's had a remarkably good time since then (last operation) with a high level of activity and minimal symptoms. On examination, his knee still looks like a battlefield with a slight fixed flexion deformity but remains relatively stable…'

As one who enjoyed being at the cutting edge of things, I was never parked in the office for long. I made the most of night school and professional courses, such as the groundbreaking Association of Personal Injury Lawyers' course on repetitive strain injury (RSI) following the Disability Discrimination Act 1995 (replaced by the Equality Act 2010), prohibiting disability discrimination in employment and other fields, in line with the rest of Europe. Such courses attracted industry experts, whose contacts came in most useful as I relied on their services to demonstrate compelling evidence when taking on tricky RSI cases, which were beginning to pile up as people realised they could seek legal recourse against employers.

To keep up with technological advancements, I attended courses such as *Computing for the Terrified* because my staff were running circles around me! I shared a wonderful work friendship with my team of staff, always catching up outside of work hours, over meals or discussing current affairs. Having formed a tight bond, it must have been awkward for some to appreciate the change in dynamics, with me now of boss rank. The shift in roles meant I was encouraged to remove my pseudo-Englishman cloak. I worried less about how I might be perceived and became more comfortable with discussing the East, sometimes, against the decadence of the West. This did not always go down well, like the time my legal cashier snapped testily, 'Why don't you go back to where you came from?' …a manner she would not have dared to use against Tony, Charles or Geoffrey. Why?

The insinuation was pretty much today's Brexit statement: You come here, take our education and benefits, our pensions, health system, social security, our women (in my case), our hospitality boxes, and now you reject us!

I deflected the topic with the staff who "challenged" me as there were others about, all fed with the same whitewashed history. There had been too much triumphalist conditioning to make them understand that much of Britain's wealth and status could be tracked to the "homes" they now flippantly order non-white people to return to… the very "homes" the empire scrambled to, to violate and enrich itself.

At an appropriate time, I called the member of staff in question to my office for a disciplinary meeting in the presence of my assistant as a contemporary note taker while I gave her a lecture on office decorum with an injection of the deep injustices caused by not knowing one's history. Everything was noted in her employment file as the issuance of a first warning.

My political views have stayed with me. If anything, I feel the situation in England has only worsened. Despite awareness that societies can no longer live in homogeneous bubbles, and even with the much-changed demographic makeup of the country, conversations imperative to curbing the rise of intolerance, xenophobia and radicalism in the face of misplaced patriotism continue to evade England. But the motivation for change cannot be forced. It has to come from within, as Germany has done with the holocaust. England's voice of education will remain lacking for as long as the nanny-raised, napkin-wearing classes, mostly benefactors of the slave trade and empire, maintain power in their grip through closing ranks.

Following the New York Marathon, it was a rough few months of pain, stiffness and lack of mobility for me. In some measure, regular visits to the gym helped my muscles get stronger and heal faster – the cue for me to take up serious cycling. I invested in a top-of-the-range hybrid Trek bicycle… a far cry from the minimalist, clean-cut ones of my boyhood. Not satisfied with cycling in my vicinity, I got in touch with a cycling adventure company in London and found out about an expedition in Vietnam, thanks in some ways to America. As a reconciliation measure, President Clinton had lifted an almost two-decade trade embargo with Vietnam post war, easing entry into the country. What a way to kill two birds with one stone: improving my wonky knee's fitness and cycling to get the true feeling of the country.

In anticipation of the gruelling two-week schedule, I decided to pamper myself by putting up in a plush

Chelsea hotel the day before leaving for Saigon (Ho Chi Minh City) and having dinner at the Indian fine dining restaurant Chutney Mary in King's Road. The dinner turned out to be an event in itself as the only two other diners at Chutney Mary's Conservatory were Britain's show business luminaries Peter Ustinov and Sean Connery. I'd already had the pleasure of listening to Ustinov's stirring speech a few years prior at a gala tribute dinner to tennis great Arthur Ashe at Grosvenor House. I told Ustinov as much, to which 007 added his affirmation of his friend's oratorical talent. What a diary entry that was for the Kajang boy who grew up watching Spartacus and James Bond in absolute awe, in an era when going to the cinema was a big affair warranting dressing up!

Sixteen cyclists met in Ho Chi Minh City, eleven from England, the others from New Zealand, America and Holland. Twelve were females. The entourage was met by locals from the organising team who took us into the city of two-wheelers. To my eye, it was a magnified Kajang of the 1960s, and it put me in my element! Like an athlete ogling state-of-the-art equipment, I was thrilled to finally be in the small nation that defeated the big superpower, a topic I took up with my first friend, American Danielle Smith.

Vietnam was no longer in economic decline and was on the reconstruction path after defeating America and fighting a further two wars; ending Pol Pot's genocidal reign in Cambodia and a violent border war with China; yet, Ho Chi Minh City reflected decades of commercial isolation owing to America's punishing trade embargo and countless bone-chilling horrors of its past. The city was chock-a-block with weary-looking low rises, stalls and vendors selling an array of things jostling out of dull-looking high street shops, crowds in traditional attire and distinctive conical straw hats bustling on bicycles, motorbikes and three-wheeled bicycle taxis.

Outside my window the next morning was a brilliant orange, and inside my head Robin Williams was shouting *Goood Mooorning Vieeetnam*! The city was already a rush of bicycles and Honda cubs. Following a briefing using detailed travel maps, we began our journey from the south to the north, from Ho Chi Minh City's Mekong River Delta to Hanoi. A backup bus followed the last rider with our luggage, supplies and three locals to assist those unable to cycle the full journey averaging about 140 miles a day from 6 am to 4 pm.

The bus was popular as most did token cycling of around thirty miles a day before seeking refuge in its air-conditioned comfort. I doggedly avoided that option, choosing instead to explore Vietnam's varied terrains, its people and cultures on my own. The landscapes and open country were reminiscent of my boyhood: towns looking like markets in session, wooden huts, tropical forests, afternoon showers, paddy terraces… The old thrill returned every time I stopped by wayside stalls for noodles or rice, gobbled down with chopsticks while being fanned by the South China Sea's bold winds.

During the three-day break in Hanoi before we flew out, I hired a motorbike and with Danielle ventured into Hanoi's hilly regions aided by four local children, one a cheeky, spirited little Coca-Cola seller with a missing arm he matter-of-factly said was blown up! On another day, I cycled the short distance north of the city to Lang Son, which borders China, to satisfy my curiosity for country borders, a fascination that probably began when as a five-year-old I craned my neck from Papa's Austin Cambridge for my first look of Singapore from the Johor Causeway. The excitement was no less when I did it at the Gambia from the border of Senegal, Brunei from Sabah or when I biked from Manali to Leh in India, into Tibet. The most visceral thrill of all by far was gazing at the Brazilian border from Argentina's spectacular Iguazu Park hosting the almighty Iguazu Falls.

I left Vietnam full of admiration for its people's vitality, optimism and friendliness despite their decades of bloodshed and persecution. It is no wonder many war-displaced Vietnamese from all over the world pilgrimage to their battered but breathtaking homeland to travel, donate, raise funds, start businesses, resettle or simply slum it with their ancestors. The trip also made me decide no more herd travels, for I enjoyed taking roads less travelled and choosing my travel partners.

In 1998, Geoffrey was approaching retirement and we decided to have a leaving party at the offices of Whiteside and Knowles. Tony set about organising it and inviting all the relevant players in the legal and financial sectors, including Geoffrey's important clients. Tony was helped by Alison, a Welsh firebrand I'd interviewed and taken on board as assistant solicitor, for she displayed the attributes of a remarkable lawyer. My partners couldn't be more pleased. None could have anticipated the minefield ahead.

The party was beautiful and befitting; so was Geoffrey's parting speech that true to form elicited sniggers and winks in equal measure to claps and cheers. Geoffrey was effusive in his fondness for me and also expressed his hope and confidence in the current partners taking his firm to greater heights.

It was the same year of the Asian financial crisis that had thrown the Malaysian currency into turmoil, and Kuala Lumpur hosted the sixteenth Commonwealth Games, the first Asian country to do so. I landed at the spanking new KL International Airport, situated not far from Prang Besar Estate, the tropical forest turned plantation turned Malaysia's new administrative capital, Putrajaya. I hired a car at the airport for the hour's drive into the city, greeted all along by impressive hoardings and billboards to mark the big occasion, as well as signboards indicating Dengkil and Sepang, both unheard-of backwaters in my time. My mind took its own journey. I was once again the proud Prang Besar Estate boy in a tee-shirt, shorts and slippers standing face to face with the loin-clothed native *sakai* transmitting an unspoken message: *Won't be long before you lose your habitat too.*

Cousin Rajan visited me at the Shangri La where I stayed for the duration of the games and sometimes accompanied me to the various venues where I watched all the athletics, badminton and cricket. Sports aside, there was much fodder for conversation as Prime Minister Dr Mahathir had sacked his deputy, Anwar Ibrahim, over accusations of corruption and sexual indecency. 'Never heard the word sodomy before but now the *whole* country knows it! Just wait and see... there's going to be a lot of drama after these games...' I remember Rajan saying.

True enough. In the weeks after the successful Commonwealth Games, headlines about Malaysia were accompanied by visuals and footage of armed riot police with water cannons, tear gas and batons battling waves of anti-government protesters. By the time I returned to Malaysia once again the following year, this time for the first Malaysian Formula 1 Grand Prix at Sepang, Malaysia's rising voice of discontent had got its rallying cry. *Reformasi*.

In the same year, Whiteside and Knowles underwent a period of tumult with the Welsh newcomer charming the partners with more than just her doubtless knowledge of the law. Alison's excellent riposte and youthful exuberance were spellbinding, and Charles was smitten. It did not escape the office grapevine, which was also up to date on Alison's poor state of marriage. I was busy with work, travels, sports and extensive socialising to be caught up, that is, until one of my legal assistants let it escape that Alison had been making coquettish enquiries about me.

'She's intrigued by your energy, Phil. Knows which gym you go to now! Charles won't like it,' came a remark.

It wasn't long before Alison began inputting in my diary. There was a reciprocal connection despite our almost twenty-year age gap, and her still being married. By the end of 1999, our entanglement was causing resentment among the staff, who felt I was being used to obtain favourable terms over them. Alison was facing its brunt and I was falling off the wire. Aggrieved Charles cited that "the conduct" was compromising office balance and decorum. Sensing warnings of an impending termination, Alison resigned voluntarily to the satisfaction of the other partners. Alongside my sadness, there was an undeniable relief because it was my first and only blotch at work and I felt like I had let Tony down.

On the eve of 2000, I had many party and concert invitations but did not feel like receiving a new millennium with crowds or noise. At 11 pm on the last day of the century, I left my Swan Yard home on my bicycle for the long, freezing journey in howling winds along my favourite cycling country in the Trough of Bowland. Timing was all-important and I'd put in months of practice to ensure I reached my target just before midnight. I ushered in 2000 at the Jubilee Tower near Quernmore before continuing via Clitheroe, Preston, Lytham, Blackpool and Fleetwood to arrive in Lancaster at about 5am on New Year's Day, having cycled approximately 125 miles – a defining moment I hold close to my heart.

The biggest highlight of 2000 for me was the Sydney Olympics. I wasn't going to miss it; besides, it was an opportunity to visit my youngest brother, Tom, and his children. Relations with Viji on the other hand were severely strained. It came to my attention that Mummy had become a prisoner under her own roof, under the control of Viji and his wife, Sara. En route to Sydney, I made a flying visit to Kerala, setting off quite a ruckus involving local community leaders and even politicians summoned by my sister-in-law to defend their case. They claimed that under local custom, the house and our land belonged to Viji as Mum's "sole caretaker". My fury was not just at the partisan *panchayat* (village council) and Viji's cruelty but also at seeing the pain on my mother's face at having history repeat itself in her life.

It was impossible to mitigate the situation in that threatening climate and I did what I had gone to do – removed my mother from that hellhole and purchased an apartment for her in Trivandrum to move into straight away. Mummy vowed to never set foot again in the village where she had been humiliated by her own son. She'd keep her word too. Hoping creature comforts would lessen her pain, I bought a car and organised a driver for her before leaving for Sydney.

Attending the brilliantly organised Sydney Olympics was one of the best decisions of my life, for I went without making prior arrangements. By a stroke of immense luck, I was approached by a ticket holder outside the Olympic Stadium on Magic Monday (nine exciting finals scheduled and tickets were sold out well in advance) offering to sell his premium ticket at face value since he had a family emergency! No tickets had been available from the touts, and I'd been hanging around desperately for hours when my angel in the form of that young Chinese Australian came with the offer, telling me he'd won the ticket in a lottery two years before the games.

From the plush centre seats at just above eye level to the athletics track, I watched Australia's Olympics darling, Cathy Freeman, in her famous catsuit, being roared to a thumping victory in the 400 metres, followed by Michael Johnson doing the same in the same event. For me, the most magical of Magic Monday's finals was the gift of watching Ethiopian great Haile Gebrselassie pip the finish line to retain his gold in the 10,000 metres race. 'That gold was from God,' Gebrselassie would say afterwards, just as my ticket for that night was for me as well as the write-up in the *Morecambe Visitor* broadsheet with my picture saying, *Sports-mad Whiteside and Knowles solicitor rubbed shoulders with Britain's elite athletes.* (I'd gatecrashed in full sports gear, my lanyard sticking out with multiple used tickets, was mistaken for an athlete and managed to chat up Linford Christie, Kelly Holmes, Colin Jackson and Darren Campbell!)

In another bizarre turn of events, sitting right behind me on that Magic Monday were the actors Meg Ryan and Russell Crowe, rumoured to have become a couple after the making of *Proof of Life*... the film's plot and settings were uncannily similar to my adventure to come in Ecuador.

Around the time I returned from the Sydney Olympics, Alison sought me out again. Her marriage was over by then and we began a serious relationship. She was eager to share my spirit of adventure and exploration and in two years we did so much worldwide travelling, including to my twin homes of Malaysia and India, where she met Mummy. 'It's not equal, this love, Mohan. I'll pray for you,' came my mother's reprimand.

I falter in love for the simple reason I give it my all when I connect with someone emotionally and intellectually, a trait that has never failed to deliver intense emotional experiences. With Alison, it was the emergence of an embryo soon after that terminated what might have been.

## TWENTY-TWO

# FULL CIRCLE

The millennium began on a stupendous note for me. In January, I was chosen to become the vice-president of the Lancaster and Morecambe District Law Society, the first person of colour to hold the position.

It was also the last year I would be living in an apartment. By December 2000, my Swan Yard penthouse was sold and I returned to the former Lancaster Moor Hospital, to move into Standen Park House, a *gentleman's residence* as my old training ground had been rechristened to erase its woeful history. Being the centrepiece of the private residences, Standen Park House had been split into two photogenic homes and given a beguiling makeover.

That I was part-owner of the building where the hospital's chief executive lived in 1972, a property once visited by no less than Charles Dickens and Wilkie Collins, felt like life was nearing full circle for the boy from Malaya swinging like a monkey as I'd been mocked for my badminton style. I cringe at the thought that I used to smile along when some thought it funny to call me Gunga Din or nig-nog; that it took me so long to recognise microaggression for what it is. Indirect discrimination. It could be because life had been relatively fair to me in this area. For instance, I once won a boundary dispute for an elderly client against her businessman neighbour, who for the three years of litigation took pleasure in calling me a bouquet of racist names, yet was respectful enough of my work to seek me out years later to be his lawyer!

Such incidents, and there were plenty, probably delayed my voice to put such "unintentional" aggressors in their place. Unlike Azeem Rafiq, who in 2021 took on the Yorkshire Cricket Club, one of England's most historic sporting clubs, calling it institutionally racist. Or Lewis Hamilton, saying, ' …if I have to be on the receiving end of that (racism) in this industry for people to become aware, then that's part of my journey.' It is the influence of such formidable personalities as Muhammad Ali and Lewis Hamilton that now sees me pursue international sports law through my participation in the Court for Arbitration for Sport (CAS)/ Tribunal Arbitral Du Sport (TAS), Lausanne, Switzerland.

In January 2001, I became the president of the Law Society. Honoured as I was with the achievement, the thought of the responsibilities that came with the position and how I would fare among my esteemed brethren rekindled the migrant spirit in me. Though a ceremonial role, the president's duties took up much time, namely presenting awards, cutting ribbons or giving out plaques, similar to what I was used to doing as trustee of a host of associations. I was soon judging an in-hand horse show near Blackburn, handing third place to the Queen's horse or deciding between prized tomatoes at the Overton Agricultural Show.

The ceremony to mark my appointment was at Leighton Hall, the magnificent ancestral home of the Gillow family, where I had to give my first speech as outgoing vice-president in front of local dignitaries, judges, magistrates, the High Sheriff of Lancashire, solicitors, barristers and guests. I lived in anxiety for weeks before that speech, taking guidance from Geoffrey (a past president) and poring over anything I could get hold of on calming nerves, preventing brain freeze, writing and pulling off an engaging speech with that all-important dry English sense of humour. That I judiciously made light of my flaws, sprinkled my speech with sarcasm and delved into satire, drew cheers and claps. Yet, I was already worrying about the big one the following year – my outgoing president's speech!

For that one, Mummy made her second visit to England, coinciding with the summer social reception at Leighton Hall that I hosted as president, with television cameras in attendance. We matched for the event: my mother in a cornflower blue saree with a matching blouse and I in a blue suit, blue sash and a heavy gold medallion. Mummy handled the attention of being the only saree-clad lady in masterly fashion, Geoffrey's constant smiles of encouragement a big support for her. Much to my amusement, and Geoffrey's, she worked through the finger buffet, wines and dancing to the West Indian steel live band without batting an eyelid! Even the expected "your father should have been here" did not come until the following day while we were watching ourselves on ITV's North West Granada News.

Papa would indeed have been very proud of the way I did things differently as president, such as staging an outdoor theatre of Shakespeare's *The Tempest* in collaboration with the Dukes Playhouse in Williamson Park's neatly landscaped gardens and natural amphitheatres. Papa would've also understood my struggles in the highly conservative set-up of the law society consisting of serious, learned members who hung their coats on Britain winning the two World Wars. There was an unmistakable air of sanctimony within the powers of the law society, stemming from a wanton ignorance of cultures and civilisations outside of their cocoon.

Throughout my tenure, I carried the feeling I was chosen as the token representative – a show of equal opportunity as I was one of the very few solicitors of colour during that period. As far as I am aware, no one of colour has attained the position in the Law Society of Lancaster and Morecambe since then, which is no surprise as only in 2021 the Law Society of England and Wales appointed *its* first non-white president.

A few days after my mother left was the September 11 terrorist attacks in America. I just could not come to grips with the non-stop television coverage of the crumbling World Trade Centre's Twin Towers in New York. It felt like a personal loss. Memories of admiring the twins from the Staten Island ferry ride, only sixpence at the time, especially at night, kept revisiting, and something in me wanted to reach out to the city I'd enjoyed on each of my many visits since 1987.

George W Bush transformed into a wartime president when he announced a *War on Terror*. Bush's approval ratings soared; Osama bin Laden, Taliban and Al-Qaeda became household words; countries cut ties with Afghanistan; America and Britain launched air and ground attacks in Afghanistan; more European countries became part of the allied forces, and by the end of 2001, most Taliban strongholds from Kabul to Kandahar had been captured. How could anyone have anticipated whatever gains made with those actions would be nullified when twenty years later America and its allies would make an embarrassingly chaotic withdrawal from Afghanistan for a swift Taliban takeover of the country, proving once again that going to war has never brought peace?

The world's deadliest terrorist attack changed air travel forever. America introduced new airport security protocols, meaning the days of easy, hassle-free airport flying were over. Three months after the 9/11 attacks, I boarded a near-empty BA 747 to find JFK swarmed by armed military personnel. You could no longer pass through security with shoes. I headed to the Plaza

Hotel, an establishment used to receiving royalty, world leaders, superstars Marilyn Monroe, Elizabeth Taylor, Frank Sinatra and more, but now hosting relief workers ploughing through a historical legacy that had shaken the world and taken the lives of citizens from more than eighty countries.

Central Manhattan was free of its former frenzy. I meandered my way through residual dust, smoky odour, people in surgical masks, unattended dogs looking for masters, cordoned-off shattered shops, before coming to the epicentre of America's biggest tragedy. A nightmarish pile of steel, concrete and general debris. For four days, I circumnavigated the bleak landscape several times, praying by photos of the MISSING taped everywhere from walls to pillars; talking to bruised New Yorkers bearing immense psychological stress; just sharing in the city's profound grief. It was an all-consuming experience and I'm glad I made that trip to understand the fragility of life. And the resilience of the human spirit.

Weeks after the trip, I briefly shared my New York experience in my outgoing president's speech, amid Leighton Hall's exquisite objets d'art, redolent of the estate's profiteering from the slave trade. Not floundering once, I worked through page after well-rehearsed page, performing like a pro for my discerning audience who in the end were charmed. Congratulations and hearty handshakes made my night. It was gratifying to feel appreciated; to be on par.

Curiously, when I got home, I slipped into feeling empty instead of fulfilled. The extraordinary effort I'd put into ensuring the night, and particularly my speech, was nothing short of perfect triggered darkness I couldn't shake off. It was completely pulling me down. To mend my spirit, I made a trip to the open blue skies of Che Guevara country, my Argentinian astrotourism, the type of travel as old as the stars, possessed of elemental energies and open to travellers of every ilk. Minus an itinerary, scouring parts unknown in the Pampas and Patagonia, sharing a steak with gauchos, stargazing in the open with a hand-crafted blanket to fight formidable draughts, it turned out to be a pilgrimage of the soul providing me with much-needed comfort and clarity.

I returned from Argentina to find new neighbours at Standen Park House. On a cold winter's morning, I bumped into Ann Haslam, who invited me into their veritable art gallery to meet her husband, Professor Ray Haslam. Their kindness, profound erudition and relatable political sensibility endeared them to me, leading to many evenings of good conversation, as you'd expect from two academics. If I delighted them with stories of the East, my devotion to sports and travel, or discussion of legal principles, Ray introduced me to their world of art, general intellectual elegance and John Ruskin. He was also visiting professor at the Ruskin Research Centre at Lancaster University. In no time at all, I came to regard Ann and Ray with the same level of affection, regard and respect as I do Geoffrey and Joan, Dave and Jean and Arthur and Eva. We became like family and it was with Ann and Ray that I spent my fiftieth birthday in 2002.

At the end of the same year, I made the instant decision to sell off Standen Park House when my dream house came on the market. For more than ten years, I'd been eyeing Clayton Bridge House, a stone-built cottage on the canal once used to store coal, right in the centre of Lancaster. If its St Peter's Road location was unbeatable, the views of the canal and cathedral right across the road took me to Kerala's picturesque backwaters. Ann and Ray were disappointed we weren't neighbours anymore, but it did not stop us from remaining in constant touch.

In January 2003, reports about my client John Buckley appeared in newspapers with headlines notifying *Irish Oil Worker May Be Dead*. That was the start of a year I regard as the most important of my career as a lawyer.

I came to find out how three months earlier John Buckley, sixty, and his Ecuadorian driver Luiz Diaz had been kidnapped near the village of Sardinas, southeast of Ecuador's capital Quito, about halfway to the Colombian border. A highly specialised technician, John was employed by the Argentine oil exploration and production company Techint to oversee its construction of an oil pipeline stretching from the crude-rich Amazon to a port on the coast. Newspapers also claimed that a ransom paid for the victims had failed to secure their release and that local police were continuing to search an area close to the notorious Colombian border.

Kidnappings of foreigners, particularly foreign oil workers, were rife in the region, suffering from perennial political instability and poverty – one of the far-reaching effects of the fall of the Soviet Union that was no longer funding Latin America's communist party activities and revolutionary movements.

John was an imposing figure, almost six and a half feet tall, bearing a strongly built body. An articulate man, he was generous with sharing his experiences right from our first meeting in the mid-'90s when a sombre John had just lost his son and wife, Ellen, whose lawyer I was. Various meetings followed over the years, John usually making fleeting stopovers in England in between overseas assignments. He signed his final will making his only surviving child, Moya Buckley, and his current wife, Bia (Portuguese with two children from a former marriage), equal joint beneficiaries to the residue of his worldwide assets. He made me the sole executor of his will.

As expected, in the first week of March 2003, Moya came to see me saying she and Bia wanted me to take the matter further with Techint, with the additional responsibility of representing her against Techint and the Ecuadorian Government. Bia had her own Portuguese lawyer.

I opened dialogue with Senior Executive Director Honorio Garcia Diaz of Techint Ltd based in Buenos Aires, who requested me to fly into Quito the following week with Moya. Considering the risks involved, I came up with certain terms, all agreed to by Techint, including a kidnapping insurance policy to the value of £10 million on my life (to be inherited by Mummy, Whiteside and Knowles and Janet in equal parts).

My partners weren't overly concerned about my decision to undertake such a complicated and dangerous case, even though I had no experience handling kidnap or cross-border matters. Had the case gone to them, they might have passed it on to a specialist London firm, but

Geoffrey understood there was no way I'd allow for such an opportunity to slip by me. 'Just don't come back in a body bag, will you?' he jested, calling it my James Bond assignment. I reminded him of Humphrey Bogart's line from *Casablanca*: 'Of all the gin joints in England and Wales (90,000 practising solicitors), this case had to land on my desk!'

On 15th March, I fetched Moya and we flew from Manchester to Heathrow for an overnight stay. Tall, with a broad frame, liberally tattooed and somewhat bohemian in appearance and soul, Moya was her father's image. Over dinner at the hotel, she filled me in on the family history – of missing her father's presence owing to the nature of his job, of fallouts and rifts, her mother's death, her brother's grief and subsequent death, and now having to deal with life as the only surviving member of her family. She wasn't enamoured with her stepmother; that was clear.

The next morning, we flew first class on American Airlines into Miami, where airport security was even tighter following Bush and his British counterpart Tony Blair's impending invasion of Saddam Hussein's Iraq "to disarm Iraq of weapons of mass destruction". When I stepped into a full-body scanner, the metal in my leg set off the alarm, causing officers to question and frisk me. Pulling up my trousers, I showed them the beauties on my right knee, whereupon a small scanner was placed directly on my kneecap containing a metal nail support. It too beeped to corroborate my story and soon Moya and I were relaxing in the executive lounge, me learning to text with my latest Nokia mobile phone.

Arriving at the crowded, noisy Quito Airport late at night, we were accorded fast-track immigration and customs clearance and were met by John from the Control Risks Group (CRG), who whisked us straight to an awaiting limousine. The driver wore dark glasses and the front passenger introduced herself as Helen, a CRG translator. The London-based consultancy employed, among other specialists, intelligence officers the likes of ex MI5/MI6 – polished public school operators trained to provide international negotiation and security services to clients with deep pockets. Quintessentially English, they lived life in the fast lane and regularly waded into the underworld.

In the limousine, Moya and I were provided with body vests and debriefed with a spreadsheet containing the next four days' well-crafted itinerary. It was a little after midnight and the forty-minute uphill drive to the Hotel Swissotel felt surreal, more so because we were weaving along the silhouetted Mount Andes.

The morning after was even more memorable, for my vast balcony overlooked the snow-clad Andes! I was up very early and, the UK being five hours ahead, I called Whiteside and Knowles to brief my legal assistant on other work matters before making my way to the hotel's gym. I'd been given strict warning, 'No running outside. It's for your safety.' I recall with embarrassment collapsing on the treadmill, possibly due to lack of sleep compounded by altitude sickness being in a city more than 9,000 feet above sea level. I came round within minutes and retreated to enjoy the Jacuzzi in my room where the large glass window splashed out the mountains.

Suited and booted, I met Moya for breakfast, and there was Bia and her team from Portugal: son, daughter and lawyer Elsa Marcelo in a sharp suit, striking quite an impression. The meeting at the large boardroom was quite an assemblage, not least dominated by a posse of lawyers. Diplomats and their lawyers from the UK, USA, Ireland, Portugal, Ecuador, Argentina and Colombia (perhaps to ensure oil production and supplies weren't put at risk due to geopolitical tussles); Techint representatives Honorio Garcia Diaz, his assistant and lawyer from Buenos Aires; Ecuador's Chief of Police Colonel Chuka and two male assistants; all four members of the CRG; the Portugal team, comprising Bia, her two children and lawyer; John's driver, Luiz Diaz, represented by his wife, her brother, her son and her daughter-in-law; and the UK duo of Moya Buckley and Philip George.

Techint's Honorio welcomed everyone in English and went around the table introducing each team and its attendees. A short DVD of John Buckley and Luiz Diaz was played, with Honorio explaining investigations were ongoing, although we were working on the basis they were both dead. It followed a discussion on conflicts of laws. John's legal matter was based on his contract with Techint and claims under the law of tort of England and Wales and the International Court of Justice (ICJ) for enforcement purposes, while Luiz's was based on Ecuador's contract law. Luiz's total claim was limited to $10k, while John Buckley's was unlimited. The blatant injustice was disregarded, although it did not sit well with me that Luiz Diaz's life was deemed not as precious as John Buckley's. For this reason, when Mrs Diaz pursued me about doing the best for her family as she could not afford legal representation, I took her on.

After Honorio, the floor was passed to Colonel Chuka, a bulk of a man like John but with a thick intimidating moustache. Colonel Chuka's assistants pinned a large map of Ecuador on a rectangular blackboard – the layout of the pipeline and the area where it was believed the kidnapping had taken place. The colonel spoke in Spanish, which Helen translated into English and Portuguese. It was followed by a slideshow of events leading up to the disappearances. In summing up, the colonel made a damaging implication. 'If John Buckley had not ventured out the compound into the cordoned-off section of the jungle, the two would still be here today with us.' He inferred that John had gone out on a "frolic of his own", persuading Luis to drive him, which allowed the bandits to spring on them. In a court of law, this act could fall under the maxim *Volenti non-fit injuria* (to a willing person, it is not wrong), and, accordingly, the employer would not be liable.

The colonel's men next played a videotape of the work done by the police thus far: the ransom paid by Techint, the capture of one kidnapper (now in custody) and his confession that John and Luiz were shot dead when trying to escape. Their explanation was supported by CRG. We broke for lunch and had our first opportunity to mingle. It was the CRG team that piqued my curiosity and we got along like a house on fire.

When the meeting reconvened, Honorio brought to our attention that subject to proof of death, Techint would receive a substantial amount from the insurance policy taken on John's life, and that the ransom payments would be taken into account towards the final figure. He explained that Techint had no legal liability but perhaps a moral obligation towards the victims' kin. Following the contractual terms of employment as agreed between John and Techint, pension was not payable to foreigners, but, Techint was prepared to pay out upon production of a death certificate. Point to note: the presumption of death in Ecuador is six months, while in the UK it is seven years.

'We need to bring matters to a conclusion and Techint want to play fair.' Honorio paused, before offering a substantial amount as ex gratia payment, with legal costs, in full and final settlement without admission of liability.

Before we adjourned, we were asked to clarify the figures and the principles of the offer with Techint's lawyers, and for Moya and Bia to choose the administrator of the compensation monies between me and Elsa, both by that evening. We were also informed to make the application using the jurisdiction of Ecuador and appoint separate Ecuadorian lawyers in Quito to act on behalf of John Buckley's executor (me), before leaving the country.

After heated exchanges, I was appointed the administrator. Elsa and her client were satisfied with Techint's offer, but I advised Moya we should go for a much higher offer and settle for a middle-ground figure. This resulted in another argument with Elsa before she relented – not for long – as my next proposal, also met with sour looks, was to incorporate the Diaz family's claim as part of the whole settlement for moral and legal reasons (avoidance of any legal action by the family for John Buckley's action of putting Luiz's life in danger). Among other matters, we agreed the compensation monies be kept outside of the estate and be paid directly to the next of kin to save UK and Portugal capital taxes; and a far bigger settlement for the Diaz family.

When we returned to the boardroom to deliver our counter offer, I began by setting out the circumstances of the case from when I knew John Buckley, to my current position as the legal rep of both families and their administrator. It went well until I thanked Techint for their generosity and kindness… and paused. Holding my nerve, I suggested, 'Could Techint raise the Buckley family's compensation, please… with costs?'

Honorio looked like he wanted to fling me to the peak of the Andes. My CRG acquaintances might have been snickering. The rest looked stumped. It followed an hour of ferocious horse trading. We settled for a significant middle figure plus legal costs for the Buckleys and a satisfactory sum plus costs for the Diaz family.

The day's meetings ended with the announcement of a helicopter site visit the next morning followed by the signing of the agreement by all parties. The chopper trip invitation was not extended to Luiz's family, while team Portugal opted out, fearing it could be a trick to blow us all up! I sought out the Diaz family in the coffee house to share the good news. Appreciation spreading on her face, Mrs Diaz gripped my hands. On the verge of tears myself, I wished the family well and hightailed it.

The next morning, the CRG team, Moya and I were

taken on a two-hour drive deep into the forest to survey the base camp where John had been posted. Moya was silent the entire trip, her face displaying despondency. From there, we boarded a helicopter for an aerial view of Techint's pipeline project stretching along the immense Amazon River. When a CRG agent pointed out to Moya the spot where her father was kidnapped, she could hold her heartbreak no longer. Seeing tears streaming down her ashen face, I placed an arm around Moya, who instinctively swung at me in flat-out rage, landing a slap on my face. Through an onslaught of sobs, her breath stuttering, Moya apologised profusely. I understood. I think everyone did.

Later that afternoon, the entire flock was driven to a jungle courthouse an hour's drive east of Quito, where we signed the originating application, paid the court fee and filed it with the judge, who gave us case management directions with hearing (for the presumption of death) three months away, in August. I also gave my power of attorney to a local lawyer as per the earlier direction.

All legal matters dealt with, it was gin and tonic time with CRG's Rob, who had some fine if bone-chilling experiences to share. A cerebral thinker, a taker of risks, an Arsenal fan, Rob had cheated death just like he had tracked, caught and brought to justice a kidnapper upon the release of his client's daughters. We became friends and from then on, with each Christmas card I received from Rob, I could not help but wonder about what must go on in the mind of one who operates in the cloak-and-dagger world.

On our last day in Quito the next morning, I was finally allowed to go out for a jog outside – with a body protection vest and a bodyguard on a bicycle toting a machine gun! It was the same arrangement when I took Moya to a mall for some last-minute shopping.

Once back at Whiteside and Knowles, Tony, Charles and Geoffrey could not believe what they were hearing. The job, of course, was only half finished. In August, our application for the presumption of death was rejected, and I instructed my lawyer in Ecuador, Jorge Paz, to appeal to the Quito Court of Appeal. There was no need for that, though, because in early September the bodies of John Buckley and Luiz Diaz were found. Moya's blood sent via the Red Cross to Quito for a DNA match came out conclusive, and a death certificate could now be obtained. A great relief for me.

Techint's lawyers summoned for a disclaimer from me and all of John's kin: Moya, Sister Carmel Buckley (John's sister and a nun), brother Joseph Buckley and his late brother Vincent Buckley's next of kin. Bia, her children and Elsa did likewise.

It called for a second trip to Quito. This time, the CRG reps were not present while Moya was accompanied by her aunt, Sister Carmel, based in New York. The first stop was to Techint's offices to finalise the release of the compensation monies. A long day of discussions produced the court application for a sealed order of the agreement from the judge, in Spanish, Portuguese and English. That night, at dinner with the families – I'd insisted on Luiz's family being there too – I briefed everyone on what had transpired.

There was a meltdown the following day when Techint passed us a CD of John's photographs and his belongings found with his body: spectacles, wallet, watch, belt… I needed all my skills gained as a psychiatric nurse and knowledge from matrimonial law to deal with Moya, Sister Carmel and Bia, who were using me as a punching bag for their grief. Only when legal matters were wrapped up, and monies had been wired by Techint to Whiteside and Knowles' account in England, was I able to breathe a little easy.

Moya, Bia and I then went to meet the funeral undertaker to select John's coffin. The same evening, we walked over to the mortuary, a single-storey bungalow by the hotel, to view John's remains and attend a service conducted by a Catholic Irish priest, in the presence of the Irish Counsel Mr Lacy and the British Vice-Consul, Ms Deeks. Ms Deeks handed me John's UK death certificate required to repatriate John's remains from Quito to Dublin and for me to administer his assets.

I can never forget my admiration for the way the priest in his words of remembrance brought to life the jungle. 'In this clear stream,' he said, 'the tigers, monkeys, wild boars and birds all came for water and to pay their respects to John and Luiz.' Next, all listened in rapt silence as Sister Carmel in her eulogy mentioned her pain at being excluded from her brother's death investigations, as well her misgivings about the early application for the presumption of death, which she felt was insensitive. For me, there was a further emotional episode when a distraught Mrs Diaz trembled and choked while thanking me before she left for their village in the mountains with her husband's remains.

Back in the hotel, Techint had kindly arranged for a clinical psychologist to provide counselling for the family members, the importance of which I realised later back in my room. While in the shower, I began to feel lightheaded, my heart raced and I grappled with a sudden, inexplicable fear of a violent attack... I desperately wished I'd had counselling too!

The next day, Sister Carmel flew back to New York. Techint organised a special dinner for the rest, attended by Ms Deeks and Mr Lacy, and a great night was had by all, with a rich exchange of bizarre stories of spies and assassins and drug barons...

There was no end to the bizarre, even on our final day in Quito. Elsa gave us oral notice that John's English will was invalid and that the forced heirship rules of Portugal would apply (overriding English law). A stunned Moya watched as I told Elsa to take a flying leap as I would deal with the will under English law and if she wanted to contest it, to issue declaratory proceedings in England. She did and that battle carried on until 2006, when I won my case and complied with the final wishes of the man who had put his trust in me to act as the executor of his will.

At the airport, the man's coffin made its way onto the tarmac. I signed for it and we made the journey home. *Così è la vita,* as the Italians say. Such is life. Four days later, John Buckley was buried in his village near Dublin. Never have I been more proud to have honoured my word.

TWENTY-THREE

# SEAT OF JUSTICE

My Ecuador feat gave me wings. I was reaping the benefits of being a dreamer, for that was all I had to spur me on in a fast-moving world. The social media juggernaut had begun with the introduction of Facebook in 2004, and I was now shooting emails to my legal assistants.

Thinking Clayton Bridge House was going to be my final home, I planned to turn it into a standout piece of construction. Without offending the historic architecture of nearby St Peter's Cathedral and Lancaster Castle, I wanted to attach a Louvre glasshouse to the ground floor of my little cottage hugging the canal. (I'd also applied for and obtained space for mooring a boat.) Geoffrey said obtaining planning permission and building control approval would be a challenge as my plan was likely to dramatically alter the external appearance of Clayton Bridge House, situated in a conservation area. I reminded my mentor of his advice from a long time ago: 'It's about whom you know, Phil.'

I got in touch with a friend from my Vietnam cycling trip who wielded authority on the English Heritage Board, London. I also had a contact I coached at badminton in the planning department who worked closely with the Canal Trustees Board, whom I needed to convince that my renovation work would not compromise the canal's structure or landscape. From then onwards, it was a waiting game for the actualisation of my stratagem.

2004 was a particularly good year for films, in my judgement. Music and films have always elicited strong emotions from me, and I often connect emotionally to the characters and situations in films, music or song lyrics, not unlike my father, whose passion included Indian music and films, other than his deep love for Hollywood's timeless productions and larger-than-life personalities. Those early trips from our Prang Besar Estate to the cinemas in Kuala Lumpur were pure euphoric stimuli, including the unfailing post-film discussion in the car as we made the long journey back, oblivious to bumps and unlit roads. Never was the memory stronger than in 2004, with two biopics that would've satiated Papa's eclectic taste.

I flew to Cannes to watch Che Guevara's *The Motorcycle Diaries* competing for the Palme d'Or award at the Festival de Cannes. The visuals evoked visceral memories of Papa jumping on his Norton or AJS for his daily trek across the vast estate to deal with his own encounters with injustice and exploitation... factors that contributed to his political and social awakening, causing his defiant spirit to reign even if it meant reprimands and demotion. I missed my father even more while watching Leonardo DiCaprio in *The Aviator* embody the complexities of Hollywood's conqueror and my father's idol, Howard Hughes. I suspect it was Papa's fascination with the abundantly rich and talented film and aeroplane maker that provided him with the gusto to hire an aeroplane to take us on a joyride on the same day that Kuala Lumpur's Subang International Airport was officially opened by the Malaysian king in 1965. It must have been at great expense. I don't know how he managed it on his salary – Papa made things happen! The whole family flew over parts of Kajang, Prang Besar Estate and Limau Manis... My intrepid energy for travels likely began on that Cessna. It would not be an exaggeration to say I have spent a large part of my earnings on jet-setting. Flying into the Nice Côte d'Azur Airport in the morning to get into Monte Carlo for the Monaco Grand Prix and returning home the same night in time to watch its coverage on the BBC, and to Nice again the following week to take in the Cannes Film Festival, wasn't unusual.

Nothing, therefore, could stop me from accepting my eighty-five-year-old client Mrs Maria Dimitriou's offer to stay with her delightful family during the historic Athens Olympics. The birthplace of the Olympics was hosting it for the first time in 2004 since the inaugural games in 1896, and there I was in Athenai, the City of the Violet Crown, wearing my prized Sydney 2000 lanyard around my neck. Weeks after the Athens Olympics, I had the opportunity to return to Barcelona, the venue of my first Olympics back in 1992. I took the overland airport train to Barcelona Sants main central station on my way to El Clot to visit a Spanish friend whom I was mentoring in commercial English and English Law. The train was full. I had to stand managing my satchel, a holdall and a bag slung across my body. Lurking on either side of me were three burly eastern European-looking men. Sensing something amiss when one made a suspiciously abrupt exit, I felt my bag and established in a cold sweat that my wallet, which also contained my passport, was missing. At that moment, the other two were leaving the carriage. I instinctively grabbed the waist of the hulking figure closer to me who wriggled and shouted in a language that wasn't Spanish, causing his accomplice to turn and also throw a volley of threats I couldn't make out. As foolish as my action might have been, I refused to release my grip. The ensuing three-way tussle (caught on CCTV cameras) caused enough commotion for the train to remain stationary. When the door opened, the guy who'd escaped first rushed in and flung my wallet at me, and all three scooted up the escalator where they were caught.

The shock remained for quite a while, even as I was being smothered by a lot of Spanish affection from fellow passengers, yet I remained very aware of how my bravado could have ended my life if my assailants had resorted to weapons. The incident, however, had no deterrent effect on my future travels.

The following month, I was in Kerala to purchase an apartment in the Kowdiar neighbourhood of Trivandrum. Mummy had just returned from her pilgrimage to Israel, a lifelong dream, and was doubly delighted as she saw the investment as my potential retirement home. We had planned to celebrate Christmas with my brother Tom in Sydney but were informed at short notice he could not accommodate us. What a blessing that turned out to be! Cancelling our Sydney tickets, I made quick arrangements to take my mother to Malaysia via Singapore as she had not travelled around the country properly from the time she left Malaysia in 1969.

There was no happy Christmas when on the day after Christmas Day, 26th December 2004, the Indian Ocean churned out a massive tsunami, killing hundreds of thousands of people and causing immeasurable damage to many coastal regions in Asia, including Kerala's fishing communities. It was all over the news on every media platform. When we flew out of Kerala two days later, the Internet, in particular, was afloat with footage of the lives, livelihoods and hopes of so many nationals being lost, resulting in a mammoth emotional aftermath.

A train from Changi Airport took us across the border into Johor Baru, where we began our adventure with a brand-new Proton Saga courtesy of Hertz Car Hire. I was fifty-two and my mother seventy-six, yet I became her little boy all over again, eager to make up for lost years. 'We're going to take the South China Sea coastal road right up to the Thai border then travel all the way south to Johor again. This way, we cover all the states, and you can never say you've not seen Malaya, okay?'

'Just like Papa.' Mummy grinned.

With her innate sociability and natural curiosity, my mother made an excellent travel partner. During the long hours cocooned in the car, I opened my heart out to her and she did a lot of laughing and a little chiding, tearing and consoling as we experienced my country of birth to our hearts' content, and I discovered my Malaysian *Lah* never left me! We took what came our way, cutting across the South China Sea, old *kopitiam* towns, paddy fields, fishing villages, rainforests; rolled into hotels and motels; and, like all Indians, "adjusted". That extraordinary bonding opportunity gives me immense solace to this day.

It was so different to the time when in the following year I finally took Dave and Jean Ashcroft for their first Kerala experience (I'd already given them the Malaya tour back in the '90s). Despite warnings and years of them revelling in my stories, it was still a shock for them to see animals road-crossing freely, vehicles speeding from the wrong side of the road or me climbing a coconut tree, drinking fresh toddy with local fishermen or using my fingers to scoop up boiled tapioca to enjoy with a spicy Keralan fish curry. I in turn was puzzled by one incident. A ragged young girl lugging a baby in a dirty cloth pouch slung around her frail body approached us outside a restaurant. I handed her ten rupees, a sizeable amount. Jean too reached into her Mulberry handbag and took out a hundred-rupee note. The shocked girl grabbed the money, turned on her heel and sped away, leaving Jean to remark loudly, 'A thank you would be very nice, young lady!'

I was troubled. Had Kipling witnessed the same to write, *Oh, East is East, and West is West, and never the twain shall meet*? I kept my counsel then, and also through Dave and Jean's "the British built the railways, set up the civil service" rhetoric, knowing full well the futility of arguing against skewed imperial history. It was much the same with Geoffrey the time we were at the London Cenotaph War Memorial when he swore at some Japanese tourists taking pictures. His ageing eyes flashed the same anger I saw the times he recounted his World War Two sufferings – reason why he would never revisit Malaysia with me. Although I was, by then, frequently testing Geoffrey over our conflicting ideologies, I could see he was in no state to spare a thought for the Western world's long history of discrimination and virulent attacks against Asia, going back to the "yellow peril" days, chiefly Britain's commercial policies against Japan's escalating trade and political influence in Africa, to keep it exclusively the white man's paradise. The thought of a power shift to Asia was as unbearable then as it is now, as can be seen from the onslaught of media attacks on China's rise and India's policies. China is aggressively equated to tyranny and lack of democracy: by the US that has materially and politically supported anti-democratic dictatorships and murderous coup-d'état, and in Vietnam alone has hundreds of substantiated claims of massacres, murder, torture and rape; as well as the UK, who from being a nation steadfastly against the Vietnam War became the US's poodle, contributing to war crimes such as in Afghanistan and Iraq that caused the deaths of hundreds of thousands of civilians and servicemen… besides having ninety-one hereditary law lords sitting in the House of Lords by their "right of birth"!

In 2006, at age fifty-four, I was recommended to join the judiciary and undertook to shadow a High Court judge in Liverpool as part of my training. Tony and Charles were pleased, although my leaving was going to considerably impact Whiteside and Knowles' income stakes. Geoffrey being Geoffrey said I'd be wasted on the bench with my easy rapport with clients and readiness to venture into different areas of the law, which in his book enhanced the firm's reputation.

My nomination to become a judge was an undeniably proud moment; my planning permission for Clayton Bridge House came through; and a comfortable, hobnobbing future beckoned. Notwithstanding, I remained restless in mind and spirit, with a feeling of coasting along without purpose. That felt strange because other than when it came to badminton, I rarely functioned with direction. I don't think I've ever had ambition, nothing was planned, there was no road map; just doing dicey, unpredictable, occasionally dangerous things on impulse. It was how I always operated… the way I went into banking or law, it was all the water finding its level.

An intuitive feel, certainly not acuity, made me look into my soul. Although I did not have it all mapped out, my retirement plans did not feature ambling into the twilight of quiet reflection, living an easy, harmonious existence. I failed to convince myself England was where I wanted to spend my post-retirement years.

I might have arrived in the country during a gloomy decade hammered by economic, political and social strife with long periods of violence and discontent, yet, there was idealism, liberalism and tolerance aplenty. In that old England of simple pleasures and lasting memories, shops and shopping in cobbled streets were unique, gifts arrived in cardboard boxes with strings and sealing wax, clothes could be altered and just about anything repaired. In the northwest of England, tuning in to *Coronation Street* was second nature, and I too watched *Corrie* avidly for years, still do on occasion, to the amusement of English friends, but none can deny how well the series depicts the essence of the north. It's a time warp I wouldn't mind returning to – when England was more welcoming and safer, qualities I feel began eroding in the divisive Thatcher era.

I was increasingly aware my spirit was being suppressed – as though I'd exhausted everything I'd come to accomplish in a country that had likely extracted the best out of me. Frustration and irritation were my foremost emotions. The charade needed to end. I wanted a release from the need to act, speak, behave in conformity with English ways... redemption for the fact I'd allowed my Eastern manners to be appropriated in the name of assimilation, of getting on with it.

I dropped out of my training to become a judge and abandoned my intended renovation of Clayton Bridge House to focus on my transition plans. As the Kop anthem goes, as John Lennon did when he crossed over the Pond to start all over, I was prepared to *walk through the storm* until I found a home converging the Western lifestyle I'd become used to with the growing Eastern spirituality tugging at my heartstrings as I approached my sixth decade.

Packing off to the Continent felt like a logical progression. I'd become too anglicised in my ways to embrace chaotic India, and it was easy to edge out a return to my country of birth, which had long distanced itself from its meritocratic past. I was appalled to follow the news of my Indian brothers and sisters in Malaysia being fired with tear gas and water cannons for taking to the streets to protest against racial and religious discrimination. Watching thousands defy a police ban to raise an international spectacle with the November 2007 rally, I could not help but reflect on my father's judgement to ship his family back to India after the 1969 riots.

For months, I made trip after trip to explore different parts of Europe, viewing properties and communes from Wengen in Switzerland and San Remo in the South of France to parts of Italy. I soon realised my heart was drawn to Italy. Its Renaissance heritage and architecture, the Latino temperament of its people (not unlike the Dravidians), healthy cuisine, sartorial elegance and dolce vita outlook to life integrated to make the hybrid environment I was searching for. Narrowing my search to northern Italy, I went on a sweeping property hunt in the Dolomites and Chianti.

'You're looking in the wrong places, Phil. I suggest you check out Garfagnana. I'm not just saying that because my family comes from there; I have a feeling you will like Garfagnana.' It was my client and friend Bruno Brucciani who said that when I enlisted his help. As I took his suggestion to heart, I recalled Bruno telling me a long time ago how his great-grandfather had done the ancient Via Francigena pilgrimage route – Rome to Canterbury – from his village in Barga, Tuscany to escape the 1920s Italian famine. That ignited something in me.

Bruno's assessment was absolutely correct. The valley of Garfagnana in the Lucca province appealed most to my lust for the outdoors and my shifting tide towards a simpler, decluttered life. The real search began in remote Garfagnana's mountainous, forested terrain dotted by gushing rivers and attractive little villages. For a house that spoke to my soul.

As the hunt was going on, I found the perfect soulmate to take with me on the next phase of my life. I'd just landed at Liverpool John Lennon Airport from Pisa one day to find an SMS from my friend Natalie asking if I could accompany her to view a Labrador puppy she'd booked with a pedigree breeder in Chorley. They were eight female and one male shimmering black beauties… such a precious moment it was. Natalie chose her Bella and I, just like that, decided to get the James Dean of the brood for myself.

'You sure, Phil? How're you going to manage him working full time?' my concerned friend wanted to know. I told her I'd take my baby to the office with me. And that was how in 2007 George became my soul partner for the next fourteen years.

I don't think my friends believed I could stick with a puppy for long; in fact, someone said outright, 'He's not a Christmas present, you know,' insinuating I'd ditch George like an unwanted Christmas gift. Couldn't blame them, could I? Me prancing around in my Jermyn Street suits and Crockett & Jones brogue shoes, taking off on frequent travels, always out and about with lady friends, running, playing sport and of course there was my work! Also, my Clayton Bridge House was immaculately furnished with expensive carpets and state-of-the-art furnishings; not at all conducive to training a puppy.

I went about like the excited new parent investing in nursery furniture and gear, only to find I couldn't bear to hear Georgie's distressing baby whines from his crate and bedding placed outside my bedroom. I got rid of both and from then on, he'd only sleep in my bed, would poop and pee just about everywhere in my pristine house until he was potty-trained, leaving me exhausted and exasperated but strangely never losing my patience. How could I when he gazed at me like I meant the whole world to him? Our worlds entangled. It wasn't about proving anyone wrong; I was well and truly smitten. George would become the greatest love of my life.

With George came stability and I carried the responsibility of parenting him very seriously. He would come on my morning runs, to all my health and recreational clubs, have a free run of my office (became Whiteside and Knowles's mascot), attend court, have meals in all types of establishments, climb mountains, trek forests, camp in the wilds and swim in the sea, lakes and rivers... and charm everyone, so it wasn't difficult to find a willing puppy-sitter anytime I needed to travel without him. When he was older, I got George a travel passport and bought a new VW Touareg to travel with him all over England and Europe. It wasn't long before Phil George came to be known as Phil & George.

It was on a journey to Pisa Airport with my estate agent that a call came about a property in the village of San Romano di Garfagnana. I wasn't in the mood to turn back, what with a throbbing headache after spending an entire weekend viewing a dozen properties up and down hilly, wooded terrains, none of which took my fancy. Was I grateful to have said a reluctant yes when the agent pleaded for "one final viewing, please"!

San Romano was a craggy settlement with a maze of centuries-old stone buildings oozing Etruscan period mystery at every turn. Standing on the edge of a winding hill on Via San Rocco was a three-level stone building so derelict and humdrum that the agent cast me an embarrassed glance. 'Unoccupied for over fifty years,' she apologised. The afternoon sun beating down on us, we took in the bleak house.

Its surrounding curtilage was unruly, making it treacherous to get into the property. Trickling down from the mountain was a little stream separating the house from its overgrown terraced gardens, and we could just about make out a rickety wooden bridge linking the two. The roof had completely collapsed and most parts of the interior were inaccessible, full of dry rot, fallen beams and withered floorboards.

All that became a blur when I set eyes on what unfolded from the foot of the rambling pile nourished by brilliant sunlight. There spread the heart of the village, the baroque church of San Romano Martire and its tall campanile ready to toll. Beyond lay layers of mountains and an endless sky looking down on the mid-Serchio Valley tucked at the feet of the white marble-covered Apuan Alps converging with the Apennine Ridge. A real treasure of the gods! My agent's words added to the magic of the moment when she said the property had access to the village of Verrucole where stood the Fortezza Verrucole, the fortress considered the most important medieval testimony of the Garfagnana valley. It was an instant pull at my heartstrings and I surrendered. What an environment for George to grow up in! I could already see him having the time of his life. There and then, I offered the full asking price to the utter disbelief of my agent. For me, it felt like the beginning of a pilgrimage.

The importance of finding home, my decision to search for it in Italy, or why I wanted to completely uproot myself when I could have invested in a vacation home in one of Italy's many elite communes was confounding to most of my English friends. To make them understand, I'd have had to go back about four decades. *Philip thought of Italy, and the whole situation was saved.* Even I hadn't realised how deeply I'd been seduced by that one sentence from my choice of senior Cambridge literature in 1969, E.M. Forster's *Where Angels Fear to Tread*. At seventeen, the line struck me immediately for the sole reason it had my name in it. I was otherwise totally indifferent to the author's or the book's deep, subversive nature. Its impact would only return more meaningfully on my first trip to Italy in the late '70s while travelling with an antiquated rucksack containing a ridge tent, living on bread, cheese and cheap red wine so I could afford just one night in a crumbling villa with stucco walls the colour of roses and a room with a view… of winding terraces of grapes and olives, overlooking the ancient walled town of Lucca. How could I have imagined I'd be a permanent resident of the same province, growing to love it as one with an ancestral connection might?

Ray and Ann understood, although they had their concerns, particularly about me undertaking such a restoration task at retirement age. When I brought them for a visit to my San Romano house for their valued opinions, it was with my Italian lawyer, Carlo Bottino, and Stefano Monti, my architect and consulting engineer. Everyone worried about the funds and engineering marvel required to turn the ruinous former agricultural building into something hospitable – for about 150 years, generations of farmers had used it to make wine, store their harvest or keep their animals.

As I was preparing my exit strategy, the practice of law in England was transforming. A legal system once regarded as the best in the world was in sad decline, alongside so much of England, where substance seemed to be taking a back seat. Whiteside and Knowles kept striving to keep the firm true to its principles and we continued to grow. In an increasingly cost-cutting, fee-worshipping environment, we remained dependent on our staff to build and retain customer loyalty and continued to provide service with a personal touch. To give an example, thanks to Tony's characteristic panache, our Christmas cards were personally designed and I hand-delivered Fortnum & Mason hampers to our elderly clients, often staying on for a cup of tea.

I truly believe I've had a career with many highlights because I uncompromisingly adhered to the Whiteside and Knowles culture of providing service with integrity and vision. Our firm ran on traditional lines and I went to lengths to understand clients' emotions and manage their expectations; to make them feel completely safe in my hands because of the all-important disclosure element crucial for judicial persuasion. I kept my client engagements frequent and explicit, reassuring them at each step of the way, often drawing diagrams to explain the legal process, legal precedents and so forth as opposed to hitting them with a sixteen-page "client care letter" containing overwhelming legal jargon. With the freedom to operate on my terms, I was constantly evolving and growing, therefore never having reason to seek pastures greener.

Whiteside and Knowles did not hit a sticky patch until after Geoffrey Knowles's demise. Geoffrey was admitted to a home in Morecambe with Alzheimer's while Joan continued to live in their house under the watch of a caregiver who came on weekdays. I visited as frequently as I could, each visit getting more painful as I watched them slipping away. The reversed dynamic, where I was now taking charge of them, was particularly difficult to come to terms with – Geoffrey's confusion and memory loss, and Joan's depression and erratic behaviour at being wheelchair-bound and living alone.

Geoffrey remained lucid on most of my visits, and I kept our old routine of sharing all the goings-on in my life, but our conversations became increasingly one-way as he tired easily and couldn't retain information. That he was listless in the face of my Italian adventures was most telling. There were no longer our high-spirited arguments and reasoning; instead, I spent a lot of time reassuring him and keeping him upbeat. For all his lethargy and absent-mindedness, Geoffrey's eyes lit up and his old exuberance lingered every time I took George or my girlfriends with me.

On a Saturday evening in April 2008, I received a call from Clive Knowles to say his mother had passed away alone and that I was the last person to have spent time with her. Upon the doctor's advice, we kept the news from Geoffrey. The following week, we went ahead with the funeral minus Geoffrey and their daughter, Janet, who could not make it from Australia.

A little over two months later, Geoffrey too left us. I felt as orphaned as Clive and Janet. At the time, I was in Kerala caring for my unwell mother and had to miss the funeral of the father figure with whom I'd spent more time and shared more bonding moments than with my biological father. Mummy and I said special prayers for Geoffrey and, between tears, my mother wondered if he might meet Papa beyond the pearly gates. I didn't know the answer to that one, but I knew for certain Geoffrey had a brother awaiting him.

As befitting his stature, Geoffrey Knowles was given a grand send-off by Lancaster and Morecambe folk. Janet Knowles gave the eulogy and a poem was read by Tony.

The "second son" takes this opportunity to eulogise Geoffrey here:

> When I came to Geoffrey Knowles a ready-made child of eighteen, I instantly noticed the gleam, rather naughty twinkle, in his eye at the prospect of shaping this boy in his mould. He had his plans. I had mine. And yet, how we intertwined our journeys for the many memories we made and escapades we had! We need no reminding of Geoffrey's abundant virtues; there cannot be anyone who knew him that doesn't know of them. I'll also spare our naughty encounters in respect of those with gentle minds. Nevertheless, I want to, and can, share this one shenanigan now that Geoffrey is out of reach of the laws of the earth. After an important Ashes cricket test match between Australia and England at Old Trafford, we'd been caught on camera exceeding the 70mph limit. We were unfortunate to have been filmed that time. Both Geoffrey and I were fast drivers and often inter-changed during long journeys, but we certainly had an inkling as to who had been the offender that time. Knowing there was a possibility of disqualification under the court's discretion rule for speeding, Geoffrey, using the reasonable doubt criminal law criteria, bamboozled the Lancaster police station staffed by many familiar faces who held him in esteem by saying the blurred CCTV image of the

driver behind my Golf GTI could not be established and therefore no summons could be issued. I recall like yesterday that triumphant glint in his blue eyes as we walked out of the station after no charges were laid, following his brilliant charade for the police and the Crown Prosecution Service, putting on the line his formidable reputation in Lancaster and Morecambe. But that's the Geoffrey we all know.

What is not as well known is that Geoffrey had put his life on the line for this beloved country of his. As a young article working for his father at their family firm, he and his twin, Donald Knowles, were conscripted into the army during World War 2 to help Britain protect Singapore from falling. As their ship *The Empress* approached the shores of the island nation, it was bombed by a Japanese aircraft and, in Geoffrey's words, he caught his first glimpse of Singapore while bobbing in the South China Sea. Their nightmare had just begun. The brothers, along with many other youngsters, were picked up by the Australian frigate *Jarrah*, which was also bombed, after which the young men were arrested, taken to the Changi prison and from there frog-marched to the Siam death railway. In his book *The Railway Man*, Eric Lomax called the Siam-Burma railway "the worst civil engineering disaster in history". Geoffrey couldn't agree more – it was there he suffered for three years until the Japanese surrendered. The twins were stationed in different camps and the only time they were together was the few weeks when Donald fell severely ill and was sent to Geoffrey to be nursed back to health. I leave it to you to imagine the pain Geoffrey experienced next when a US aircraft in friendly fire dropped a bomb, killing Donald in his camp. News only reached Geoffrey some weeks later.

On his return voyage to England, Geoffrey's heart was broken another time to find out his fiancée, thinking he was dead, had married an American captain. The ring was returned to him with one final tea dance with his lady love before saying goodbye forever. It was on the back of such sorrow that Geoffrey returned to Morecambe to rejoin the family business… bearing a pain that never left him. Nevertheless, Geoffrey wasn't one to allow suffering and demoralisation to get the better of him. If anything, from the time I first knew him, I only saw, and benefitted from, his immense propensity for kindness, loving and living the good life. Geoffrey Knowles might have had his nightmares in the East, yet his big heart always rose to shelter me from the nightmares of the West. I have not known a braver heart in England than this man I hold most dear to my heart.

## TWENTY-FOUR

# HOME

My strongest association with England died with Geoffrey. During that period of reckoning, it dawned on me I had never felt a sense of belonging to England.

It came on the heels of the 2008 financial crisis when I lost a lot of money and my plans for my San Romano house had to wait, also because the cost of building materials had shot up. Yet, never once did I regret my investment; my heart in fact was already longing to be surrounded by all things Italian. I targeted construction work to begin in 2009 with the aim of moving in after my retirement in 2012.

From the time he was a few months old, I began taking George running with me on the canal towpaths, the Trough of Bowland and Morecambe Promenade. Our absolute favourite times, though, were being up in the core of the Bowland Fells, running, walking through fields and valleys; fleeing from angry bulls on Nicky Nook; trekking, scrambling through unmarked tracks, woods or streams all the way to Littledale, a spectacular haven that made John Ruskin write, *I do not know in all my country, still less France or Italy, a place more naturally divine or a more priceless possession of the true Holy Land…* Two things were assured: a good time was had by the boys, and both would be absolutely bushed from their wanderings by the time they got back to the car by the cattle grid near Little Cragg. I loved introducing this part of my world to George as I'd spent decades exploring every nook and cranny by myself without the benefit of Wainwright's Fell maps covering the Lake District.

George was a handsome boy of two, sturdy and full of boundless energy when I started conditioning him for the 1,350-mile road journey from Lancaster to San Romano, which we would do countless times over the next few years. For each trip, I prepared George's food using a bespoke recipe book for dogs and packed his meals in three Tupperware containers. Similarly, my sandwiches, pies, rice and curry would go into an Indian tiffin holder, along with coffee in an aluminium thermos flask and George's water with his two blue and orange Alessi bowls. I certainly took food preparation as seriously as I did ensuring my Golf GTI was always serviced and road-ready, as the trip averaged thirty-two hours over two days, with one layover in the car.

We hit the M6 motorway at either 5 am or 10 pm depending on the timings of the Chunnel ferry crossing from Folkestone or Dover respectively taking around six hours without any stops. I'd refuel my tank, go on a toilet break, take George for a walk around the woods nearby, then tuck into our food. Once on the ferry, I'd settle George in the car before going upstairs to the passengers' cabin as required, for the ninety minutes' crossing to Calais. Following very minimal border checks in Calais, I would drive for around six more hours before the next break at whichever town or city on the way along the four routes I could take. If I took the scenic South of France route, it was Reims in the Loire Valley, or if it was via Brussels, which offered three options, it would be anywhere in Germany before entering Italy via Austria or Switzerland. George and I travelled extensively on each route, learning, exploring and enjoying the experiences, whether driving along the Ligurian Sea or parked at motorway service stations among large HGVs criss-crossing the Continent. We slept in the car, me in my sleeping bag with the recliner on full setting, George in his, content in the back seat.

The routine would continue: up at 4 am, walk George, shower and change clothes, with my mate outside tied up by his red lead, with stylish blue collar and trademark bright pink Liberty scarf. We often shared a McDonald's breakfast before getting into the GTI to head down the Italian Riviera to Genoa, then La Spezia for the next brief break. The final lap to San Romano via Aulla, a historic little village linked to the Via Francigena pilgrimage road, was a pleasantly circuitous hour-and-a-half drive.

In the three years of construction work, George and I would check into a pre-booked dog-friendly Bed and Breakfast by a ranch near Villetta, the next village downhill from San Romano di Garfagnana. We went running first thing in the morning after George had said his hellos to the horses, then set about overseeing building works. George was part of the whole process. He came to choose building materials at places recommended by my architect and builder: windows and doors from Estree in Filicaia, steel and iron from SRL in Pontecosi, local chestnut and other wood from Bertoncini and stones, sand and cement from Matinelle, both in Camporgiano.

My soul cried each time I had to leave San Romano, such was its hypnotic hold over me. It became harder and harder to settle back into life in England. George and I became so familiar with our home-to-home routines and routes… and San Romano folk began to identify with the *Indiano avvocato* and his loyal wingman. George found his own mate too when Sciusci, the cat belonging to Debora, a kind primary schoolteacher who lived on the upper terrace of my house, came nosing into our unfinished house. It was strange to see the two hit it off straight away – nothing cats and dogs about them at all.

In 2012, I rang in my sixtieth birthday with George, contemplating my journey going forward with the potential psychological impact of retirement as I wasn't just leaving my job, I was leaving England altogether. After forty-two years.

On the eve of my birthday, George and I trekked up Helvellyn via Striding Edge, where we cooked and snuggled inside our tent, heavy spring fog and incessant drizzle clamping us in. I told George how the misty night reminded me of the time he strayed away from me along the River Lune; how scared I was when I didn't find him waiting outside Clayton Bridge House like other times he'd done the same; how for hours I tore around shouting his name; and our absolute joy at that moment he smashed through the mist somewhere along the viaduct bridge straight into my arms. We'd had many conversations, George and I, so much so that I'm confident I'd be able to give a TED talk to an audience of canines!

That same year, I formed a real estate company called HIT (House in Tuscany), specialising in the iconic Cinque Terre perched idyllically on the Italian Riviera, with my English friend Geoff Dixon. Geoff operated mainly from Morecambe but we had satellite offices in Lucca, about thirty miles from my village. After years of scouring Tuscany, looking at hundreds of houses in various shapes and styles, and then being so deeply engaged with the transformation of my San Romano home, I became quite the connoisseur of buildings – in any case, I've always taken great pleasure in admiring buildings, their forms, locations, materials used, designs, colours, etc., which was what prompted me to explore a new career, albeit a short-lived one.

Taking advantage of my position, I invested a part of my pension funds and savings in a house on a cliff with a vineyard overlooking the Ligurian Sea and the colourful town of Riomaggiore, possibly in the best location in Cinque Terre. I eventually lost the stunning property to trickery… you know what happens when a lawyer gets tricked. I launched a meticulous legal offensive, driving my Italian lawyers all the way despite not being familiar with Italian law or the language, to eventually recover my investment.

Friends find my whimsical spirit exasperating, particularly when juxtaposed with my legal rationality and efficiency, but that has been my life – never smothered by pastels or dictated by normality; neither do I moan nor harbour regrets – not for me the "what if I'd taken precautions, what if I'd been more guarded…"

2012 was also the period when Whiteside and Knowles began undergoing changes from the time Charles proposed a merger of our firm with Jobling and Knape (J&K) where his wife worked. As both Tony and I were winding down and had long stopped singing from the same hymn sheet with Charles, we did not object. I only realised what a big disservice we'd done to Geoffrey the moment Craig Hollingdrake and Ian Gee (partners of J&K) came to inspect our office. The disdain on Craig's face upon seeing George under my desk was the first red flag of impending conflicts and confrontations. The merger was concluded in the summer and Whiteside and Knowles became JWK Solicitors. Being head of civil litigation, I moved to our office in Fenton Street, Lancaster, while Tony and Charles, who focused on general legal matters, stayed on in Morecambe.

JWK Solicitors was about aggressive marketing, time recording and cash flow projection. Geoffrey would've boxed my ears for letting it happen! Things quickly came to a head between me and Hollingdrake, who was also the managing and financial director, when he requested me to transfer money from a client's account into the company account without the client's authority. Keeping to the Whiteside and Knowles template, I was having nothing of it. My refusal stoked Hollingdrake's anger and polite language went out of the window... a backhand flip with my favourite Yonex racket would not have gone amiss. From then on it was downhill, but I did not care for the firm's new direction. It had already lost its soul. Foremost in my mind was to tolerate whatever came my way since there was only a year to go before my retirement. In accordance with the agreement, my retirement was in July 2013, one year after the merger. I was offered a position as ambassador for the firm on a yearly contract for three years after retirement, which I accepted.

Around 200 colleagues, peers, staff and friends attended my retirement party, where Tony made a generous speech outlining my journey from the time I began as a shy articled clerk to becoming an inseparable member of Whiteside and Knowles; about my constant travels, man about town dalliances, readiness to embrace change and new ideas... I had no idea then that the firm, started in 1888, only had another five years of shelf life.

I put Clayton Bridge House on the market and began the months-long process of giving away stuff to charities, transferring my belongings to my new house bit by bit and bidding farewell to friends. The unspoken consensus among my English network was that I had "made it" and ought just to be grateful. Not ruffle their polite society by reasoning with them as to why they are distrusted by other nationalities or how their perception of Britannia ruling the waves is about as flawed as their notion of superiority.

The times, they were certainly a-changin'. For one who had forged his path through hard work and considerable ingenuity, also inheriting Papa's hindsight, I could see that the more the face of the English nation changed, the more pervasive the intolerance throughout its society. A consolation for me by then was being armed with the knowledge to counteract such tendencies of "unintentional" aggressors used to getting away with their "stance" or "joke" …unlike decades ago at Central Pier's Miami Bowl nightclub where I served beer for pocket money. 'Hey Sambo! What're you doing here?' Britain's famous comedian Bernard Manning hollered from the stage, putting the spotlight squarely on me as the packed audience roared. I could tell it was something demeaning from the stony reactions of Geoffrey and my company of friends at a nearby table.

'Slang for someone of colour. Never mind it, lad…' a red-faced Geoffrey explained to me in a manner rather circumspect. The fact is, I'd spent too long in England never minding.

For that reason, I wasn't interested in having a foot in two camps. I sold off not just Clayton Bridge House but also my apartment in Kerala. It had to be a clean break. That I did it on my own terms, and before the messy Brexit bent on making life even more difficult for "outsiders", gives me a great degree of comfort.

Naïve and excited, I'd arrived in England with great expectations, thinking the country was all about great music, great football, great culture and a place that mooted great things, whose leaders set the agenda for the rest of the world. It was, for the most part, all that, which was why for a long period of time, I excused the innuendoes of class and ethnic stratification I encountered... until I set about critically exploring England's troublesome history, and that of Europe's. I also firmly believed English institutions – namely education, media, legal and government – were the best in the world, only to find they could also be the very agents perpetuating discrimination and division. Or worse, protecting white supremacy.

If in 1970 my father, KP George, was my only family member in Malaysia to see me off to England, in December 2013, when I left England for Italy, George was my only family to make the journey with me. It wouldn't be an overstatement to say I was physically fit and agile at sixty-one; I certainly possessed the same fire as I did at eighteen when I left Malaysia. And in George I had a sturdy, reliable co-traveller. If Malaysia provided for twenty pounds in my pocket as I left her, big money at the time, England afforded me enough for a comfortable retirement in Europe's dolce vita. George and I departed Lancaster on a grey morning, with Christmas just around the corner. George on the front passenger seat, belt fastened, a festive red scarf around his neck, we set off to Dover in a large Ford Transit van piled with our final belongings. To our new home, for a new life, a better match.

The dizzying array of travellers and freight vehicles freely passing through the English Channel to and from the Continent (under the 1992 Maastricht Treaty pre-

Brexit days) were greeted by the welcoming sight of Christmas lights. We alighted to stretch our limbs and fill our stomachs by the busy seaport's great white cliffs. Dawdling in Dover, thinking over my transition, I knew the die was cast: there was no turning back.

My departure coincided with the start of Brexit dominating national debate and the then Home Secretary Teresa May's Home Office vans pasted with the words *Go Home* going around the UK creating deliberate fear and allowing racial hatred to flourish. An act that would've immediately prompted my father to say, *When India said the same to the British as it fought for independence, they ripped the country into two, leaving both sides crippled.*

At the time, it didn't look like Britain might vote for independence from Europe... but if in the unlikely event it did, would it cripple not just trade and freedom of movement but also the United Kingdom's vaunted unitedness with Scotland, Wales and Northern Ireland? This was the thought running through my mind looking across the Channel, readying for my own Brexit.

Today, when I look at the upheavals caused by Brexit – the misgovernance by shifty politicians, a right-wing press relentlessly stoking an already divided, ill-informed country, a government brazenly hostile towards foreigners (Clause 9 under the Nationality and Borders Bill containing deprivation powers affecting minorities), I bear no regret for leaving behind the elite lifestyle England would've afforded me.

It was in complete excitement that I left my first country in 1970. Leaving my second country after four decades, there was only a latent sense of weariness. If anything, the moment felt like shaking hands with a business partner once a difficult deal had come to a mutually beneficial end. By every measure, as much as I contributed to it, England shaped my thinking, afforded me creature comforts and its people accepted me into the fold. Importantly, England provided me with the liberty and opportunity to observe, question and challenge received wisdom from any source; to look beyond the narrow confines of identity and stake my claim wherever I went. What better illustration of this than an invitation to Royal Ascot? In the summer of 2005, I'd attended the races with a titled lady friend, dressed in my morning suit, top hat to boot, for I could only match up to England's elite with their dress code, not their language or attitudes. Never mind. This member of the hoi polloi from Kajang munching on Cadbury's Whole Nut chocolate (in 1970), reading *This station* (London Euston) *was opened by Her Majesty The Queen* found himself at the heart of the club that controlled England's realm, cheering Queen Elizabeth II as she did that special wave for her torrent of buoyant northern subjects. Casting my eye over it all now, I remain fond of England for the solid friends, lessons and memories it has provided me in abundance, and my Eastern values will not allow me to judge the masses of the island for the vices of its elite class of rulers.

In that spirit, when George and I converged at England's busiest trade route, still labouring in heavy traffic from across the country and the Continent, I left without a backward glance, aware of a lump in my throat and a deep sensation in my heart. Yet acutely committed to the adventure ahead. If I had my racket to navigate England, for Italy, I carried with me the realisation I was no longer skydiving without a parachute.

After two days of driving through countries with an Italian cultural origin – France, Belgium, the Netherlands, Germany and Switzerland – halting by lakes and sleeping in the cabin of the van, we entered Italy via Lake Como in Milan. We arrived at San Romano with the sun above our heads, to snow-clad mountains, a light bluster, the sky a brilliant Argentinean blue.

It was Christmas Eve, my fridge was empty, and as soon as the unloading was done, George and I hit the local supermarket a short drive away in Gallicano that flat put to shame Lancaster's and Morecambe's supermarket chains with just its selection of bread, cheeses, olive oils, and wine, of course. To think Italy's ubiquitous piazzas, the heart of Italian society "where history, architecture, and social relations become one" offered even better selections, as I already knew, my house being right off *il corso* (high street) and round the bend to the lovely Piazza Pelliccioni, San Romano's open-air common living room, its very soul, its venue to be. It was where the church congregation turned up on Sundays and other religious occasions and where fairs, pop-up markets and concerts took place at any time of the year.

Using wood I'd collected on my last visit to the house, I started a bountiful fire and settled down with George to our first Italian Christmas. No noise, surrounded by mountains and wilderness, it remains my most solitary, tranquil, almost medieval-level Christmas ever.

The scene was set for the months to come: there was no heating yet, so I had to commit much time and energy to foraging, collecting, chopping, stacking up piles of wood for the wood burner, which was the main source of heating and hot water to withstand San Romano's highland winter conditions in my large, three-level house, to which I had adventurously added twenty-two small wood-framed windows from its original three and four Velux skylight windows for daylighting, ventilation and aesthetic appeal. A far cry from the luxury of staff sorting out my lunch to withdrawing money from the ATM for my personal expenses!

By an effort of will, I began my routine early the next morning with fog veiling the mountains, fighting wind and snow all along as I ran the three kilometres uphill to Fortezza Verrucole, my *Stairway to Heaven*. San Romano's winters are long and harsh and my first winter was particularly challenging since it wasn't until spring the following year that work began on underfloor heating and injecting anti-earthquake protection to all stonework and steel membranes to reinforce my house. No challenge, however, was insurmountable when I looked at the views from each section of my sensitively restored house, knowing my terraced gardens led to the Santuario della Madonna del Bosco, a religious shrine immersed in the woods within Garfagnana's other treasure, the vast Orecchiella Natural Park. The Lady of the Woods drew reverent gift-bearing pilgrims from all over San Romano to her little church during its annual festival.

Despite the lack of fences, gates or any form of barricades in the inter-connected village served by a winding maze of cobblestone roads and alleys, there was no need to feel insecure. I never locked my main door when going on my runs. Protection came from the mountains, forests and the good nature of San Romano residents. Anyone could peek into my clear-glass doors and windows, and on occasion, some did tap on them to gain my attention, like Gretcha, my next-door neighbour Tino's niece, when she brought me a palm leaf blessed in church on Palm Sunday.

George became a conversation starter from the time we walked into the local church, which we attended regularly, always sitting in the back pew. One and all were blown over by his beauty and character, and it became common for locals to greet us, *Ciao*, Filippo! *Ciao*, George!, or stop us on our daily run. Boys from the local primary school would often descend on George and I headed home on my own for him to trot back when the adulation stopped. Such was George's freedom, he no longer wore a collar, nor was he housebound.

Making friends was not at all difficult despite the language barrier. I got away with basic salutations and plenty of arm-waving. Besides, a number spoke reasonable English, though not members of the older generation, such as my nonagenarian neighbour Tino, who did not speak a word of anything other than Italian. That was no hindrance for us to striking up a bond, and I loved that Tino loved spoiling George. Gretcha, who also lived in the vicinity, came early every day to take care of her

Uncle Tino's morning needs. Then she wheeled him out (a former soldier, he'd lost both legs to the Second World War) in well-pressed trousers, shirt and jacket, tie, scarf, peaked cap and, if the sun was shining, his sunglasses, for a stroll to the piazza to be in the company of regular old boys for a game of cards on the verandah of our local family-run Rewind Bar.

The Rewind Bar quickly became my people-watching haven, to appreciate the flurry of local customers enjoying a Stanley Tucci-worthy ritual of espresso or spritz, Garfagnana wines and beer or great pizzas, meat platters and cheeses. George soon became George Clooney to regulars, the actor being a Tuscany dweller. It was much the same at the Il Grotto restaurant in nearby Villetta, our other favourite haunt, where the reception from the staff and the quality of its food were as gratifying as any of Italy's culinary marvels.

I began building relationships with the locals, openly curious but easily accepting of its first, *not* lawyer from England but *Indiano avvocato* and *postino* (postman, because of my running). They couldn't figure out why I had chosen to settle in San Romano di Garfagnana instead of Florence, Venice, Rome, Milan or the Chianti but were very pleased I had converted a former eye-sore into a respectable piece of real estate, especially since my house strategically bordered the finest corner of the village.

My strolls at the collonaded shops of San Romano's piazza – and others in surrounding villages – made me understand Italy's enduring art of slow living. I'd put it down to the Italians' sclerotic connection to nature and community and inherent pride in their heritage. The magic of Italy unleashed powerful emotions within me and, at long last, I felt a sense of belonging to western soil, albeit in Tuscany. It had much to do with the enchanting call of the phallic-inspired Etruscan spirit, a subject introduced to me by DH Lawrence.

It was a definite full-circle moment for me looking at the piazza's balconies and arched terraces, inspiration for Shakespeare's famous line, *Many a morning hath he there been seen with tears augmenting the fresh morning's dew adding to clouds more clouds with his deep sighs* from *Romeo and Juliet* that my class was made to memorise in 1969 and which never left me.

It is not possible for anyone to feel lonely or unwelcome in an Italian village's piazza, as exemplified by one of my first friends in the village, Fausto, a tender-hearted, spiritual, middle-aged bachelor with a colourful past living on his own. Fausto routinely walked around the village, sometimes washing up at the village's public spring water tap or wandering into the piazza's shops making a friendly nuisance of himself, yet was treated with love and care by locals. Then there was Tano, one of George's many fans, who lived a stone's throw away from our house and spoke good English but for some reason preferred Italian with George, who seemed perfectly fine with it.

It filled my heart with joy to see the young and old flock to the piazza, far more beneficial and fun than the alarming isolationism of hogging behind screens. Every fair held at the piazza was a unifying moment where everyone got their hands dirty setting up woodfires, baking, cooking or roasting (the chestnut harvest fairs hosted by all villages in turns was a big custom), and the most endearing part of all for me was watching the mountain people sharing stories and legends with the young ones.

People took two-hour lunch breaks for a long sit-down meal, a far cry from my days of sitting in Lancaster's traffic, downing a sandwich or pie during lunch breaks. Being a well-connected region, it wasn't uncommon even for those working outside of San Romano to return for lunch or even a siesta. Serenaded by mountains, post-lunch life in San Romano came to a standstill, not unlike Prang Besar Estate back in the day.

Three months into settling down in San Romano, my mother fell seriously ill and was hospitalised. It called for a long trip to Kerala and I left George in the care of Tano, who by then was familiar with the layout of my house and George's routine. I spent a month with my ailing mother, mostly reminiscing our great Malaya road trip, talking about my new life and how I hoped to take her with me to San Romano when she was better. One month after my return, my mother breathed her last in May 2014. I'd had my moment with Mummy and did not return for her funeral. Kerala no longer felt like home now that I'd been orphaned, and in part, I was still harbouring anger at the way my mother had been turfed out of my father's house. Attended by my siblings, Mummy was buried a hundred miles away from her husband's Kalayil House family burial ground in Thekkemala. You might have guessed how I spent my mother's funeral day. I called on my Racket Boy spirit, tied up my shoelaces and took off for a very long run, making a stop at the Madonna Bosco shrine to say a prayer.

*Piano, piano* (slowly, slowly), George and I worked our way from the periphery to the forefront of the story. We began with a lot of slow travelling with trips to the mountains, pristine lakes or the rugged coastline of the Italian Riviera, enjoying Italy's deep appreciation of food, fashion, history, culture, family and worship. There was no shortage of crosses even in forests, valleys or mountains, my favourite being the magnificent wooden cross outside the pilgrim church of San Pellegrino in Alpe, a hamlet sitting right on the border between Tuscany and Emilia Romagna, about an hour's drive from my village taking the provincial mountain road, cutting across the Corfino Massif and the Orecchiella Park.

We took full advantage of San Romano being a vantage point for travelling around not just Italy but also Europe: a three-hour drive to Monaco, Switzerland, Austria or Venice, four hours to Rome, two hours to Milan, an hour and a half to Florence, all well connected by trains. With pre-Brexit Europe being so accessible, travel was easier with our British passports, and George too travelled with me around the Continent. Everything was easily reachable, like Papa driving the family from KL to Singapore!

San Romano embraced us as part of *la famiglia* over church fellowships similar in nature to the Syrian Orthodox service, coffee meets, dinner invitations, Sunday lunches, treks in the wild or opera dates in Castel Nuovo three miles down the valley or in Lucca, for a feel of Puccini's birthplace. At most gatherings, I'd be the only non-Italian in a room flowing with wine and coffee, full of loud, lively hosts, guests, children, pets, liberal with hugs and kisses, talking at the same time on a range of subjects, butting in, arms flailing, cutlery clanking… It was the best way to find out where to enjoy the best wines, the best wood-fired pizza or the best local river trout, or whose children needed English coaching or general mentoring. Naturally, I'd be offering legal counselling.

I built a network of local lawyers, some of whom became my associates when I set up *thelegalangel*, a pro bono legal consultancy service to supplement my relaxed existence. This meant travelling to different parts of the region to meet new contacts or clients, a very enjoyable way of learning about and embracing Italian culture and customs – not unlike the way I operated in Middle England when hitchhiking all over for badminton. I noticed immediately the comfort level and trust my new Italian network shared with me, with many commenting on how approachable and "like them" I was because of my openness, Asian ancestry and gullibility, and were ever so eager to benefit from my broad range of legal knowledge, my dedication to sports and my fondness for travel. It was all going on until 2018, a year I'll always remember for one thing. Curtains.

If in Malaysia the coalition party that had ruled the country since its independence in 1957 was finally toppled after sixty years, in England the curtain came down on my former firm after 130 years. Geoffrey had instilled in me that the behaviour of a company's representative was an extension of the company's beliefs and values, the wisdom of which I witnessed in JWK's downfall. Hollingdrake and another partner, Peter Bujakowski, dragged the firm into disrepute when they got involved in a failed multimillion car park investment scheme with a client whose customers lost millions of their pension funds, resulting in JWK being investigated and the two directors being reprimanded and fined for misconduct by the Solicitors Disciplinary Tribunal. Not too long after, owing to poor client care, mismanagement and cash flow problems, JWK was bought over for a pittance by Simpson Millar, a national law firm. Even from the seclusion of my mountain abode, my heart sank trying to come to terms with the fact that the Knowles' legacy had been wiped out by greed and injudiciousness. I dare say had I still been an active partner at the time, I'd have used my vigilance and thought to at least prevent the shame that befell the firm; such were my troubled emotions.

By withdrawing into Italy's embrace, I might have loosened my connection to England, but the tragic demise of the firm I considered my workplace, classroom and refuge brought home a startling message. I hadn't cut adrift. The old moorings remained.

EPILOGUE

# TRANQUILLO

Before I had time to raise a glass of red for having pulled my weight equally for the completion of my book, my next adventure announced itself like a dreaded telegram from back in the day.

2023 had just been born and I was sharing the merriment with my English friends Ray and Ann Haslam and Tony Collinson at the Red Well Country Inn, situated in the beautiful countryside of the Lune Valley on the edge of the Trough of Bowland.

In all the excitement, I missed one wee, which set the dominoes in motion. I found myself in A&E at Blackpool Victoria Hospital, thighs apart, for two doctors and two nurses failing to insert a catheter into my bladder because

– this is the telegram moment – I had an enlarged prostate refusing to let them perform their task. The ordeal began at around midnight, and it wasn't until 4 am, on the fifth attempt, that a urologist finally succeeded. I like to think my prostate relented on seeing that she was a Malay doctor wearing a headscarf from Malaysia with whom, through my pain, I had a delightful conversation about *nasi lemak* before she worked her magic on my waterworks.

All of a sudden, my brief holiday turned into an opportunity to enjoy my decades of investment in England. The NHS functioned with gusto, notwithstanding ongoing strikes crippling many industries in the UK, including its hospitals, and, I was humbled by the way my English network responded with visits and very comforting WhatsApp messages. I felt truly grateful for the company of my friend Suzie, with whom I was staying on the trip, and for the hospital visit of David and Jean Ashcroft, friends from the week I landed in England in 1970!

A few days later, I fled England's fresh wave of strikes for follow-up treatment in Tuscany, still fitted with a catheter and a urine bag – no good for my street credentials but at least I knew I wouldn't be facing the NHS's lack of staff or red tape causing "bed-blocking", among other problems.

Driving up the mountain road to my San Romano village, I realised what an honour it was to be telling my stories. To be sharing the lessons learnt and the benefits gained from standing on the shoulders of giants over the course of my three lives, knowing perhaps they might provide the balance sheets for younger generations. If a born wanderer with pretty average grey matter like me, growing up with a mind not working the way the Asian mind was supposed to work, somehow made it to the shore, there is certainly hope!

I rode on my badminton skill with passion, which complemented my wielding in an English society that valued sports on a par with academia. The positive mentoring that came with badminton greatly helped me shed my rough edges and, within a short time, I found myself in the haven of class and privilege, from the "gentleman's entrance" of the Marylebone Cricket Club (MCC) to watching the hunting/shooting classes in hats, scarves, field coats, braces and breeks lugging rifles as they moseyed into the Red Well Country Inn for lunch before returning to their exquisite countryside estates. Unfailingly, I would be the only non-white patron, as I was on the afternoon in the Red Well just before my prostrate acted up when it felt as if nothing had changed. It's not unusual in the Red Well to meet people I've known from as far back as the 1970s – English people happy to see me back, who can recall my "Young Turk" times when I would place bets on winning my squash matches at the Concorde Racket Club in return for orange juice because I couldn't afford it. The same people who used to give me a jolt with their cutting quips and dry humour that flat shut me up… but would eventually share their deepest emotions and feelings with me! What was all that about? *Saki boy has gone through the ringer*, Geoffrey used to say. It was his endearing epigram of me, using the old British term *saki* for *sakai a* and referring to the oft-repeated story of my childhood meeting with the Malayan native. And how right he was. I didn't possess finesse, neither was I a brainbox; all I had was spirit and, like the *sakai,* the ability to sponge off my surroundings and benefit from wandering the earth, taking a deep interest in things, valuing every detail of life's experiences, gathering evidence, making contemporaneous notes.

I cannot forget my mother's welling eyes upon seeing my name on the shiny brass plate outside of Whiteside and Knowles' Skipton Street office, along with an expression I took to be bewilderment at how far her "only fit for climbing coconut trees" eldest son had come. Upon my retirement, I unscrewed the plate and took it with me in its pristine state – I'd never known it not to be cleaned and polished every week. I wasn't in any way more deserving of having my name embossed on it just because I had made it against greater odds than my fellow partners, but I was certainly the one that most longed to be in possession of the plate, for it to join my sports trophies and medals; a conversation piece when I embarked on a good chinwag, as is my force of habit.

Growing up in Prang Besar Estate's colonial set-up of divide and administer, I was aware of life's privilege cards in their many variables. I realised too that I hadn't been dealt a bad card, just a tricky one. My biggest privilege card has been to be in the right place at the right time with the right people.

Growing up in England, I began to properly understand, through personal experiences, the nuances of how privilege worked, the underlying factors that contributed to it and how deeply embedded it was in

English culture. It is a fact most of my wholly English circle are blind to, accept quietly or flaunt openly as if winning the lottery. I played along to gain merit and also because it felt like the only game in town to get into the inner sanctum. What a grand feeling it was to be using the gentlemen's entrance of the MCC or to hear Geoffrey remark, 'The garnets of this world would welcome you through the front door of their mansions (instead of the tradesman's entrance).' A combination of my immigrant energy, chancer spirit, intense curiosity and sheer luck contributed to my breaching English society's social hierarchy, where many of my white friends could not survive the tricks of the game and had to settle for the "tradesman's entrance".

How ironic it is to hear in this day and time my fellow economic migrants and selfish beneficiaries as it would appear – Rishi and Suella – currently waging an all-out war against migrants/ "illegal" asylum seekers flocking into Britain, even at the expense of violating international human rights legislations. 'Enough is enough,' insists the prime minister, whose hardline bravado vanishes when fed-up former colonies scream the same slogan, demanding reparations, a return of stolen wealth and territories, official apologies for Britain's colonial atrocities or, God forbid, a Nobel-worthy Willy Brandt-style dropping on knees, as the German chancellor did for the Warsaw victims – a moment he described in his memoirs as *feeling the burden of millions of murders, I did what people do when words fail*. How can Rishi and Suella dare dream of executing any of the above when they have to abide by English social attitudes and the white mischief of the heavyweight machinery above their heads, namely the Conservative Party, the Women's Institute and the Protestant church embedded in Anglo-Saxon virtues?

I'd been holding my tongue for more than forty years in England, putting up with facetious dispositions. In the early days, I did it because I did not have the courage to speak up owing to my lack of knowledge to strip it to the bare bones to prove a *res ipsa loquitor* point, as was my style of case preparation to ensure easy passage for a judge to hit the high bar of beyond reasonable doubt/balance of probability. I continued it in the latter part of my life for not wanting to antagonise friends, lest I be labelled a troublemaker.

By the end of my life in England, my soul was in protest knowing the wealth, status and standing of the inner sanctum I so revered and aspired to be like, more likely than not, had its roots in blood and woes the result of impoverishing others to enrich themselves. My ancestors included. I could no longer put up with the emptiness and pain of farce privilege. In Yeats's words, *changed, changed utterly: a terrible beauty is born.*

Having no kin to be impacted by my decisions, I could up sticks at will to become a resident of Italy. The search for the house after my heart was undertaken hell for leather, but then, I've always enjoyed adrenaline and cramming – might even have deliberately distanced myself from tranquillity! I certainly did not set out to the mountains for seclusion or a slower pace... better ventilation and insulation for sure, as I have sued hospitals for giving my clients chronic respiratory infections; also because I detested air conditioning. Much of my growing up in England had been in the Trough of Bowland, which carried my pain and passion, my turmoil and bliss, and I must have carried those feelings in my hunt for a home. It had to be the mountains.

Living on my own at my age, I am acutely aware of the demands of maintaining a big house, and the importance of an active, healthy lifestyle to take me to my deathbed with dignity. San Romano provides me with the security blanket for this, along with the tantalising pursuit of learning and cultivating patience. In an environment where language remains a hurdle, just going to the pharmacy to get my prescription is a success story for me now, and I enjoy it since I've always operated with no security. Instead, I create my own chances and have cultivated a healthy relationship with failure. Perhaps this is why I approached retirement choosing to restore a building in a ruinous state, learning to fix a snow tyre or strimming the steep slopes of my terraced gardens.

With the same zeal, I managed three weeks with a catheter and having to pop pills – something I abhor as much as feeling sorry for myself. Instead of seeing the urine bag as a vehicle of doom, I micromanaged my situation by turning it into a "friend" – a mindset developed from badminton, instilling in me the value of intense practice towards executing even a simple thing, like hitting the shuttlecock straight. It takes a hell of a lot of hard work, just like the deceptively simple-looking clean cuts of Giorgio Armani clothing I so admire because I appreciate how much effort must have gone into their production.

I also gamely dealt with hitherto unknown medical terms such as benign prostatic hyperplasia (BPH), digital rectal examination (DRE), PSA levels, cystoscopy, etc., as well as putting myself in Italy's efficient healthcare system. In what was certainly a period of uncertainty, there was only one way to respond – place faith in my strengths, which in this case were my obsessive compulsion for good personal hygiene and forensic thinking. I seek solutions by collecting knowledge, facts and data to totally understand a problem, a skill I cultivated when studying for the law exam professional paper. Similarly, for my appointments with the urologist, I read up on prostate-related issues and consulted friends with knowledge to ensure I went well prepared, not to challenge the doctor but to ensure I could ask the correct questions and verify I was on the right track.

On the day I was relieved of the catheter and urine bag, I was told of some ugly cancerous-looking lacerations to my bladder, which didn't bother me one bit because, at the back of my mind, I knew I could rely on my loyal remedy to break the hard luck chain. After one month of sedentary living, admittedly a respite for the mind and body, I jumped into my neon running gear and took Walt Whitman with me, feeling afoot and light-hearted for a reunion with the mountains, my open road. My old self was soon knocking for entry.

I owe much to the aura of San Romano di Garfagnana for imparting wisdom and life lessons. Melancholia-tinted bliss of mountain life aside, there is a vibrant ecosystem in San Romano and its surroundings to sustain my energetic spirit, because it wasn't a hermit's living that I came seeking, or that gives me proper joy. Sharing does. When people share is when you know you have loved. I share easy warmth with a network of Italian friends who give their time and counsel generously: Sandra, my Italian translator during doctors' appointments as she's a nurse; Leo, my general troubleshooter and tech support; Matteo, also a translation assistant and drink buddy at the village bar; Valentina and Manuel, exemplary hosts and owners of the Selva del Buffardello Adventure Park, one of our village's biggest attractions. I also share a good friendship with Mayor Raffaella Mariani, who has contributed admirably towards the upkeep of the San Romano commune, besides readily making time for people despite the demands of her position.

The Italian word *campanilismo* can be viewed in several ways, my favourite being "the spirit of village cohesion and loyalty to those who live within the sound of the village church bells". I feel this every time I find freshly plucked tomatoes, zucchini or courgettes left outside my front door when I return from my run, when the eighty-something Alice band connoisseur Sandrina, who runs a small grocery shop around the corner with her daughter, affectionately brings out only the sweetest of peaches and the freshest of bread for me, or knowing my neighbour Debra would kindly turn on my underfloor heating and bring out a frozen dinner each time I was returning from my travels. I last experienced such devoted neighbourliness in my estate and *kampung* days of Malaya: the barter of dishes between families; soups, ointments, herbs rushed to anyone ill; families getting together during festivities to make a cauldron of *dodol* to be shared. Is it any wonder I view Italians with uncritical affection?

If I've taken on an ambassadorial role for San Romano, it's because my village so aptly fits Cesare Pavese's description of a country: *…means not being alone, knowing that there is something you have in people, plants and earth, that even when you're not there, it's still waiting for you.*

In many ways, I see the Italian spirit as a cross between India and Malaysia. It bothers me immensely to see Malaysia losing its soul by sticking to its inherited divisive policies… to think how far the country could have come had it kept to the spirit of Tunku's Malaya, when the three main races were clearly demarked yet were more respectful and eager to embrace each other's cultures and heritage. In the same way, it upsets me to see the decline of many of England's key institutions and the country's post-Brexit return to its sick-man-of-Europe status of the 1970s. It's a situation I equate to England's disastrous shift from respect-inspiring buttoned-up businesswear with immaculately polished brogues to the current *work-from-home-type* sloppy comfort attire which nevertheless is an optical nightmare. No surprise shoe-polish brand Kiwi did a Brexit on England or why more of Britain's young are exiting the country to make their lives in more attractive countries.

I feel privileged to have been part of that generation in England who had a fair chance at building decent careers and affording nice homes and holidays despite me coming from a background of chowing down steak pie and mushy peas with piss on fingers while screaming my lungs out at the Kop! What an irony then when the same notion of a privileged, easy existence in England became one of the reasons for my escape to rugged Italy. *Cabut*, as we say in Malay.

What I have not been able to totally escape from is the practice of law. I still receive plenty of requests for legal advice or help, which I find difficult to turn down. I suppose I can never extricate myself from the profession, although I certainly do not approach it as work anymore. This a different lawyer to the one that retired – a problem solver rather than the rottweiler snarling to score a point over the opposing lawyer. As a result, I mostly hand over cases to my vast network of lawyer friends.

Retired and with no pressure of dealing with the perplexities of domestic life, I take pleasure in doing a lot by myself in San Romano. I must register my gratitude to technology and social media for making my mountain life that much more fulfilling, seeing that I love good conversations and never fear taking myself out of my comfort zone. Smartphones and fast Internet service, I admit, are a huge godsend. Tools that help me with everything from translating languages and keeping up with current affairs, being the inveterate news/sports/movie junkie that I am, to tuning in to BBC Radio 4 and the House of Commons live. Also, very importantly, WhatsApp, FaceTime and email enable me to perform my responsibilities for the Lancaster Association of Boys and Girls Club (LABGC), the only trustee position I've held on to post-retirement as I strongly believe in youth empowerment; as well as keep tabs on the Eden Project Morecambe, a brilliant initiative that promises to inject renewed life into my old world.

Now that *Racket Boy* has been released, I want to just lock up and start wandering around the globe again to where my story takes me. Already in the pipeline is a camper van drive around Argentina, a long-time bucket list item to do before I kick the bucket!

As it happens, *Racket Boy* had already set the standard for my future travels from that momentous return to Malaysia in 2022 when I first met Geetha. During that trip, Janet Knowles, Geoffrey's daughter, who left Lancaster in the 1970s to settle in Australia, wondered if I'd accompany her to spread her father's remaining ashes on the grave of his twin, Donald Knowles. I would never have declined the honour.

From Kuala Lumpur, I flew to Bangkok to meet Janet, arriving directly from Perth via Changi, Singapore. Janet and I received each other with familial tenderness, not having seen each other in ages, and I could not hold back memories of the time years ago when I flew to Perth while Geoffrey was visiting Janet for a very special holiday, which delighted Geoffrey so much he dubbed us "two Morecambe guys roaming down under"!

Janet used to be a keen badminton player, like her mother, the key factor that intertwined my journey with her family, so there were delicious reminiscences centred around my badminton adventures all over England.

I checked into the River Kwai Hotel, popularised by the woefully fictionalised Hollywood film *Bridge on the River Kwai*, with *Merry Christmas, Mr. Lawrence* ringing in my head.

My mind travelled to the many sombre exchanges with the man whose mental and emotional fortitude I had great respect for, but my exploits with Geoffrey weren't the only thoughts occupying my mind at the River Kwai Hotel. The trajectory also included my father's stories about how 'far more of our people went to Siam, suffered and died than the white men...'

The Kanchanaburi trip produced many moments of revelatory insights. If strolling along the graves, reading the inscriptions at the well-kept Kanchanaburi Death Railway War Cemetery was troubling, the total lack of recognition of Asians, particularly the Tamils, who were the largest casualties by a huge margin, was far more disturbing for me. Another poignant moment was when Janet recalled one of her last father-daughter moments on a walk around Bungendore Park when Geoffrey had made a characteristic remark: 'I don't want any bloody crying at my funeral. I've had a *very* happy and productive life and don't want anyone feeling sorry for me as I lie in my wooden overcoat, because I won't be giving a shit.' Geoff was right. His was a grand ship that had gone on utterly splendid voyages.

Janet and I also visited Geoffrey's camp in Chungkai, where I immediately felt a connection to the man like never before since his death... I'd long harboured disappointment at not being in England for Geoffrey's funeral. That night, my moleskin received emotional jottings but I went to bed with lightness, feeling proud that by assisting Janet I'd fulfilled a debt owed to Geoffrey.

I am now at the age when my father died. People I've been following since the '70s are dropping like flies – Christine McVie, Jeff Beck, David Crosby – all during my prostate scare. Cue to think about dying matters! My rackets have discharged their duty and I have stretched my life to great limits, which gives me immense fulfilment.

My only wish now is to taper my possessions to zero and go the way my father and Geoffrey did – retaining their brilliant minds and unique wit right up to their ends. If my maker has other plans, I abide by my faith. I'm tranquil.